The MAILBOX
IDEA MAGAZINE FOR TEACHERS®

2005–2006 YEARBOOK

The Education Center, Inc.
Greensboro, North Carolina

The Mailbox® 2005–2006 Preschool Yearbook

Managing Editor, *The Mailbox* Magazine: Kimberly Brugger-Murphy

Editorial Team: Becky S. Andrews, Kimberley Bruck, Karen P. Shelton, Diane Badden, Sharon Murphy, Karen A. Brudnak, Hope Rodgers, Dorothy C. McKinney

Production Team: Lori Z. Henry, Pam Crane, Rebecca Saunders, Jennifer Tipton Cappoen, Chris Curry, Sarah Foreman, Theresa Lewis Goode, Clint Moore, Greg D. Rieves, Barry Slate, Donna K. Teal, Zane Williard, Tazmen Carlisle, Marsha Heim, Lynette Dickerson, Mark Rainey, Margaret Freed

ISBN10 1-56234-723-3
ISBN13 978-156234-723-9
ISSN 1088-5536

Printed in the United States of America.

The Education Center, Inc.
P.O. Box 9753
Greensboro, NC 27429-0753

Look for *The Mailbox® 2006–2007 Preschool Yearbook* in the summer of 2007. The Education Center, Inc., is the publisher of *The Mailbox®*, *Teacher's Helper®*, *The Mailbox® BOOKBAG®*, and *Learning®* magazines, as well as other fine products. Look for these wherever quality teacher materials are sold, call 1-800-714-7991, or visit www.themailbox.com.

Contents

Departments

Bulletin Boards and Displays 5

Busy Hands 19
      Lovely Leaves 20
      Lots of Dots...22
      Special Delivery 24
      Fabulous Feathers! 26
      Start Your Engines! 28

Arts & Crafts for Little Hands 31

Get Moving! 47

Management Tips & Timesavers 61

It's Circle Time 67

Kids in the Kitchen 79

Learning Centers 93

Our Readers Write 107

Songs & Such...115

Science Explorations 125
      Same and Different 126
      Investigating Thumbprints 128
      Amazing Evaporation! 130
      Mixing Up Colors 132

Storytime..135

Features

Book Units 149
      The Napping House...150
      Jamberry 154
      Mouse Paint 158
      Fish Eyes 162
      If You Take a Mouse to School 164

Center Units..167

    Gobblin' Good Centers!..168

    All Aboard for Centers!...173

    A Rainbow of Centers...178

    Send In the Clown Centers!...182

    Wild About Watermelon Centers...187

    "A-peel-ing" Birthday Centers..192

Literacy Units..197

    A "Purr-fect" Time for Rhyme!...198

    A Sequencing Smorgasboard..204

    Fun With Beginning Sounds...210

    Bananas About Letters!..214

    Literacy in the Forecast..219

    Learning Letters and Sounds..224

Math Units..229

    Patterning in Preschool..230

    Shapes on Parade..234

    Counting With Mice..237

    Exploring Measurement...242

    Recognizing Numbers!...246

    Get Ready for Graphing..250

Thematic Units..253

    Making a Splash in Preschool!..254

    All About Apples...260

    Plentiful Pumpkins..264

    Bear Necessities..270

    Gifts Galore!...276

    Families Are Fabulous!...281

    Hooray for Valentine's Day!...285

    Plentiful Puddles!..290

    Fine-Feathered Friends!...294

    Beautiful Farm Babies!..300

    Let's Go Camping!...305

    A Boat Bonanza!...310

Index..315

Bulletin Boards and Displays

Our Family Quilt

Youngsters look to this family-friendly bulletin board to find familiar faces! Have each child's family send in a family photo. Attach each photo to a square wallpaper sample. Then mount the samples on a bulletin board to resemble a quilt and add the title shown. If desired, use a permanent marker to add stitching details. This cozy quilt is sure to be a comfort to your little ones!

Patricia Hill
First Baptist Pleasant Grove
Pleasant Grove, AL

Add this vivid display to your study of colors, and your students will be tickled pink! Send a note home requesting that youngsters bring in a small object (or magazine picture) in the color currently being studied. When a child brings in an object, have him tape it to a matching piece of bulletin board paper labeled with the appropriate color word. At the end of your color unit, you'll have a collection of class-made collages!

Deborah Luke, Fairmount Nursery School, Syracuse, NY

Preschool Is a Hoot!

Have each child color a copy of the owl pattern on page 16. Instruct her to glue torn pieces of brown paper to the owl to resemble feathers. When the glue is dry, cut out the owls and display them as shown.

Mandi Bordeau, Plattsburgh City School District, Plattsburgh, NY

Provide a selection of colorful cutouts and encourage each child to choose one. Then have students glue their cutouts to a piece of bulletin board paper titled as shown. When the glue is dry, display the paper on a bulletin board. Then gather youngsters around the board and play the traditional game of I Spy, having students locate chosen cutouts. I spy with my little eye the number 2!

Cherie Rissman
Meredith Drive Preschool
Des Moines, IA

Have youngsters use white tempera paint to make fingerprint snowflakes on a strip of bulletin board paper; then attach the paper to a wall. Instruct each child to decorate a bird cutout to resemble a cardinal. Have her brush glue on a twig and then sprinkle silver glitter over the glue. Then mount the cutouts and twigs on the paper.

Patti Bernstein and Ellen Pastuch, Rolling River Day School, East Rockaway, NY

This nifty holiday tree is made from recycled phone book pages! Tear out pages from an outdated phone book and have youngsters paint them green. When the paint is dry, fringe-cut the pages and display them to resemble a tree. Embellish the display with student-made decorations.

Tiffany Garner and Mindy Waddell
Buttons and Bows Child Care, West Monroe, LA

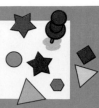

AND DISPLAYS

Hats Off to a Happy New Year!

Hats, noisemakers, and streamers—this New Year's display has it all! Have each youngster decorate a hat cutout. Display the hats on a wall along with noisemakers, streamers, and the title shown.

Sarah Booth, Messiah Nursery School, South Williamsport, PA

Commemorate Martin Luther King Jr. with a display dedicated to friendship! Have each child color a personalized copy of the pattern on page 17 to resemble himself. Cut around each pattern. Then display the cutouts on a board decorated as shown.

Jodi Montel, Mentone Elementary, Mentone, IN

Combine equal amounts of nonmenthol shaving cream and white glue; then use food coloring to tint the mixture pink. Have each child spread the mixture on a cloud-shaped cutout. Allow at least 48 hours for the clouds to dry. Next, have each child color and cut out a personalized flying-heart pattern similar to the one shown. Then display the clouds and hearts as indicated.

C. Welwood, Learning Experience, Calgary, Alberta, Canada

Send a note home with youngsters encouraging parents to send in labels from the packaging of familiar food items. When each child brings in his labels, have him glue them to a piece of bulletin board paper. Then post the paper in your classroom with the title shown. Youngsters have a terrific time identifying familiar environmental print!

Kristi Kirinch
Miami Valley Child Development Centers and Head Start
Dayton, OH

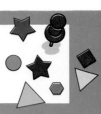

Our Preschool Pot of Gold

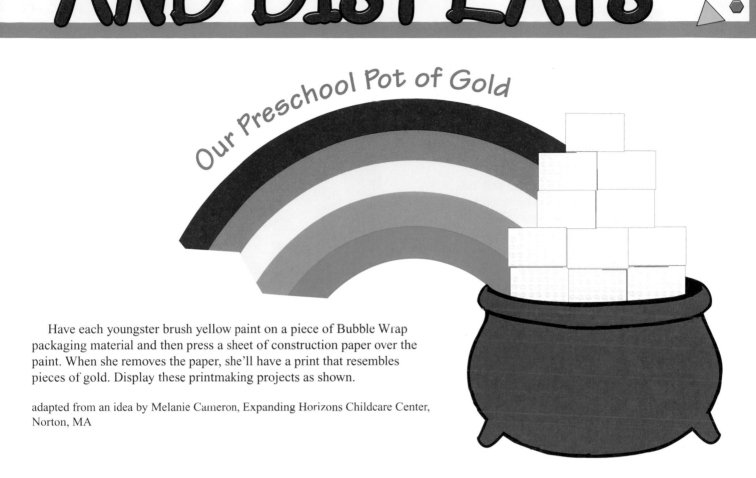

Have each youngster brush yellow paint on a piece of Bubble Wrap packaging material and then press a sheet of construction paper over the paint. When she removes the paper, she'll have a print that resembles pieces of gold. Display these printmaking projects as shown.

adapted from an idea by Melanie Cameron, Expanding Horizons Childcare Center, Norton, MA

The Birds Are Back!

Celebrate the return of songbirds this spring with a fun display! Mount on a bulletin board a branch, a bird feeder cutout, and the title shown. Have each child glue a simple bird body pattern to a sheet of paper. Then instruct her to make hand-prints on either side of the body with tempera paint. Have her add eyes, a beak, and feet to her bird. Then cut out the birds and attach them to the display.

Deborah Ellis, M.S.S. Child Enrichment Center, Magnolia, AL

Get youngsters' families involved with this spiffy Easter display! Send home with each student a large egg cutout along with instructions asking parents to decorate it with their child. When the eggs are returned to school, mount them on a display similar to the one shown.

Christina Bainbridge
Hansel and Gretel Preschool
Centreville, MI

Have an "Egg-cellent" Easter!

Keep Our Earth Sparkling Clean

Have each child sponge-paint a white construction paper circle with green and blue tempera paint to resemble the earth. Then encourage each child to sprinkle glitter over the wet paint. When these pretty planets are dry, display them on a bulletin board with star stickers and the title shown. What a lovely Earth Day display!

Laurie Taivalmaa, The Ark Christian Childcare and Learning Center, Bessemer, MI

Have each youngster dip a toothbrush in gray paint and then run his finger over the bristles to splatter-paint a white cloud cutout. Display the resulting storm clouds with blue curling ribbon to resemble rain. Trim pieces of aluminum foil to resemble puddles. Then add the puddles and the title shown to the display.

Here's a unique display idea for youngsters' springtime paintings! Mount finished paintings in a row. Then transform the paintings into a caterpillar by adding a head cutout and several leg cutouts. Finally, title the display as shown.

Joanne Fusco, Tutor Time Child Care, Wappinger Falls, NY

Use a pencil to draw lines on a class supply of white circle cutouts so the lines resemble the lacing on a baseball. Have each child personalize a baseball and then glue pieces of red yarn to the lines. When the glue is dry, display the baseballs with the title shown.

Erica Avila, Wee Care Learning Center, Festus, MO

For this sunny display, cut a large circle from yellow bulletin board paper. Place the circle in an extra large box and drop several paint-covered marbles in the box. Supervise each child as he gently shakes the box. Remove the circle and allow it to dry. Next, trace each child's feet on yellow paper. Help each child cut out the tracings. Then mount the circle and tracings on the board to resemble a sun and rays. Finish your display by adding the title shown.

Kimberly Dessel
Pixie Preschool
Spotswood, NJ

Kelly Martin
Weatherly Children's Learning Center
Alabaster, AL

Preschoolers Stand Tall for Their Country

| Alex | Jayne | Lee | Aaron | Sarah | Ashley | Misty |

Cut a length of adding machine tape to the exact height of each preschooler in your class. Have each child sponge-paint stars in red and blue along his tape. Then mount the lengths of tape on a bulletin board and add student names and photos as well as the title shown. What a unique patriotic display!

Cindy Clements
Mack Benn, Jr. Elementary
Suffolk, VA

Have each child draw a self-portrait on a copy of the racecar pattern (page 18) and embellish the car as desired. Then use a permanent marker to add a fun racing-themed name to each car. Mount the cars on a board with signs displaying skills the students have worked on throughout the year and title the board as shown.

Sarah Booth, Messiah Nursery School, South Williamsport, PA

TEC41021

Racecar Pattern

Use with "Ready...Set...Learn!" on page 15.

TEC41025

BUSY HANDS

BUSY HANDS

Creative Learning Experiences for Little Hands

LOVELY LEAVES

Orange, yellow, red, and brown—autumn leaves are falling down. That means it's the perfect time of the year to jump into this pile of leafy explorations!

ideas contributed by Roxanne LaBell Dearman
Western NC Early Intervention Program for Children
Who Are Deaf or Hard of Hearing
Charlotte, NC

FROM BARE TO BEAUTIFUL!

Cut a basic tree shape from brown paper, omitting the foliage. Then tape the tree to a flat surface. Make a variety of colorful leaf cutouts and several squirrel cutouts. (Patterns on page 30.) Place the cutouts in a container and set them near the tree. A youngster places leaves on the tree, making sure to scatter a few at the bottom to show that some have already fallen from the branches. Then he adds squirrels on and around the tree to make a lovely autumn scene.

LEAFY LACING

Cut large leaf shapes from colorful plastic canvas. For each leaf, cut a length of yarn and dip an end of each length in glue to make the lacing process easier for little fingers. After the glue is dry, tie the remaining end of each length to a different fall leaf. Then place the cutouts and yarn lengths in a container. A child chooses a leaf and then laces the yarn through the leaf to give it fall flair!

HIDDEN LEAVES

Gather fall leaves in different shapes and sizes and tape them to a tabletop. Then tape a length of white bulletin board paper over the leaves. Provide a supply of unwrapped crayons in fall colors. Children rub the crayons over the paper to reveal the hidden leaves. When all the leaves have been revealed and the paper is covered with fall colors, remove it and tape down a clean length of paper for more leaf-rubbing fun!

PRESTO CHANGO!

Make sponge painters by hot-gluing each of several sponge pieces to separate film canisters. Place the sponge painters at your art table along with shallow pans of yellow and red paint and a supply of green construction paper leaves. Encourage youngsters to transform the green leaves into colorful fall leaves by dabbing on yellow and red paint. When the paint is dry, use the leaves to add fall pizzazz to a bulletin board or display.

A BIG BASKETFUL

To prepare for this simple idea, scatter a variety of autumn leaves or leaf cutouts in a traffic-free area of your room. Provide a big basket and encourage youngsters to find all the leaves and place them in the basket. When all the leaves have been collected, encourage youngsters to toss them back on the floor with great enthusiasm. The leaves fall—and fall again!

BUSY HANDS

Creative Learning Experiences for Little Hands

LOTS OF DOTS

Here a dot, there a dot! With explorations featuring bingo daubers, your little ones are sure to see lots of dots!

ideas contributed by Ada Goren, Winston-Salem, NC

FLIPPIN' FOR PANCAKES!

Place at a table a blue bingo dauber, a supply of tan construction paper pancakes, and pancake-related dramatic-play items, such as a skillet, a spatula, an empty syrup bottle, and plastic plates and forks. A youngster uses the dauber to make blue dots on several pancakes to resemble blueberries. Then he uses the props to cook up some breakfast-themed dramatic play!

DOUBLES AND TRIPLES

Use thick rubber bands to bind pairs of bingo daubers together. Then place the daubers and a supply of paper at a table. Encourage youngsters to explore making dots with these unique painting tools. When each student has had ample opportunity to investigate the dauber pairs, bind groups of three daubers together. These colossal painting tools are triple the fun!

KWANZAA CANDLES

Cut a strip of white bulletin board paper and tape it to a tabletop. Then place at the table glue, yellow bingo daubers, a shallow container of water, and a supply of nine-inch construction paper strips (candles) in the following colors: red, green, and black. Each child glues several candles to the paper. Then she dips the tip of the dauber into the water and presses it above each candle to make the flame. Look at all the glowing lights!

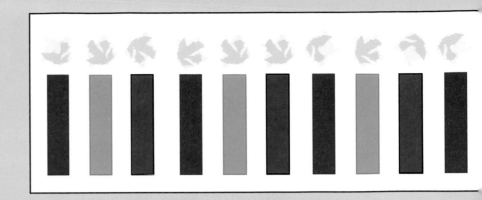

DOT-TO-DOT

Place drawing paper, markers, and a selection of bingo daubers at a table. A child uses a bingo dauber to make several dots on a sheet of paper. Then she uses a variety of colorful markers to connect the dots. What a unique piece of modern art!

BEAUTIFUL BERRIES

Tape a length of bulletin board paper to a tabletop. Provide access to the following items: glue, a red bingo dauber, and a supply of green holly leaf cutouts. A youngster uses the bingo dauber to make a cluster of three berries. Then he glues holly leaves near the berries. When the paper is filled with holly and the glue is dry, attach the paper to a wall to make a festive decoration!

BUSY HANDS

Creative Learning Experiences for Little Hands

SPECIAL DELIVERY

With cards, envelopes, and other mail-themed items to explore, these ideas are sure to get your little ones' stamp of approval!

ideas contributed by Ada Goren, Winston-Salem, NC

LOTS OF ENVELOPES!

In advance, save used envelopes that have transparent windows, such as those shown. Then place the collection of envelopes at a table along with colorful paper, pencils, and crayons. A youngster visits the table, writes a letter to a desired person, and places it in an envelope. She can take her envelope home to give to a loved one or she can deliver it right away to a friend in the classroom!

Vicki Ault
Guiding Hand Preschool
Cheshire, OH

LOVE LETTERS

To prepare for this exploration, label a supply of 4½" x 6" pieces of construction paper with different alphabet letters; then add simple stamp details to each piece of paper as shown. Place the resulting love letters at a table along with a supply of tissue paper squares. Also provide a bowl of white glue and a paintbrush. A student chooses a letter and identifies it, with help as needed. Next, he brushes glue on the letter and places crumpled tissue paper squares on the glue. Then, if desired, he repeats the process with a different love letter.

Noelle Lawrence
Pixie Preschool and Kindergarten
Spotswood, NJ

FANCY CLASS CARD

Place an extra large tagboard card at a table along with glue sticks, scissors, and a variety of craft items, such as heart cutouts, pieces of lace, doilies, and tissue paper. Invite students to visit the center and glue craft items to the front of the card as desired. After each child has had an opportunity to add to the card, have students help you compose a message to your preschool director or principal. Write the message inside the card and then help youngsters deliver the card to the deserving individual.

SUPER STAMPS

Use fancy-edged scissors to cut out a supply of construction paper rectangles to resemble large stamps. Place the rectangles on a protected tabletop along with watercolor paints, brushes, and small containers of water. A visiting student uses the watercolors to paint unique, colorful stamps!

PLEASANT PACKING

Place at this center a supply of boxes and packing materials, such as Bubble Wrap packaging material, paper shreds, newsprint, and tissue paper. Also provide several items for youngsters to place in packages. To begin, explain that it's important to place packing material around items being sent through the mail to keep the items protected. Then encourage youngsters to visit the center and pack some Valentine's Day presents!

BUSY HANDS

Creative Learning Experiences for Little Hands

FABULOUS FEATHERS!

Feathers aplenty! Feathers galore! Feathers sure are lots of fun to explore!

ideas contributed by Ada Goren, Winston-Salem, NC

BEAUTIFUL BRUSHES

Gather several large craft feathers and place each feather in a shallow pan of tempera paint. Place the pans at your art table along with a supply of construction paper. A youngster writes his name on a sheet of paper. Then he glides the paint-covered feathers over the paper until a desired effect is achieved. How lovely!

FUN FEATHER SORT

To prepare for this exploration, make four copies of the bird pattern on page 297 on different colors of construction paper. Cut out the birds. Then gather several craft feathers to match each bird and place them in a container. Place the birds and container at a center. A child visits the center and sorts the feathers on the matching birds!

WRITE ON!

Place at a table containers of tempera paint, paintbrushes, a supply of white construction paper, and several large craft feathers. A child brushes paint over an entire sheet of paper. Then she holds the feather as if it were a pen and "writes" on the paint, making sure not to press down too hard on the tip of the feather. Look at all of those wonderful looping lines!

SNIP, SNIP, SNIP

To prepare for this fine-motor investigation, place several supersize feather cutouts at a center along with a supply of scissors. Youngsters practice their cutting skills by making small snips along the edges of the cutout to resemble a real feather. (Depending on youngsters' fine-motor abilities, you may want to draw lines on the cutouts for them to follow.) If desired, use these fabulous feathers on a bird-themed bulletin board or display.

FIND THAT FEATHER!

Gather a supply of craft feathers and place them in a plastic tub, including only one red feather (or another color of your choice). Invite youngsters to the tub to explore the soft fluffy feathers and to find the red feather. There it is!

BUSY HANDS

Creative Learning Experiences for Little Hands

START YOUR ENGINES!

No doubt youngsters will race to these explorations that feature toy cars and trucks!

ideas contributed by Roxanne LaBell Dearman
Western NC Early Intervention Program for Children Who Are Deaf or Hard of Hearing
Charlotte, NC

BATHTIME!

To set up this squeaky clean car wash, place a tub of sudsy water and a variety of scrubbers and sponges at a table. Place a variety of toy cars and several towels nearby. Children wash and scrub the cars and then use the towels for drying and buffing. Those cars are sparkling clean!

LOAD THE TRUCK

Place several small stuffed animals around your room. Provide access to a large toy truck. Then explain that the animals are having a party and they all need to be picked up from their different locations. Encourage a child to roll the truck around the room, finding each animal and placing it in the truck bed. It looks like everyone is coming to this party!

READY...SET...PAINT!

Tape a length of bulletin board paper to a table. Then draw a large oval racetrack with a start and finish line on the paper. Place a shallow container of tempera paint at the table, and place a car in the paint. Have a youngster remove the car from the paint and then "drive" it from start to finish. Invite other youngsters to visit the center and repeat the process, adding more prints ot the racetrack.

MAKING TRACKS

Place a supply of play dough at a table along with a rolling pin and several toy cars and trucks in different sizes. A student rolls the rolling pin over the dough to make a smooth surface. Then he "drives" the toys over the play dough, observing the tracks made by the wheels. Some tracks are large and some are small!

BUMP, BUMP, BUMP!

Gather a variety of items with different textures, such as corrugated cardboard, sandpaper, bubble wrap, and cellophane. Glue each textured item to a separate sheet of tagboard; then tape the sheets together to make a road. Place the road on the floor along with a container of toy cars. A youngster visits the area and rolls the cars over the different textures.

Arts & Crafts for Little Hands

Arts & Crafts for Little Hands

"Tee-rific" Apples

When little ones make this "a-peel-ing" craft, they're sure to have a ball! Press a foam ball onto a tabletop to flatten it slightly to prevent rolling. Insert a golf tee (stem) into the top of the ball. Then paint the ball red, holding the stem to steady it as you paint. Allow the paint to dry. Remove the stem; then dip it in green paint and insert it into the ball as before. Glue a personalized leaf cutout next to the stem. (You may need to tape the leaf in place as the glue dries.) After the project is dry, place the finished apples in a bushel basket and add the basket to a fall display!

Amy Andrews
Jack & Jill Preschool
Leavenworth, KS

Nifty Noodles

The "pasta-bilities" are endless with this simple art technique! Place cooked, cooled spaghetti noodles on a sheet of colorful construction paper until a desired effect is achieved. When the spaghetti is dry, it will remain attached to the paper. Now that's using your noodle!

Melissa Talasky
Asbury Elementary
Fairview, PA

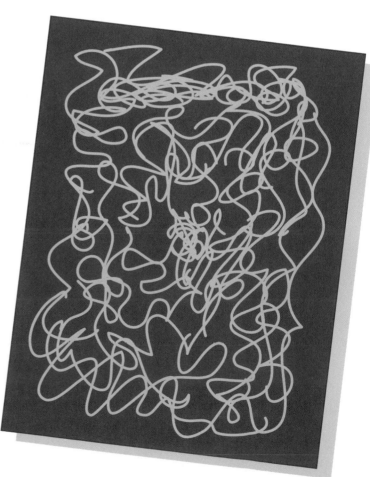

Hickory, Dickory, Clock

Little ones use this cute craft as a prop when they recite the traditional nursery rhyme "Hickory, Dickory, Dock." Copy the clockface and mouse patterns (page 45) onto white construction paper. To make the craft, cut out the clockface and glue it to a seven-inch paper plate. Glue the plate to the top of a 6" x 12" brown construction paper rectangle. Then glue a yellow strip and a yellow circle to the rectangle to make a pendulum.

Next, color and cut out the mouse. Punch a hole in both the paper plate and the mouse. Tie a length of yarn to the mouse and insert the remaining end of yarn through the hole in the plate. Recite the rhyme and use the string to move the mouse up and down the clock. Hickory, dickory, dock!

Jody Steed
La Vega Primary Center
Waco, TX

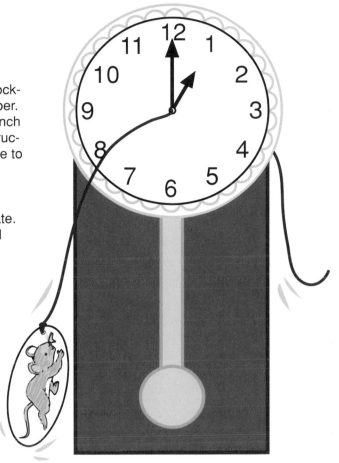

On a Roll!

This twist on marble painting is sure to be a hit with your little sports enthusiasts! Place a cut-to-fit piece of construction paper in the bottom of a lidded shoebox. Use a spoon to dip a golf ball in tempera paint and then transfer it to the box. Place the lid on the box. Then tilt the box back and forth, rolling the golf ball across the paper. Remove the lid to reveal an interesting, textured print. If desired, add to the masterpiece using other golf balls and colors of tempera paint!

Angi Meyer
Ebenezer Elementary
Lebanon, PA

Do the Mash!

To create a festive atmosphere for this print-making project, play a recording of the classic song "Monster Mash." Then, while grooving to the music, press a potato masher into a shallow pan of tempera paint and make a print on a sheet of paper. Blot the masher on a paper towel. Continue in the same way with different colors of paint until the desired effect is achieved.

Jill Stemple
Rock Cave Elementary
Rock Cave, WV

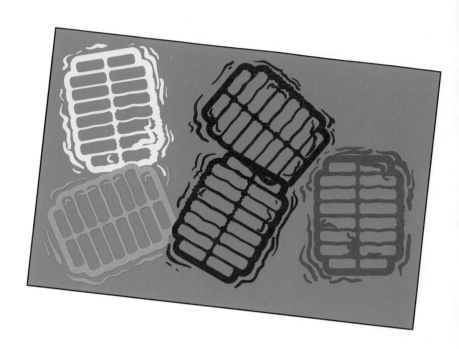

Mmm...Pie!

To make a pie slice that looks good and smells good, paint a paper plate wedge orange and then sprinkle pumpkin pie spice over the paint. When the paint is dry, brush glue over the outer edge of the slice. Then crumple squares of brown tissue paper and press them in the glue to resemble piecrust.

Tonya Jensen
Heartland Child Development
Council Bluffs, IA

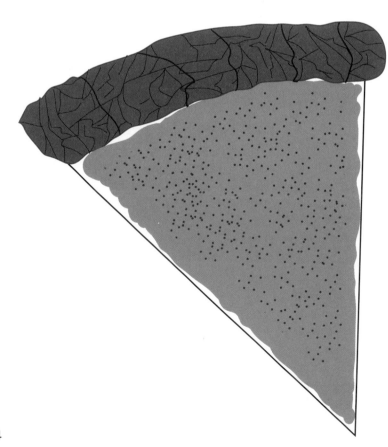

Leafy Turkey

Press an assortment of fall leaf cutouts on the sticky side of a Con-Tact paper circle. Then carefully place a second Con-Tact paper circle over the first circle. Next, color and cut out a copy of the turkey body pattern on page 170. Then glue the body to the Con-Tact paper. Now that's "unbe-leaf-ably" cute!

Cynthia Thurman
Montezuma Elementary
Stockton, CA

Snoozing Ladybugs

Your youngsters may be surprised to learn that many kinds of ladybugs hibernate, choosing areas under leaves and logs for their long seasonal snooze. To make a snoozing ladybug craft, color and cut out a copy of the log pattern on page 46. Glue one end of the log to a 9" x 12" sheet of construction paper to make a flap as shown. Glue red construction paper circles under the flap; then decorate the circles to resemble ladybugs. Finish the craft by gluing fall leaves around the log. When the glue dries, lift the flap to peek at the snoozing ladybugs!

Charlet Keller
ICC Preschool
Violet Hill, AR

Arts & Crafts for Little Hands

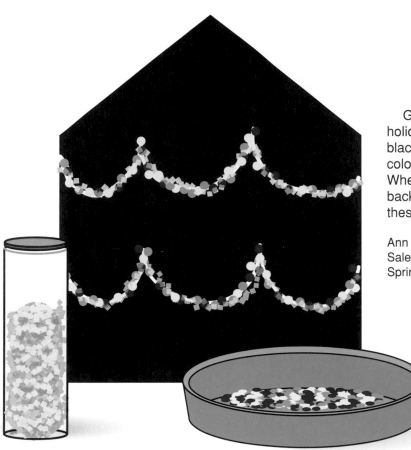

Lovely Lights!

Glitter and hole-punched dots create twinkling holiday lights! Squeeze draping lines of glue on a black construction paper house cutout. Sprinkle colorful hole-punched dots and glitter over the glue. When the glue is dry, display the houses on a snowy background below a black nighttime sky. No doubt these projects will earn lots of oohs and aahs!

Ann Zelter and Jenny Knoll
Salem Lutheran Preschool
Springville, NY

Spinning Dreidels

Here's a brush-free painting idea sure to brighten your youngsters' Hanukkah celebration! Hold a dreidel by its handle and dip it into a container of tempera paint. Then spin the dreidel on a large colorful sheet of paper that has been placed in a shallow box. Repeat the process with other dreidels and different colors of paint.

Angela Lenker
Montgomery Early Learning Center
Pottstown, PA

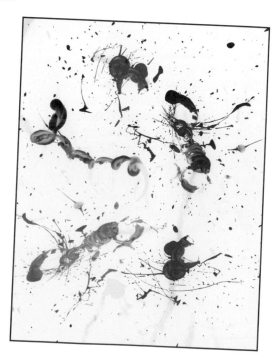

Frosty Windows

These frosty windows look so realistic, your little ones are sure to feel a chill in the air! Add Epsom salts to a container of warm water, stirring the mixture until no more salts will dissolve. Then brush the mixture over a sheet of black construction paper. Allow the paper to dry overnight, which will give it a frosty appearance. Have youngsters add construction paper strips to their projects, as shown, so they resemble frost-covered windows.

Sherri Howard
Cornerstone Baptist WEE School
Greensboro, NC

A "Berry" Pretty Wreath

How do you add pizzazz to a holiday wreath? Why, simply add cereal! Cut out the center of a white paper plate to make a wreath. Paint the wreath green. Then glue trios of Cheerios cereal to the wreath. When the glue is dry, dip a brush in red paint and then dab it over the Cheerios so they resemble holly berries. Finally, embellish the wreath with a gift bow!

Sarah Booth
Messiah Nursery School
South Williamsport, PA

Nancy Jandreau
Kids Corner Day Care
Potsdam, NY

Mazao for Kwanzaa

Mazao, or fruits and vegetables from the harvest, are part of a traditional Kwanzaa display. To make a mazao project, cut out the center of a construction paper bowl shape to make a frame similar to the one shown. Tape a piece of plastic wrap to the frame. Brush a mixture of half glue and half water on the plastic wrap and then press pieces of red, black, and green tissue paper onto the mixture. Brush more of the mixture over the tissue paper if needed. Then sprinkle gold glitter over the project. Finally, glue fruit and vegetable cutouts so they peak out of the bowl.

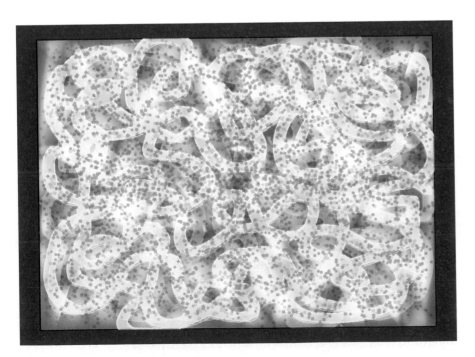

Finger Skating

Lightly tape a piece of aluminum foil to a tabletop. Place small spoonfuls of white tempera paint onto the aluminum foil. As you listen to a recording of upbeat music, swirl two fingers through the paint as if they were ice-skating. When the paint has been spread around the foil and a desired effect is achieved, sprinkle fine glitter over the paint. Then mount the finished project on colorful construction paper. That's some fancy finger skating!

Arts & Crafts for Little Hands

Lovable Mouse

This cute little mouse is full of love! Glue two black construction paper circles (ears) to a red construction paper heart (body) as shown. Use a black marker to draw eyes and a nose. Then attach a length of yarn to the underside of the heart to resemble a tail. How cute!

Tammy Ward
Learning Journey Home Childcare
Roy, WA

Splendid Shamrock

Homemade puffy paint turns an ordinary shamrock cutout into an extraordinary one! Place equal parts of nonmenthol shaving cream and white glue in a resealable plastic bag. Add a few drops of green food coloring to the mixture. Then gently squeeze the bag to mix the ingredients. Next, snip off the bottom corner of the bag. Squeeze the paint onto a large shamrock cutout. Finally, sprinkle green glitter onto the mixture. Allow at least 48 hours for the project to dry.

Kim Montanye
Glyndon United Methodist Preschool
Glyndon, MD

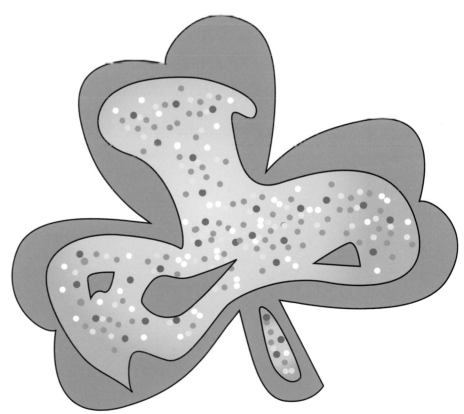

Roller Rainbow

When youngsters use a paint roller to spread dollops of paint, the result is an artsy rainbow! Place dollops of red, yellow, and blue paint in a row near the edge of a sheet of paper. Then use a small paint roller to spread the paint across the paper. Watch as orange and green appear between the primary colors!

Reba Barfield
Marietta First United Methodist Preschool
Marietta, GA

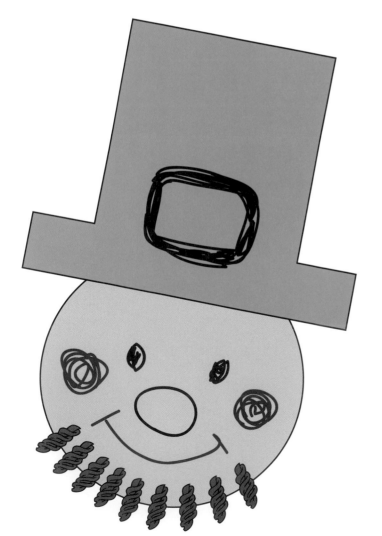

Lucky Leprechaun

This leprechaun pal is sure to spread lots of St. Patrick's Day cheer! Dye a supply of rotini pasta by combining the pasta, a small amount of rubbing alcohol, and several drops of orange food coloring in a large resealable plastic bag. Seal the bag and shake it until all of the pasta is dyed orange. Spread the colored pasta onto a piece of waxed paper to dry. To make the leprechaun, draw a buckle on a green construction paper hat. Then glue the hat to a six-inch tagboard circle. Draw facial features on the circle. Finally, glue rotini pasta to the leprechaun to resemble a beard. What a jolly fellow!

Heather Campbell
HCDS
Pennington, NJ

Arts & Crafts for Little Hands

"Egg-cellent" Easter Card!

To make a card, fold a sheet of 9" x 12" construction paper in half. Cut an egg shape from the card, leaving the fold intact. Use a marker to label the front and inside of the card with the words shown. Then decorate the front of the card to resemble an Easter egg. Next, press a finger in yellow tempera paint and make several fingerprints inside the card. When the paint is dry, use fine-tip permanent markers to decorate each print to resemble a chick. Finally, write your name inside the card.

Gayle Newman
Divine St. United Methodist Church Preschool
Dunn, NC

Up, Up, and Away!

Wallpaper samples are the key to this uplifting art experience! Cut several diamond shapes (kites) from a variety of wallpaper samples. Also cut several lengths of colorful curling-ribbon tails. Glue the kites to a sheet of blue construction paper. Then glue one end of each tail to each kite so that the tails dangle freely. Finally, pull and stretch cotton balls and glue them to the paper to resemble clouds.

Barb Stefaniuk
Kerrobert Tiny Tot Playschool
Kerrobert, Saskatchewan, Canada

41

Pom-Pom Pals

Brighten your classroom with these colorful caterpillars! To begin, make a green leaf cutout and then use fancy-edged scissors to cut a bite shape from the leaf. Draw a line on the leaf and then squeeze glue on the line. Place a row of colorful pom-poms on the glue to resemble a caterpillar. If desired, glue construction paper eyes and antennae to the caterpillar. When the glue is dry, display the leaves on a tree shape cut from bulletin board paper.

Lisa Migliaccio
Buffalo Hearing and Speech Center
Buffalo, NY

Fabulous Flower Garden!

Here's an artsy garden filled with beautiful blooms! Brush brown tempera paint on a sheet of 9" x 12" green construction paper. Drag a toy rake or a hair pick over the wet paint to make lines that resemble rows in a garden. After the paint is dry, crumple squares of brightly colored tissue paper and glue them to the garden to resemble flowers. If desired, embellish the scene with cut paper worms or insects.

Arts & Crafts for Little Hands

Buzzy Little Bees

A potato masher is the key to making these adorable bees! Dip a potato masher into a shallow pan of black tempera paint. Then press the masher on a yellow sheet of construction paper. Continue in the same way to make several bees. When the paint is dry, glue tissue paper wings and a construction paper eye to each bee. Then use a black marker to further embellish the scene. There's sure to be quite a buzz about these cute projects!

Sandy Barker
Early Childhood Family Education
Cottage Grove, MN

Beautiful Bubbles

After an experience making bubbles with bubble solution, invite students to make these lovely pieces of art! Gather yarn in different shades of blue; then snip the yarn into different lengths. To make a bubble picture, brush a thick layer of glue on a sheet of tagboard. Then place pieces of yarn on the glue, carefully shaping the yarn into circles to resemble bubbles.

Michelle Freed
Peru State College
Peru, NE

Fabulous Fireworks!

Cut a supply of cotton swabs in half. Place red, white, and blue tempera paint in separate containers. Mix a small amount of white glue with each color of paint. To make fabulous fireworks, dip the end of a prepared cotton swab in a desired paint color; then place the swab on a sheet of black construction paper. Continue in the same way, placing the swabs in an arrangement similar to the one shown to resemble fireworks. When a desired effect is achieved, sprinkle gold glitter over the swabs. What a fantastic fireworks display!

Camille Cooper
Emporia State University Center for Early Childhood Education
Emporia, KS

Cool Castle

Use building blocks to make two-dimensional sandcastles! Place several building blocks in a shallow tray of brown tempera paint. Then remove a block and press it on a sheet of construction paper. Continue in the same way with other blocks to make a castle. Then sprinkle sand over the wet paint. When the paint is dry, brush off the excess sand. Waves won't be able to knock down this splendid sandcastle!

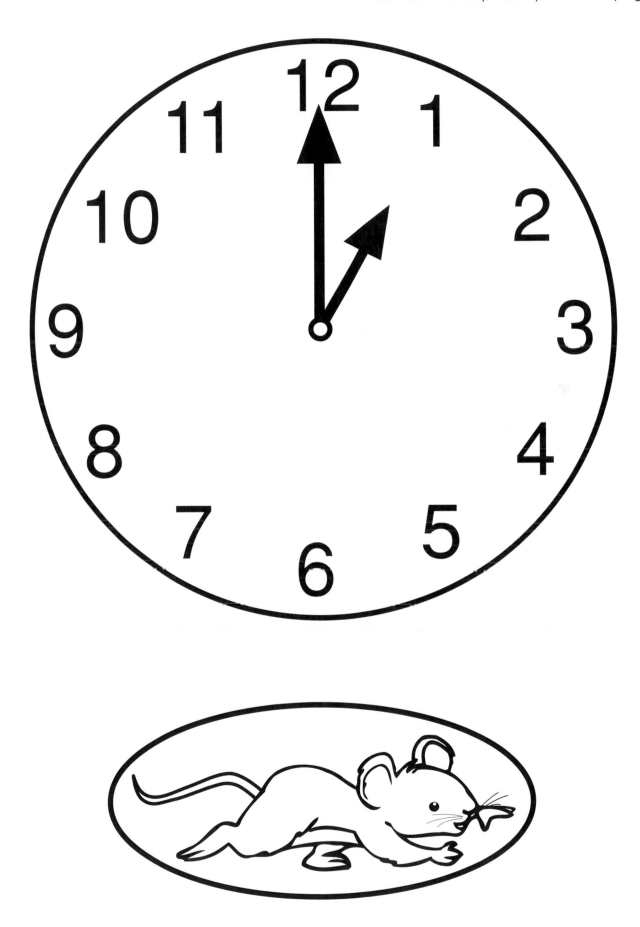

Log Pattern
Use with "Snoozing Ladybugs" on page 35.

GET MOVING!

Get Moving!

Movement Ideas for Preschoolers

Action Spinner

This spinner is labeled with different actions for lots of movement fun! Mount a copy of the spinner pattern (page 59) onto tagboard. Gather youngsters in a circle and place the spinner in the center. Arrange a pencil and a jumbo paper clip in the center of the spinner as shown. As you hold the pencil, encourage a child to spin the paper clip. Name the action the spinner lands on; then encourage the youngster to name a number from 1 to 10. Lead the students in repeating the action the chosen number of times. Then invite another child to spin the action spinner!

Ann Bruehler
Immanuel Lutheran Early Childhood Center
Charleston, IL

Awaken the Animals!

Little ones pretend to be animals with this engaging song and activity! Have youngsters pretend to be sleeping cats as you sing the song shown. After the final line of the song, prompt the students to wake up and move around like cats. Repeat the activity several times, substituting a different animal each time!

(sung to the tune of "Twinkle, Twinkle, Little Star")

[Cats] are sleeping on the floor
By the bookcase, near the door.
Sleeping here and sleeping there,
[Cats] are sleeping everywhere.
Now it's time, there's no mistake:
Time for all the [cats] to wake!

Peg Piepenburg
Woodson YMCA
Wausau, WI

Whimsical Walking

Whether youngsters are moving around the classroom or walking through the halls, they're sure to enjoy these holiday-related and seasonal inspirations.

- For fall, encourage youngsters to drift along like quietly falling leaves.
- At Thanksgiving time, have students quietly strut like turkeys.
- For winter, encourage children to float like drifting snow-flakes.
- For St. Patrick's Day, have students tiptoe like leprechauns secretly moving their pots of gold.
- For spring, invite youngsters to creep like quiet little caterpillars.
- For summer, have students glide silently like sailboats on a lake.

Krista Vilbig
Kristagarden
Idaho Falls, ID

Moving to Music

This activity alleviates youngsters' wiggles and trains their ears to hear different pitches! Have students crouch low to the floor. Then play a xylophone from the lower pitches to the higher pitches. As you play, encourage students to stand slowly. Reverse directions on the xylophone and prompt the students to gradually return to their crouching positions. Repeat the activity several times, adding interest by reversing directions in the middle of the scale and by increasing and decreasing the tempo.

Christina Lynch
Corpus Christi School
Rochester, NY

Get Moving!

Movement Ideas for Preschoolers

A Circle of Friends

Stand in a circle with your youngsters in a large open area. Toss a beach ball up in the air and say, "My friend, [student's name]," naming the child standing next to you. Encourage the child to pick up the ball, come back to the circle, and repeat the process, calling out the name of the next child in the circle. Continue in the same way with each remaining youngster, having the final child name you as his friend!

Marcia Buchanan
Philadelphia, PA

My friend, Taylor!

1, 2, 3, 4!

Reach the Teacher

Hopping, walking, or crawling. With this activity, youngsters travel across the floor in a variety of ways! To begin, stand in an open area several yards away from your youngsters. Encourage the children to chant, "Teacher, teacher, far away, how will we get to you today?" Call out a number and a type of movement. For example, you might say "four jumps" or "six tiptoe steps." Then have youngsters complete the given movement. Repeat the process, calling out different numbers and types of movement until the youngsters reach you. Then designate a child to be the teacher and join your students for another round!

Lois Otten
Kingdom Kids Preschool
Sheboygan, WI

Find Your Nest!

This idea not only gets your little gobblers moving, but also helps them identify colors! Make a class supply of colorful construction paper circles to represent nests. Laminate the nests for durability. Then scatter them on the floor around your room. Play recorded music and have youngsters strut around the room pretending to be turkeys. After they've had ample strutting time, say, "Turkeys, turkeys, sit on a nest!" Then encourage youngsters to find a nest and sit on it. Ask each student what color his nest is. After each youngster has had an opportunity to respond, instruct the students to stand and then play another round!

GOBBLE! GOBBLE!

A Rhythmic Rainbow

Tie lengths of colorful ribbon to each of several ponytail holders. Then give each youngster a holder and have her place it on her wrist. Play recorded music and encourage each child to move to the music as desired. Students will be fascinated by the beautiful rainbow of color that follows them wherever they go!

Marie Warren
Kids Time Preschool
Clearwater, FL

Get Moving!

Movement Ideas for Preschoolers

Candy Cane Lane

If youngsters aren't careful when they walk down Candy Cane Lane, they just might end up stepping in the caramel quicksand! Glue candy cane cutouts on a length of bulletin board paper as shown to make a meandering path. Draw areas of caramel quicksand near the path. Then laminate the bulletin board paper and place it on the floor. Have a youngster carefully walk down Candy Cane Lane. If she veers from the path and gets "stuck" in the quicksand, encourage a classmate to help her out of the sticky situation!

Patricia Wythe
Peace Lutheran Christian Preschool
Galloway, NJ

A Short Winter's Nap

This mellow movement idea is sure to have little ones relaxed and ready to focus! To begin, have students stand. After you turn out the lights, sprinkle each child with imaginary sleeping dust. Then encourage him to gently lie down and pretend to fall asleep. After several moments, turn the lights back on and encourage little ones to yawn, stretch both their arms and legs, and then stand up. Continue in the same way for several rounds.

Floating Flakes

Simple hand puppets make nifty props for this open-ended movement activity! Have each child seal a business-size envelope. Then encourage him to cut the envelope in half and glue a snowflake cutout to each half. When the glue is dry, have each child slip the resulting puppets onto his hands. Play a recording of festive music and encourage youngsters to move their snowflakes and bodies to the music to create a blizzard right in the classroom!

Toss It In!

Give a beanbag toss a seasonal twist with a Santa hat! Gather a small group of youngsters and give each child a beanbag. Hold the Santa hat upside down and have each child toss his beanbag into the hat. When students are comfortable with this activity, have children take turns holding the hat while the remaining youngsters toss the beanbags.

Nancy Jandreau
Kids Corner Day Care
Potsdam, NY

53

Get Moving!

The Telephone Hop

At this center, youngsters practice phone numbers and develop gross-motor skills! Write each number from zero to nine on a separate sheet of 9" x 12" construction paper. Use Con-Tact paper to attach the numbers to the floor to resemble a telephone keypad. Write each child's name and phone number on separate index cards and place the cards near the keypad. A child finds his name, reads his phone number aloud, and then hops from number to number in sequence on the keypad.

Marilyn Kellen
MMN Elementary
Madison, MN

Catch the Lovebugs!

Your classroom is infested with lovebugs! No doubt your little ones will delight in catching them all. Make several red construction paper copies of the lovebug cards on page 60. Hide the bugs near a center; then provide access to a butterfly net and a container with a lid. (You may wish to punch holes in the lid as you would do if the bugs were real.) A youngster sneaks up on a lovebug, catches it in the net, and then places it in the container. He continues in the same way until he has caught all of the lovebugs!

adapted from an idea by Krista Vilbig
Kristagarden
Idaho Falls, ID

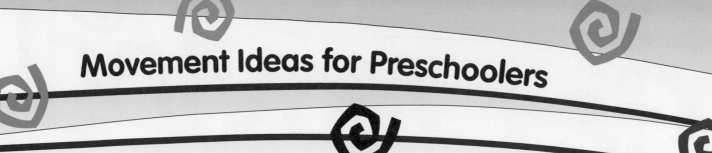

The Rainbow Pokey

Reinforce colors with this vivid version of The Hokey-Pokey! Cut lengths of crepe paper streamers in at least three different colors to make a class supply. Then give each child a streamer. Lead youngsters in singing the song, encouraging students with red streamers to complete the actions. Next, repeat the song, substituting the underlined words with the word *rainbow,* prompting all the students to join in. Continue in a similar way for several verses, changing the color word or substituting the word *rainbow* for each repetition.

(sung to the tune of "The Hokey-Pokey")

You put the [red streamer] in.
You put the [red streamer] out.
You put the [red streamer] in
And you shake it all about.
You shake your colored streamer(s) cause you know without a doubt
[Red]'s what it's all about!

Camille Cooper
Emporia State University Center for Early Childhood Education
Emporia, KS

Shakin' Shamrocks

Gather youngsters around a parachute (or a large bedsheet) and place a supply of shamrock cutouts on it. Have each child grab an edge of the parachute and then shake it up and down, causing the shamrocks to bounce in the air and scatter on the floor. Have the students put the parachute down, gather up the shamrocks, and then place them back in the parachute. No doubt little ones will want to play another round of Shakin' Shamrocks!

Sharon King
Center City Child Care
Amarillo, TX

Get Moving!

Fast and Slow

With this exciting little chant, youngsters practice a variety of movements at different speeds!

Flap, flap, flap your arms as slowly as you can.
Flap, flap, flap your arms as quickly as you can.

Nod, nod, nod your head as slowly as you can.
Nod, nod, nod your head as quickly as you can.

Stomp, stomp, stomp your feet as slowly as you can.
Stomp, stomp, stomp your feet as quickly as you can.

Continue with *bend your knees, shake your hands,* and *shrug your shoulders.*

Judie Wetherby
Breezy Point Day School
Langhorne, PA

Buzzing Bracelets

Your busy little bees will love zooming around the room with these adorable bracelets! Give each youngster half of a small cardboard tube and encourage her to paint black and yellow stripes on it, as shown, to resemble a bee. Have the child glue construction paper antennae and tissue paper wings to her bee. When the projects are dry, cut each tube open to make a cuff-style bracelet. Play a recording of upbeat music. Then have students don their bracelets and "fly" their bees around the room. For a more mellow variation, have students make butterfly bracelets in a similar way and move to a recording of slower music.

Marie Warren
Kids' Time Preschool
Clearwater, FL

Catch the Fly

Little ones develop number recognition skills with this fun frog activity. Label each of ten lily pad cutouts with a different numeral from 1 to 10. Use Con-Tact paper to attach the lily pads to your classroom floor, in order, in a meandering row. Two youngsters visit the area. One child places a black pom-pom (fly) on one of the lily pads. His partner hops from lily pad number 1 to the lily pad with the fly as she recites the numbers. After she has retrieved the fly, she hops back to number 1. Then the partners switch roles. The students continue in the same way for several turns.

Christy McNeal
Hudson, IA

Awake.

Asleep, Asleep, Awake

Have students play this game in a way similar to the traditional game of Duck, Duck, Goose. Arrange youngsters in a circle. Choose a volunteer and then encourage the remaining youngsters to pretend to be asleep. Have the volunteer walk around the outside of the circle, saying, "Asleep," as she lightly taps each child on the shoulder. She continues in this way with several classmates. Then she taps a child and says, "Awake." The child who is now awake leads all the others in a simple exercise, such as toe touches, jogging in place, or stretching. Have all the youngsters sit down. Then choose a new volunteer to begin another round.

Michele Story
Shandon Weekday School
Columbia, SC

Get Moving!

Pop! Pop! Pop!

Youngsters experience the sights and sounds of the Fourth of July with this fun activity. Use masking tape to attach a large piece of bubble wrap to the floor. Invite a small group of youngsters to the bubble wrap and give each child lengths of red, white, and blue streamers. Then softly play a recording of patriotic music while youngsters march over the bubble wrap and wave their streamers. That sounds just like fireworks!

Erica Avila
Wee Care Learning Center
Festus, MO

Between the Lines

Attach two parallel lines of tape to your floor. Have half of your youngsters stand on one line and the remaining half on the other line. Invite a volunteer to travel between the lines doing any movement he wishes. As he travels, lead the remaining youngsters in singing the song shown and clapping to the beat. When he is finished, have the youngster join his line once again. Then repeat the process with other youngsters, changing the name and pronoun in the song appropriately.

(sung to the tune of "The Farmer in the Dell")

Who's moving down the street?
Who's groovin' to the beat?
Yes, [Justin]'s got some groovin' feet
As [he] moves to the beat.

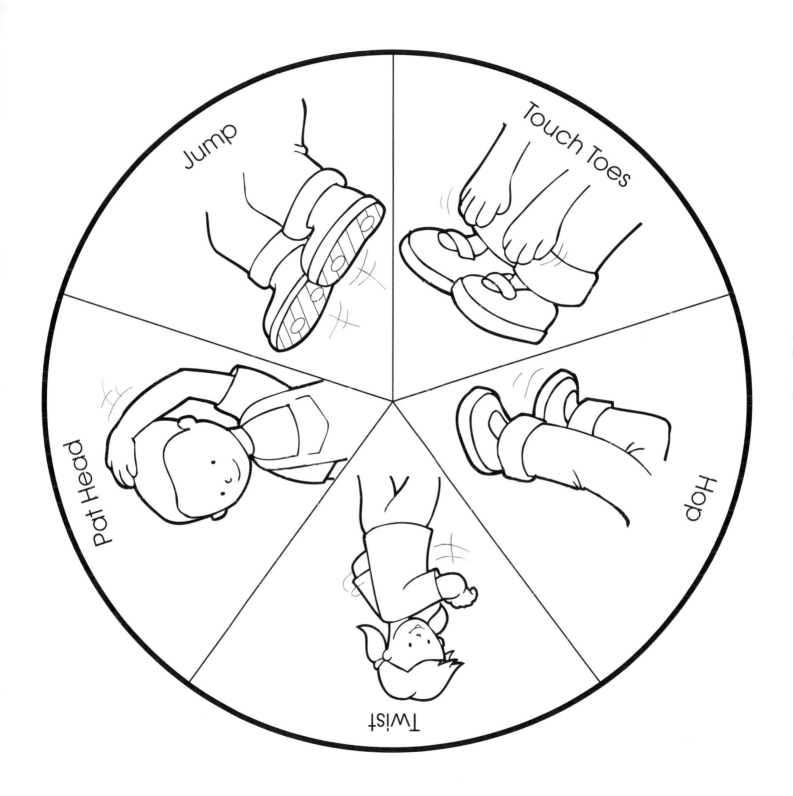

Lovebug Cards
Use with "Catch the Lovebugs!" on page 54.

Management Tips
& Timesavers

Management Tips & Timesavers

Crayon Holders

Keep crayons neat and organized with soap containers! Gather a class supply of soap containers, plus a few extras for youngsters who arrive midyear. Place a set of crayons in each container and close the lid. Then use a permanent marker to label each lid with a different child's name. *Sarah Booth, Messiah Nursery School, South Williamsport, PA*

Not-So-Permanent Writing

It's easy to remove permanent marker from laminated nametags and reproducibles. Simply spray whiteboard cleaner on the laminated surface and then wipe off the writing with a paper towel. Those markers weren't so permanent after all! *Starla Johnson, Discovery Elementary School, Brigham City, UT*

Preschool Portfolios

Use binders and page protectors to make simple portfolios for your youngsters! Label each binder with a child's name and then place several page protectors in each binder. When a student completes a piece of work for her portfolio, have her slide the work into a page protector in her binder. No doubt parents will be delighted to receive this portfolio as a gift at the end of the year! *Patty Young, Fun-N-Games, Inc., Haymarket, VA*

Teacher Tote

A gardening tote makes a terrific teacher bag! The extra wide opening allows you to find papers and books in a snap. Plus the handy outside pockets hold everything from markers to scissors! *Michele Knoth, Allisonville Christian Preschool, Indianapolis, IN*

Bonus Bulletin Board

When you need an extra bulletin board, try this simple tip! Purchase a trifold display board (the kind commonly used for science fair projects) from your local office supply store. Attach desired papers and artwork to the board. Then display this mobile bulletin board where desired. When the school year is at an end, remove any papers from the board, fold it, and then store the board for the next school year! *Nancy Goldberg, B'nai Israel Schilit Nursery School, Rockville, MD*

Management Tips & Timesavers

Waiting to Wash

Ease crowding in front of your classroom sink with colorful shapes. Use Con-Tact paper to attach a row of shape cutouts to the floor in front of your sink. When children stand in line to wash their hands, you can direct each youngster to stand on a specific shape! *Dorothy Stein, Christian Beginnings Preschool, Prince Frederick, MD*

The Sharing Snowball

With this snowball prop, youngsters learn to take turns sharing information! Let a child hold the snowball (a large foam ball) when he shares information during circle time. When he is finished sharing, encourage him to gently toss the snowball to another child who wishes to talk! *Catherine Brubaker, Girard Head Start, Coldwater, MI*

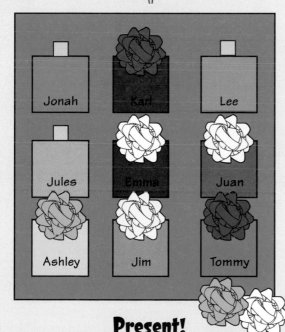

Present!

To make this holiday attendance display, attach to a board a personalized present cutout for each child. Place the hook end of a Velcro fastener above each present and each corresponding loop end on the back of a separate gift bow. At the beginning of each school day, have each child attach a bow to his present! *Beth Baranowski, Roselle Park, NJ*

Beat the Buzzer

Set a kitchen timer for a few minutes directly before youngsters get ready to go outside. This discourages dawdling and youngsters have a great time trying to beat the buzzer. As students improve, set the timer for fewer minutes. *Hilarie Hutt, Summit School, Summit, SD*

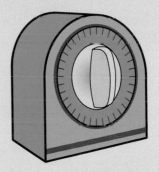

Imitating Animals

Inspire good behavior with animal imitations! To settle youngsters in for circle time, encourage them to be "as quiet as a mouse" and to listen with their "big elephant ears." Finally, when it's time to move to another activity, have them walk with "slow turtle feet." Now that's more fun than a barrel of monkeys! *Jana Sanderson, Rainbow School, Stockton, CA*

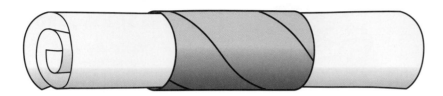

Totally Tubular

Cardboard tubes make handy holders for youngsters' artwork. Simply roll up the artwork, slip it in a tube, and send it home with the youngster. The artwork stays nice and neat so it can be admired at home! *Marisol Rodriguez, Little Learners, Hammond, IN*

Glue on a Stick

Here's an easy method for using white glue with your little ones. Pour a small amount of glue on a paper plate. Then have each child use a craft stick to scoop up the glue and place it on her project! *Trystahjill Harns, Lakeside Christian School, East Lansing, MI*

Simple Flannelboard Cutouts

For quick and easy flannelboard cutouts, simply place felt in your die-cut machine and punch out pieces just as you would when using paper. What a simple way to make props for youngsters' favorite songs and stories! *Michele Barry, USD 506 Mound Valley Grade School, Mound Valley, KS*

Personal Plates

How can youngsters keep track of small pieces needed for projects? They simply place them on personalized plates! Then, when the child is finished with the project, he can place it on top of the plate and you automatically know who the project belongs to! *Sharon A. Beintema, St. John Vianney Preschool, Wyoming, MI*

Soothing Music

While students work on an art project, play a recording of classical music by a well-known composer. Encourage youngsters to talk quietly while the music is playing. After several art experiences, your youngsters just might begin requesting favorite composers! *Dorothy Hsu, Grace Brethren Preschool, Westerville, OH*

Management Tips & Timesavers

Storing Calendar Pieces

Organize and store numbered calendar cutouts by placing them in an index card file with monthly dividers. No more lost calendar pieces! *Cathy Gorman, Montgomery Kid Connection, Skillman, NJ*

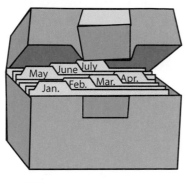

Who's Here?

Instead of calling youngsters' names to find out who is present for the day, recite their addresses. What a nice way to combine a daily task with a required preschool skill! *Linda Bille, Riviera United Methodist Preschool, Redondo Beach, CA*

On a Roll

Transition youngsters from circle time to their next activity with this quick chant. Simply say the first two lines of the chant below and then roll a ball to the child named. Then recite the final two lines and have her roll the ball back to you before she moves to the next activity.

[Jasmine, Jasmine] sitting
  straight and tall,
Can you catch the rolling
  ball?
[Jasmine, Jasmine], you have
  the ball!
Now roll it back and leave
  us all.

Cindy Farnham, Boothbay Headstart, Boothbay, ME

Our spring open house is tonight at 6:30!

Don't forget our field trip to the zoo on Monday!

Handy Bracelets

Send home important reminders on easy-to-make student bracelets. For each child, make a paper strip displaying the information. Then tape a strip around each child's wrist. Parents can read the note while youngsters proudly show off their new jewelry! *Donna Bunn, Crystal River Primary School, Crystal River, FL*

"Eggs-tra" Special Behavior

Encourage kind behavior in the classroom with a bunny display! Post an Easter basket cutout filled with eggs. Then mount a bunny cutout several feet from the basket. Each time your students show kind behavior, move the bunny closer to the basket. When the bunny reaches the basket, celebrate with youngsters by sharing a special treat! *Susan Luengen, Makalapa Elementary, Honolulu, HI*

Management Tips & Timesavers

PRESCHOOL

On the Level

To place letters in a straight line on your bulletin board, measure down from the top of the board to the level where you want the lettering to begin. Make a mark on the board. Then repeat the process to show approximately where you want the lettering to end. Tack a length of elastic from the first mark to the second. Then use the elastic as a guide for placing your lettering. When you're finished, just remove the elastic and tacks. *Louise Younger, Wee Friends Preschool, Hays, KS*

Lips and Hips

This rhyming reminder helps little ones remember to be quiet and listen. Simply say, "Lips and hips," and have each youngster put one hand on her hips and the pointer finger of her other hand against her lips. This gives little hands something to do while they're waiting for directions. *Sara Doty, Brockport Child Care Center, Brockport, NY*

Cups for Cuttings

Give each child a clean cake frosting container (or other flat-bottomed container) when it's time for cut-and-paste projects. The child cuts out the necessary pieces and then places them in her container for safekeeping until it's time to glue them down. *Susan LaBrie, New Life Christian Preschool, Maple Valley, WA*

Joshua

All Hands to the Sink!

When youngsters are completing a project that involves making handprints, set up your art station near your classroom sink. Then students can make prints and wash up afterward all in one location! *Karen Cummins, Catholic Social Services of Monroe/Head Start, Temperance, MI*

Title Page Tip

To remember which classroom books have coordinating activities in your files, label the title pages with star stickers. When you open the book you'll be reminded right away to check your files for engaging activities. *Kara Coffman, Newfield Elementary, Newfield, NY*

It's Circle Time

It's Circle Time

Names and Faces

What do you get when you add photographs to a name recognition activity? A learning opportunity that's picture-perfect! Tape a photo of each child to a sheet of poster board. Laminate the board for durability. Then place the hook side of a Velcro fastener next to each photo. Place each remaining loop side on the back of a different student nametag. Gather students for circle time and hold up a nametag. Have the corresponding child take his nametag and place it next to his photo. Continue in the same way with each remaining nametag. Not only do students become more familiar with their own written names, but they also link classmates' names to their faces!

Staci Peterson
Voyager Elementary
Alexandria, MN

What's the Weather?

There's sure to be a downpour of excitement when you combine dress-up time with a discussion of the current weather! Collect clothing and accessories appropriate for various types of weather; then place the items in a box. During the weather portion of your morning routine, help a volunteer choose items from the box to use to dress and accessorize for the current weather. Encourage youngsters to explain why the items chosen are appropriate. Then have the child place the items back in the container. That rain slicker keeps clothing dry!

Jennifer Drewnowski
Peekaboo Playhouse
Cranberry, PA

Friends Forever

Celebrate friendship with an action chant that's perfect for circle-time sharing! Help each child sit facing a partner. Then lead students in reciting the chant, encouraging each youngster to shake hands with his partner during the second, fourth, and sixth lines. Repeat this activity several times, making sure each child has a new partner each time!

Friends are for sharing and friends are for caring.
I'm so glad we're friends!
Friends are for singing and friends are for swinging.
I'm so glad we're friends!
Friends are for sliding and seeking and hiding.
I'm so glad we're friends!

Cynthia Holcomb
Education Service Center XV
San Angelo, TX

Shape Safari

When you take little ones on a shape safari, they're sure to roar with approval! To enhance the experience, make binoculars for each child by hot-gluing pairs of cardboard tubes together as shown. To begin, display a rectangle cutout and help students identify the shape. Then lead them in reciting the chant shown before they use their binoculars to look for rectangles in your classroom. If desired, keep a tally of the rectangles found. Go on future shape safaris with your little ones, encouraging them to search for circles, triangles, and squares!

We're going on a shape hunt.
We're looking all around.
There are so many [rectangles]
Waiting to be found.

Allison Covington
Alexandria Country Day School
Alexandria, LA

Feeling Familiar?

Youngsters familiarize themselves with the classroom with this twist on a traditional five-senses activity! Take an item from each of several areas in your classroom, such as a block from the block center, a clean paintbrush from the art center, and a book from the bookcase. Place the items in a feely box. Invite a child to reach into the box and feel an item. After he attempts to identify the item, have him pull it out for everyone to see. Next, explain to youngsters where in the room you found the item and what can be done with the item when students visit that area. Repeat the process for each item in the box. What a neat way for youngsters to get in touch with their surroundings!

Peggy Wieck
Litchfield Prekindergarten
Litchfield, IL

It's Circle Time

Rhyme Time!

Gather a beanbag for yourself and for each of your youngsters. After you give each child his beanbag, say, "I can rhyme. Yes, it's true. This word rhymes with part of you!" Place your beanbag on your head and say, "Bread." Encourage each child to place his beanbag on his head and say, "Bread, head." Continue in the same way, placing the beanbag against different body parts, such as your knee, ear, foot, and tummy. This activity is sure to make little ones giggle!

Amy Spencer
R.B. Stewart Elementary
Leoti, KS

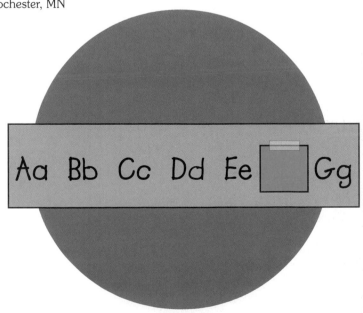

Bread, head!

Faces and Feelings

Encourage youngsters to share their emotions with help from a pumpkin pal! Gather a few small pumpkins. Use a permanent marker to draw a different face on each pumpkin to represent different emotions. Then display the pumpkins near your circle-time area. Encourage students to describe each pumpkin's feelings based on its facial expression. Then invite a volunteer to describe her emotions as she holds the corresponding pumpkin. Continue in the same way with other student volunteers.

adapted from an idea by Renee Bakken
Head Start
Rochester, MN

Mystery Letter Sing-Along

Encourage children to close their eyes as you tape a piece of paper over a letter on your classroom alphabet display. Have youngsters open their eyes and guess what the letter might be. Then lead students in singing "The Alphabet Song" as you point to each letter on the display, stopping directly before the covered letter. Have children identify the letter. Then remove the paper and continue singing the song. The mystery letter is *F!*

Gail Marsh
Pacific, MO

Aa Bb Cc Dd Ee ☐ Gg

It's the Shape Monster!

To make a shape monster, cover a sturdy box with colorful paper; then use a craft knife to cut a hole in the box to resemble a mouth. Embellish the box as desired to complete the monster. To begin, give each child a colorful shape cutout. Recite the chant below with your youngsters. Then encourage all the children with purple triangles to place them in the monster's mouth. Continue in the same way with other shapes. Yum!

Shape monster, shape monster, munch, munch, munch. How about a [purple triangle] for lunch?

Amy Aloi
Bollman Bridge Elementary RECC
Jessup, MD

Howdy, Partner!

Little ones practice following directions with this partner activity! Make pairs of colorful cutouts to match the current season. To begin, give each child a cutout. Then encourage each youngster to find the classmate with the matching cutout. Have the resulting sets of partners stand together and place their cutouts on the floor. Then give the partners directions to follow, such as those provided.

Suggested directions:
Look at your partner and say, "Howdy, partner!"
Shake hands with your partner.
Link arms with your partner.
Tell your partner your name.
Make a silly face at your partner.
Smile at your partner.
Wave and say, "See you later, partner!"

Paulette Shupak
Gregory Gardens Preschool
Pleasant Hill, CA

It's Circle Time

How Many Stars?

Make ten star cutouts and ready them for flannelboard use. (If desired, add glitter details to each star.) Invite a child to place any desired number of stars on your flannelboard. Count the stars with your students. Then lead them in reciting the rhyme shown, substituting the appropriate number in the first line. Continue in the same way with different student volunteers.

I see [five] stars shining oh so bright,
Twinkling in the chilly sky on a winter's night.

adapted from an idea by Sue Fleischmann
Waukesha County Project Head Start
Waukesha, WI

Five!

Jingle All the Way!

This activity combines counting practice with some timely accompaniment! Have students count as they pass a jingle bell bracelet around the circle, stopping at the fifth child. Encourage the child to shake the bracelet enthusiastically. Then continue in the same way, beginning another round with the next child in the circle!

Melissa Rose
Early Childhood Alliance, Fort Wayne, IN

Santa's Cookies

Here's a fun seasonal twist on a traditional rhyme! Make a class supply of cookie cutouts and label each one with a different child's name. Provide access to a large decorative plate. Hold up a cookie and have students identify the name. Then lead them in reciting the chant shown. At the end of the chant, have the child place her cookie on Santa's plate.

All: Who will add a cookie to Santa's plate?
All: [Child's name] will add a cookie to Santa's plate.
Child: Who, me?
Teacher: Yes, you.
Child: Okay, will do!

Lori Sazinski, The Villages Charter Early Learning Center, The Villages, FL

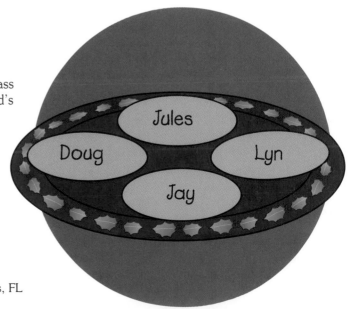

Squish and Bake

Here's a fun way to have little ones make cookies this holiday season! Pour a package of dry sugar cookie mix into a large resealable plastic bag. To begin, have students watch as you add any additional ingredients required in the package directions. Have students guess what they might be making. Then, after reinforcing the bag opening with tape, encourage each child to take a turn squishing the bag to mix the ingredients. When the ingredients are well blended, snip off a corner of the bag and squeeze individual cookies onto a baking sheet. Have students decorate the cookies with colorful sprinkles. After baking and cooling the cookies, invite little ones to have a snack!

Susan Schoelkopf
Centralia College Children's Lab School
Centralia, WA

I'm your friend!

Who's My Friend?

For this fun group game, have a volunteer stand with her back to the rest of the class. Prompt the child to ask, "Who's my friend?" Then point to a student and encourage her to say, "I'm your friend!" Invite the child to turn around and guess the friend's identity. Once she guesses correctly (with some hints from you, if needed) have her return to the group. Then invite her friend to become the next volunteer!

Eve Dutkiewicz
Chavez Learning Station
Kenosha, WI

It's Circle Time

Lucky's Feelings

Discuss an emotion each day with Lucky the Leprechaun! Make a simple construction paper leprechaun similar to the one shown, omitting the facial features. Laminate the leprechaun and post him in your classroom. Before youngsters arrive, use a wipe-off marker to draw facial features on the leprechaun that reflect a specific emotion. To begin, ask students to identify how Lucky is feeling. Then discuss situations that might make him feel this way. After youngsters have left for the day, wipe off the features and then draw new features on Lucky to represent a different emotion!

Katie Horton
St. John School
Seattle, WA

Mystery Noises

Preschoolers focus on their sense of hearing to guess common sounds! In advance, make a recording of common sounds, such as a telephone ringing, popcorn popping, a door closing, water running, and ice being dropped into a glass. Play the first sound; then stop the recorder and give youngsters an opportunity to guess what it is. After several guesses, reveal the name of the sound. Then continue in the same way with the remaining sounds.

Sharon J. Young
Bright Start
Greer, SC

Pop! Pop! Pop!

Getting Warmer!

This letter-recognition activity is sure to cause lots of giggles! Gather youngsters around your alphabet display. Choose a letter, such as *p*, and point to a letter near letter *p* on the display. Ask youngsters whether the letter you're pointing to is *p*. After students confirm that the letter is not *p*, point to another letter nearby and ask students whether you are getting warmer (closer to the letter *p*) or colder (farther away from the letter *p*). Continue in the same way until youngsters lead you to the correct letter. There it is!

Linda Bille
Riviera United Methodist Preschool
Redondo Beach, CA

NOPQR

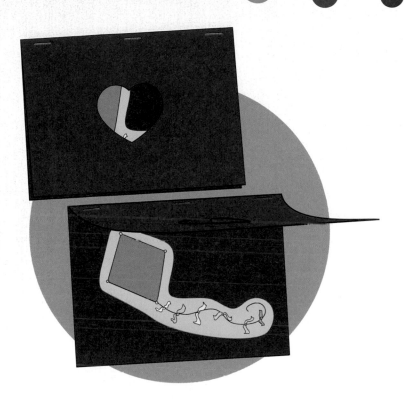

Hidden Pictures

Cut a picture from a magazine; then attach the picture to a 9" x 12" sheet of construction paper. Cut a small heart from the center of an identical piece of paper. After stacking the papers with the heart on top, staple them together as shown. Make several more viewers in this same way. Have students try to identify each picture by looking only at the portion that shows through the heart. Then reveal the picture. It's a kite!

Amber Baker
Learn a Lot Christian Preschool
Mooresville, IN

Whose Valentine?

Prepare a class supply of heart cutouts, each one labeled with the phrase "Won't you please be mine?" On the back of each heart, write a different child's name. To begin, hold up a heart so students can't see the name. Then lead them in singing the song below. During the fourth line of the song, flip the heart over to reveal the child's name. Then guide students to sing the final line. Finally, give the heart to the child to take home. Repeat the process with each remaining heart.

(sung to the tune of "Clementine")

It's so lovely.
It's so lovely.
It says, "Won't you please be mine?"
Wonder who it could belong to?
It is [child's name]'s valentine!

It's Circle Time

Student I Spy

This fun twist on a traditional game incorporates photographs of class activities! Glue to a sheet of poster board photos of activities and events taken throughout the year; then display the poster board in your circle-time area. Give youngsters a clue such as, "I spy a picture of Lee on the slide." Then invite a child to find on the poster board the picture you've described. When students are comfortable with this game, encourage them to supply the clues.

Joanne Monroe
Prince of Peace Lutheran Church and Preschool
Orlando, FL

Vivid Butterflies

Cut from felt a green butterfly body and several matching pairs of hearts (wings). Place the body on your flannelboard. Next, ask a volunteer to make a butterfly by adding wings in a specific color, such as red. Encourage the volunteer to find the red hearts and then place them next to the body, as shown, to make butterfly wings. Continue in the same way with the remaining hearts.

Rachael Knight
Little Hands Daycare
Alton, IA

Sing a Song of Letters

Print the letters *EIEIO* on a large index card. Also print other five-letter groupings on separate index cards, such as *SMSMA*. Lead youngsters in singing the traditional song "Old MacDonald Had a Farm," holding up the *EIEIO* card and pointing to each letter when appropriate. When students are comfortable with the song, introduce them to a new letter grouping. Then lead youngsters in singing the song, replacing *EIEIO* with the new set of letters.

Jennae Snow
Snow Preschool
St. George, UT

Watering the Flowers

Your little gardeners are sure to love this whimsical letter-recognition idea! Write a different letter on each of several flower cutouts. Scatter the flowers on the floor in your circle-time area. Then have youngsters sit in a circle around the flowers. Give a child an empty watering can, and encourage him to pretend to water one of the flowers. Help the child identify the letter on the chosen flower. Then encourage the child to give the watering can to another child in the circle. Continue in the same way until all of the flowers have been "watered."

Kelly Ash
Head Start
Waukesha, WI

An "Egg-cellent" Match

Gather a supply of plastic eggs, and label matching halves with identical numbers. Hide the bottom half of each egg in your classroom and place the top halves on a table. Have each youngster search for the bottom half of an egg. When she finds one, have her take it to the table to find the matching upper half. After she reattaches the halves, have her say the name of the number and place the egg in a basket in your circle-time area. Then encourage her to begin a search for another egg half!

Jennifer Gillis
Fair Acres Country Day School
Marstons Mills, MA

Ant Invaders

To prepare for this alphabet game, make a class supply of ant cutouts and label each one with a different letter. Spread a tablecloth on your floor and then scatter the ants on the cloth. To begin, explain that you want to have a picnic but all of these ants have invaded the area. Encourage a child to find an ant labeled with a specific letter and then give it to you. Repeat the process with each remaining child until all the ants have been removed. Then bring out a simple snack for everyone to enjoy— picnic-style!

Erica Crowder
Laurelville Head Start
Laurelville, OH

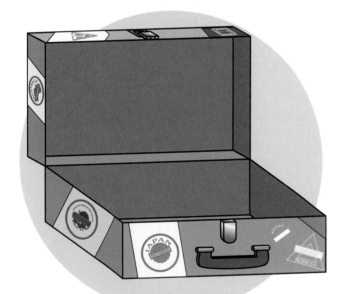

Going on Vacation

What would your little ones pack if they were going on a trip? Find out with this catchy rhyme and activity. Gather youngsters around an empty suitcase. After leading them in reciting the rhyme below, invite a child to name an item she would pack. Have her pretend to place the item in the suitcase. Then repeat the process several times, calling on a different child each time.

We're going on vacation to a far-off place.
What should we pack in our big suitcase?

Beth Mickle
First United Methodist Preschool
New Castle, PA

Getting Closer...

Your little ones will love this active game that reinforces letter sounds. Have a volunteer close his eyes while another youngster hides an object, such as a stuffed bear. Have the child open his eyes and then slowly search for the object. As he searches, encourage little ones to repeat the beginning sound of the item's name, saying it quietly when the child is far away from the object and increasing in loudness as he moves closer. Congratulate the child when he finds the item. Then play another round of the game, choosing new volunteers and hiding a different object.

Stephanie Schmidt
Lester B. Pearson Public School
Waterloo, Ontario, Canada

KIDS IN THE KITCHEN

KIDS IN THE KITCHEN

Put on your apron and step into the kitchen—with your kids, of course! What's on the menu? A generous portion of learning opportunities served up with a batch of fun!

Here's what to do:
- Collect the necessary ingredients and utensils using the lists on one of the recipe cards below.
- Photocopy the step-by-step recipe cards on page 81 or 82.
- Color the cards; then cut them out.
- Display the cards in your snack area.
- Follow the teacher preparation guidelines for that activity.

Pumpkin Spread

Ingredients for one:
slice of bread
2 tsp. spreadable margarine
2 tsp. canned pumpkin
⅛ tsp. sugar
cinnamon

Utensils and supplies:
pumpkin-shaped cookie cutter
measuring spoons
paper cup for each child
plastic spoon for each child
paper plate for each child
plastic knife for each child

Teacher preparation:
- Use the cookie cutter to cut each slice of bread into a pumpkin shape.
- Arrange the ingredients, cups, plates, spoons, and knives near the step-by-step recipe cards (page 81).

Ada Goren
Winston-Salem, NC

"Bear-y" Cute Cupcake

Ingredients for one:
chocolate cupcake
chocolate frosting
miniature pretzel
3 M&M's Minis candy pieces

Utensils and supplies:
paper plate for each child
plastic knife for each child

Teacher preparation:
- Arrange the ingredients, plates, and knives near the step-by-step recipe cards (page 82).

Kenya Leao
School of Nations
Brasília, Brazil

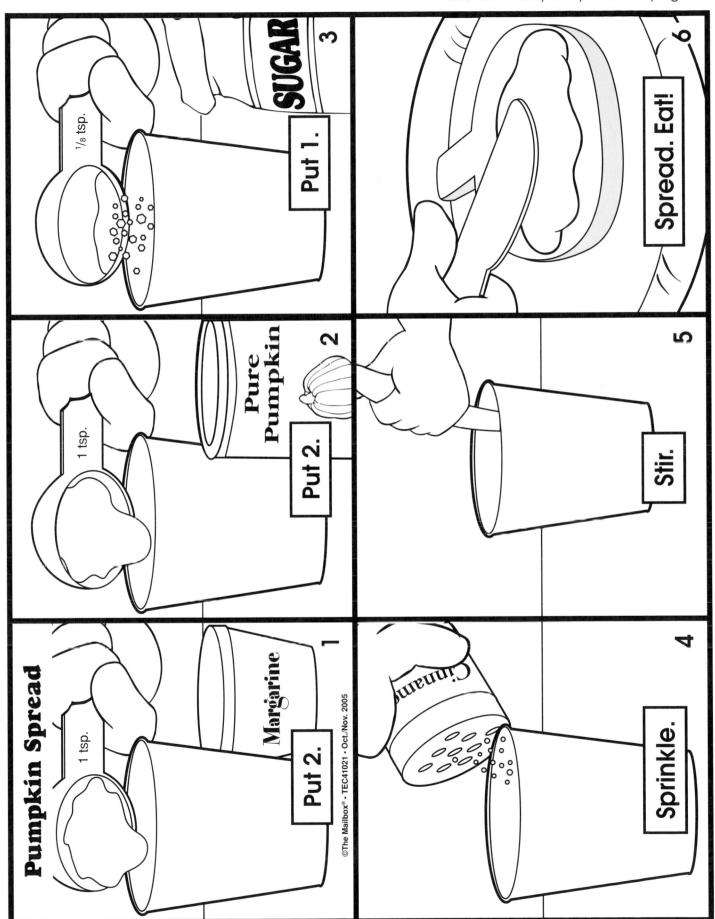

Pumpkin Spread

1 tsp. — Margarine — Put 2. — 1

1 tsp. — Pure Pumpkin — Put 2. — 2

1/8 tsp. — SUGAR — Put 1. — 3

Sprinkle. — Cinnamon — 4

Stir. — 5

Spread. Eat! — 6

©The Mailbox® · TEC41021 · Oct./Nov. 2005

Recipe Cards

Use with "'Bear-y' Cute Cupcake" on page 80.

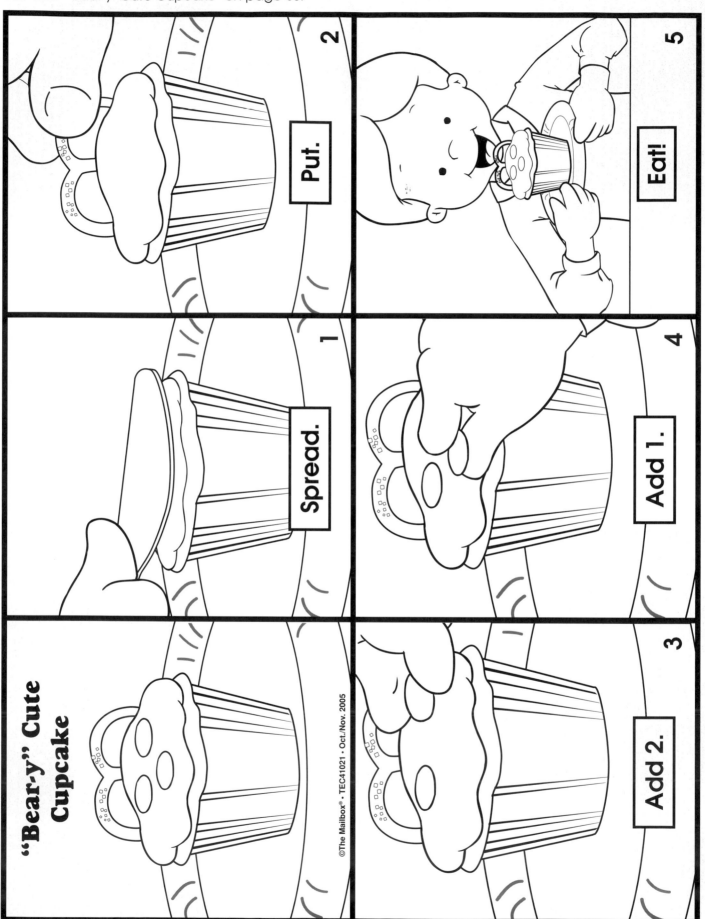

"Bear-y" Cute Cupcake

Spread.

Put.

Add 1.

Add 2.

Eat!

KIDS IN THE KITCHEN

Put on your apron and step into the kitchen—with your kids, of course! What's on the menu? A generous portion of learning opportunities served up with a batch of fun!

Here's what to do:
- Collect the necessary ingredients and utensils using the lists on one of the recipe cards below.
- Photocopy the recipe cards on page 84 or 85.
- Color the cards; then cut them out.
- Display the cards in your snack area.
- Follow the teacher preparation guidelines for that activity.

Christmas Cake

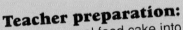

Ingredients for one:
small slice of angel food cake
green-tinted whipped cream (see below)
cherry pie filling

Utensils and supplies:
green food coloring
knife
plastic cup for each child
plastic knife for each child
napkin for each child
plastic spoon for each child, plus two extras

Teacher preparation:
Cut an angel food cake into small slices. Use food coloring to tint a container of whipped cream green. Place a spoon in both the whipped cream and pie filling. Arrange the ingredients, cups, napkins, and remaining utensils near the recipe cards (page 84).

Snowshoe Hare

Ingredients for one:
2 round crackers
cream cheese
2 thin apple slices
3 M&M's Minis candy pieces
6 shoestring potato pieces

Utensils and supplies:
paper plate for each child
plastic knife for each child

Teacher preparation:
Arrange the ingredients, plates, and knives near the recipe cards (page 85).

Recipe Cards

Use with "Christmas Cake" on page 83.

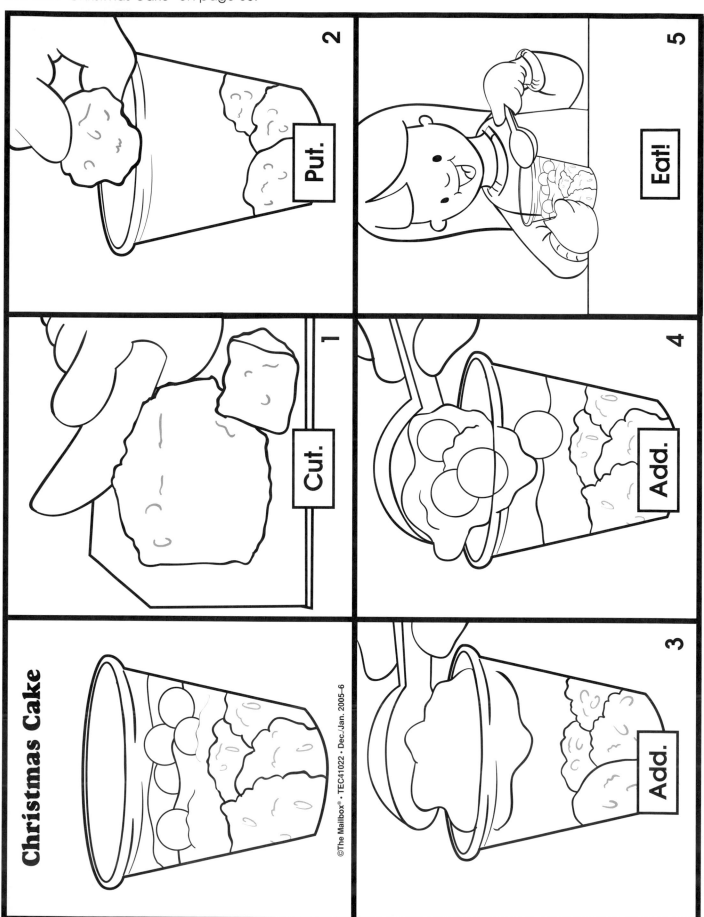

Christmas Cake

Cut. 1

Put. 2

Add. 3

Add. 4

Eat! 5

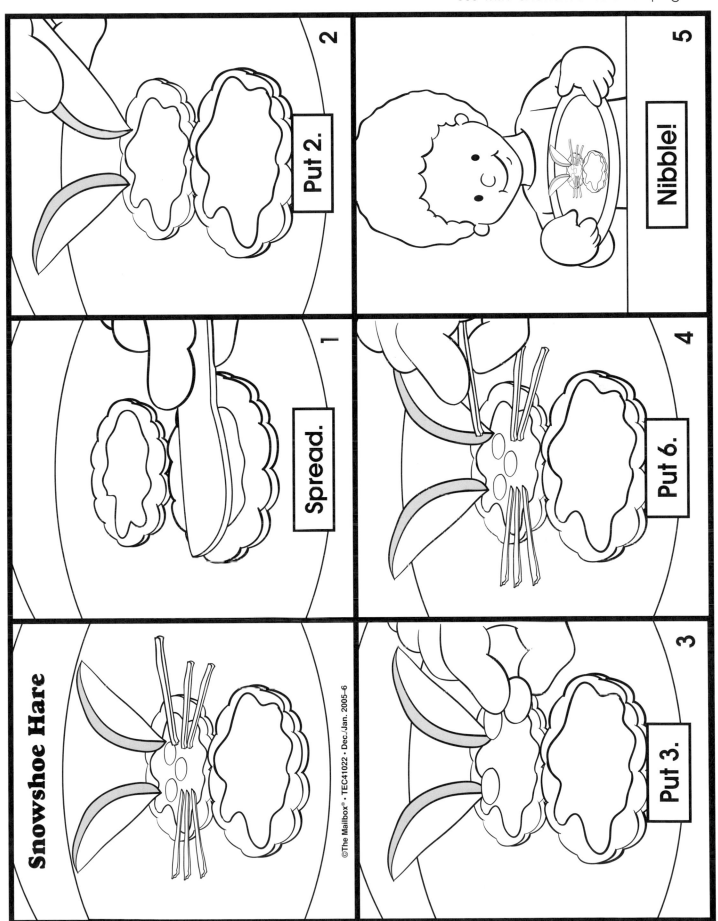

2 Put 2.

5 Nibble!

1 Spread.

4 Put 6.

Snowshoe Hare

3 Put 3.

KIDS IN THE KITCHEN

Serve up a batch of fun with a recipe that's just perfect for March! Then follow up the tasty snack with the activity shown below. It's worth its weight in gold!

To prepare for the snack:

- Collect the necessary ingredients and utensils using the lists on the recipe card.
- Photocopy the step-by-step recipe cards on page 87.
- Color the cards; then cut them out and display them in your snack area.
- Follow the teacher preparation guidelines for the snack.

Magic Leprechaun Pudding

Ingredients for one:
½ cup vanilla pudding
drop of green food coloring
E.L. Fudge sandwich cookie
   (leprechaun)

Utensils and supplies:
½ cup measuring cup
plastic cup for each child
plastic spoon for each child

Teacher preparation:
- Arrange the ingredients, utensils, and supplies near the step-by-step recipe cards.

Trudy McGowan
Loring-Flemming Elementary
Blackwood, NJ

Name _Tera_   Fine-motor skills
Lucky's Gold

Listen for directions.

After the Recipe

Now that your little ones have caught a leprechaun in their pudding, he's sure to lead them to his gold! Give each child a copy of page 88. Have her trace the dotted lines on the pot and then color the page as desired. Then have her press a film canister in a shallow pan of yellow paint and make prints above the pot to resemble gold!

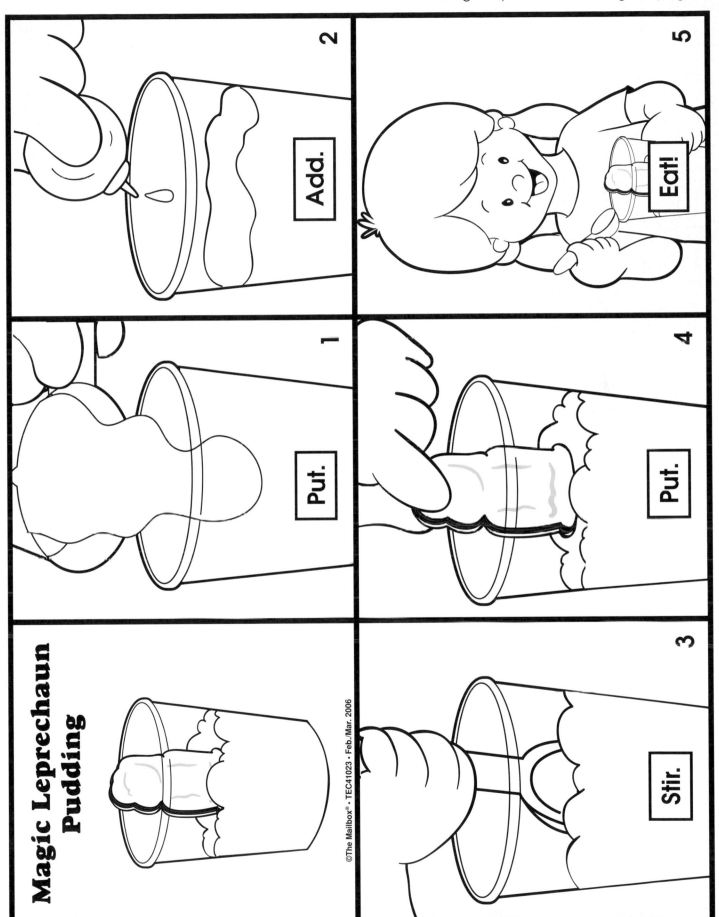

Magic Leprechaun Pudding

Put.

Add.

Stir.

Put.

Eat!

Name _____

Lucky's Gold

Listen for directions.

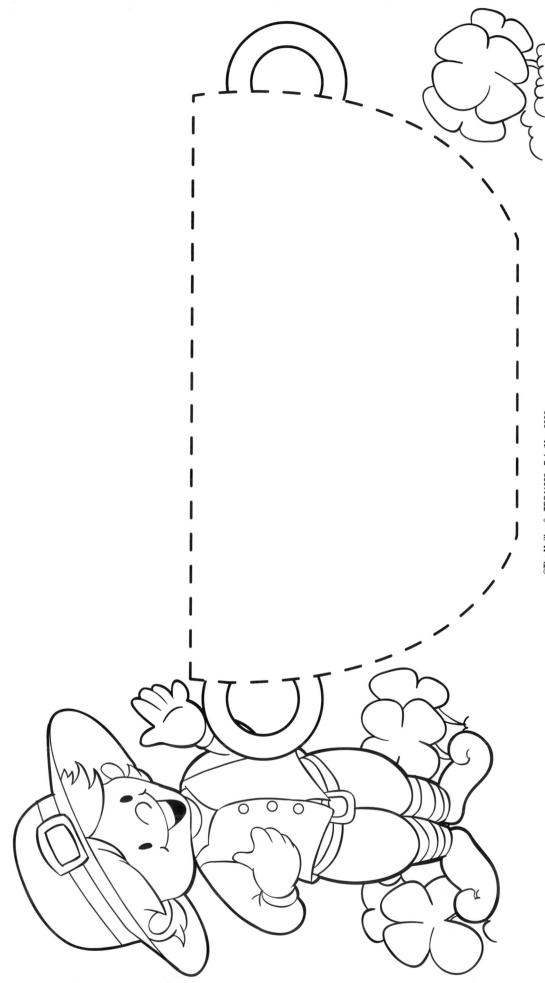

©The Mailbox® • TEC41023 • Feb./Mar. 2006

Note to the teacher: Use with "After the Recipe" on page 86.

Serve up a batch of fun with a recipe that's just perfect for spring! Then follow up the tasty snack with the activity shown below. No doubt your little ones' imaginations will take flight!

To prepare for the snack:

- Collect the necessary ingredients and utensils using the lists on the recipe card below.
- Photocopy the step-by-step recipe cards on page 90.
- Color the cards; then cut them out and display them in your snack area.
- Follow the teacher preparation guidelines for the snack.

Beautiful Butterfly

Ingredients for one:
small piece of celery
flavored cream cheese
2 oval-shaped crackers
pretzel stick, broken in half

Utensils and supplies:
napkin for each child
plastic knife for each child

Teacher preparation:
Arrange the ingredients, napkins, and knives near the step-by-step recipe cards.

Susan Burbridge
University United Methodist Day School
San Antonio, TX

After the Recipe

Now that your little ones have eaten their tasty butterfly snacks, they're ready to learn how butterflies get food! Use Con-Tact paper to attach several large flower cutouts to your floor. Place colorful scarves near the flowers. Then explain that butterflies fly from flower to flower to drink nectar, a sugary liquid that flowers produce. Invite a youngster to visit the area and hold a scarf in each hand to resemble butterfly wings. Then encourage her to "fly" from flower to flower, pretending to sip nectar.

Recipe Cards
Use with "Beautiful Butterfly" on page 89.

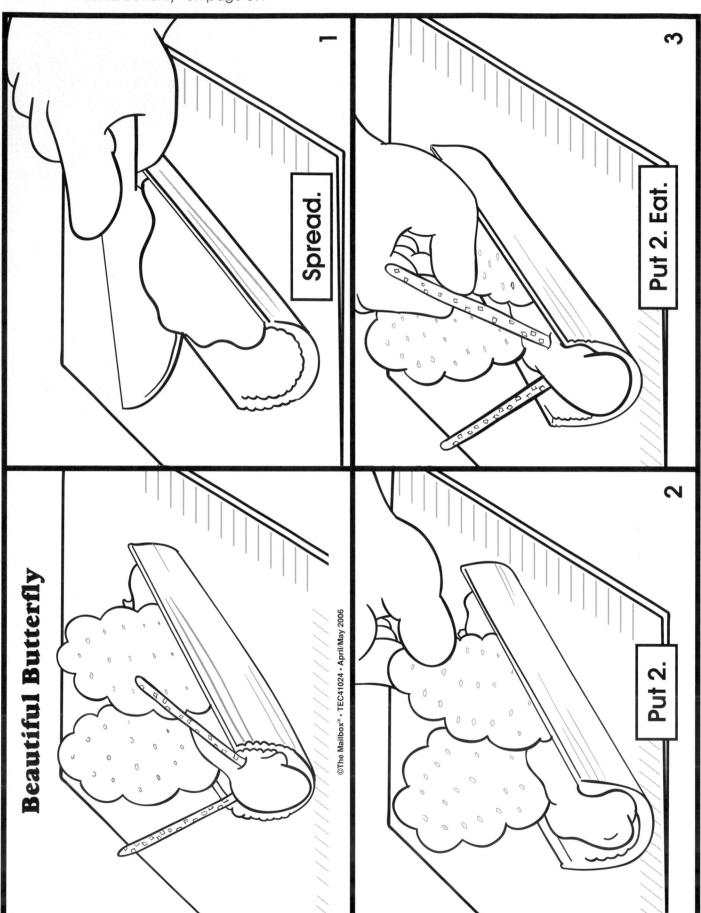

1

Spread.

3

Put 2. Eat.

Beautiful Butterfly

2

Put 2.

KIDS IN THE KITCHEN

Serve up a batch of fun with a recipe that's just perfect for summer! Then follow up the tasty snack with the activity shown below. These ideas are sure to make your little ones curious about these cute little garden-loving critters!

To prepare for the snack:
- Collect the necessary ingredients and utensils using the lists on the recipe card.
- Photocopy the step-by-step recipe cards on page 92.
- Color the cards; then cut them out and display them in your snack area.
- Follow the teacher preparation guidelines for the snack.

Snail Snack

Ingredients for one:
small flour tortilla
whipped cream cheese
jam

Utensils and supplies:
paper plate for each child
plastic knife for each child

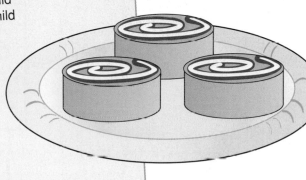

Teacher preparation:
- Warm the tortillas slightly so they are soft and flexible.
- Arrange the ingredients, utensils, and supplies near the step-by-step recipe cards.

Telvon

After the Recipe
In advance, roll a piece of modeling clay into a snake shape and then coil it to resemble a snail. Let it harden overnight. Then place the snail and a shallow tray of paint at a center. Have a child press the snail into the paint and make several prints on a sheet of construction paper. When the paint is dry, add details to each print with a fine-tip marker.

Recipe Cards

Use with "Snail Snack" on page 91.

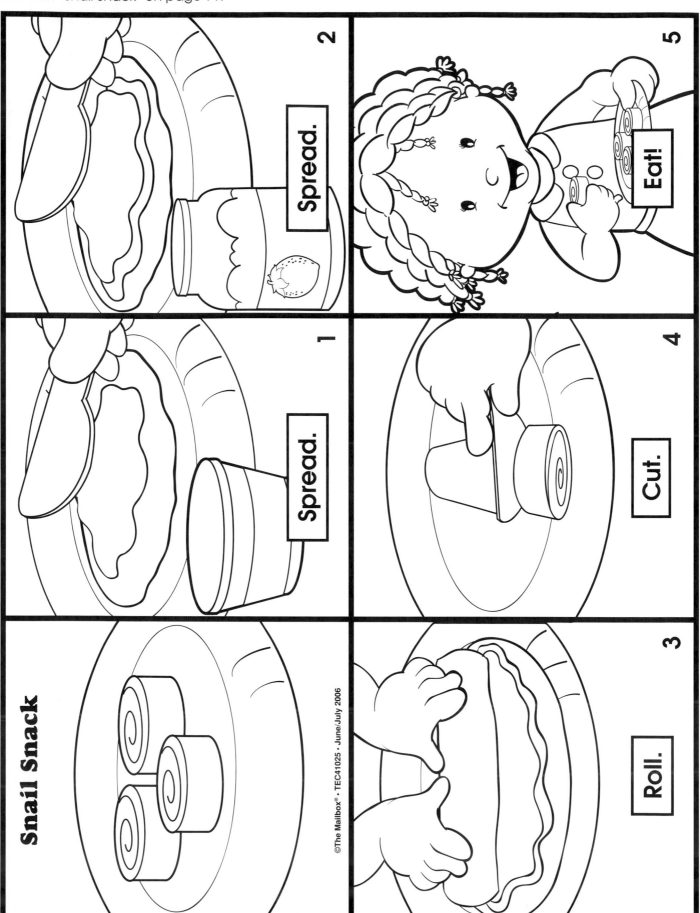

2

Spread.

5

Eat!

1

Spread.

4

Cut.

Snail Snack

3

Roll.

©The Mailbox® • TEC41025 • June/July 2006

LEARNING CENTERS

Learning Centers

Beaming Blocks
Block Center

Space creatures! Robots! There's no telling what youngsters will build with these shiny blocks! Cover a variety of boxes with aluminum foil. Use a permanent marker to add facial features to some of the boxes; then place the boxes in your block center. When little ones build at this center, you're sure to see beaming smiles!

Beth Baranowski
Roselle Park, NJ

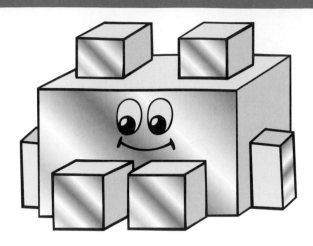

What's on the Menu?
Dramatic Play

This picture-perfect menu will add zest to restaurant-themed dramatic play! Make a menu by attaching photos or magazine cutouts of food to a sheet of folded construction paper as shown. Label each picture and the front cover. Then laminate the menu. Place the menu in your dramatic-play area along with plastic tableware and a pen and notepad for taking orders. Youngsters visit the area to order, serve, and eat at the restaurant. The special today is a heaping helping of center fun!

Anna Katrina Enverga
Alphabits Learning Center
Manchester, NH

Shaking the Seasons
Science Center

At this center, little ones can experience the characteristics of trees in each of the four seasons! Gather four shallow clear plastic containers with lids, such as those found in a deli. Glue a brown tree cutout, minus foliage, inside each container. Place snowflake confetti in one container, fall-colored leaf confetti in a second container, and flower confetti in a third container. Glue green leaf confetti to the tree in the final container. Place a lid on each container and tape it in place. Then place the containers at a center. A child visits the center and shakes each container to see trees in fall, winter, spring, and summer. Those leaves stay right on the tree during summer!

Sandra C. Bendickson
The Salvation Army Child Care Center
Peoria, IL

Digging for Dinosaurs
Literacy Center

With this name recognition idea, your little archaeologists dig for their very own personalized dinosaurs! Make a class supply of dinosaur cutouts. Label each cutout with a different child's name. Laminate the dinosaurs; then bury them in your sand table. A visiting youngster digs through the sand to find the dinosaur with his name. Then he places it back in the sand for future digging adventures!

Sue Reppert
Widening World Preschool
Mentor, OH

See-and-Feel Shapes
Math Center

Students feel these triangles with their fingers and then make colorful rubbings! Draw several triangles in a variety of sizes on a sheet of poster board. Trace over each triangle with a thick line of glue. When the glue is dry, tape the poster board to a tabletop in your math center. Provide a supply of copy paper and unwrapped crayons. Students run their fingers over the triangles as they say the name of the shape. Then they use the supplies to make shape rubbings. No doubt students will want to repeat this activity with other basic shapes!

Brooke Beverly
Julia Bancroft School
Auburn, MA

Guess Who!
Games Center

This matching game helps transform classmates into familiar faces! Take a full-body photograph of each child. Cut each photo in half. Then glue the lower half of each photo to a sheet of poster board, making sure there is enough room for the upper halves of the photos as well. Place the poster board and the remaining photo pieces at a center. A child matches the halves to reassemble his classmates. It's a match!

Lois Bellhorn
Flickinger Elementary
Utica, MI

Learning Centers

One Giant Pizza, Please!
Math Center

Cut a large circle from brown bulletin board paper and decorate it to resemble a pizza crust. Place the crust at a center along with a variety of colorful shape cutouts to represent toppings. A child visits the center and decorates the pizza crust with toppings as desired, naming the shape of each topping chosen.

Michele Michalski
Oak Hill Nursery School
Howell, NJ

Sarah Reed
Davison, MI

Bunches of Bugs
Art Center

Any spider would be delighted with this web full of colorful bugs! To make a web, attach lengths of double-stick tape to a Hula-Hoop toy (or a circle of tagboard) as shown. Display the web at children's eye level near your art table. Place glue and scissors at the table along with a variety of craft items, such as colorful construction paper, tissue paper, and pom-poms. A child visits the center and uses the supplies to create a bug. When the glue is dry, he attaches his bug to the web.

Jennifer Hernandez
WVUH Child Development Center
Morgantown, WV

Not So Soft!
Sensory Center

Place in a plastic tub a variety of soft objects, such as tissues, cotton balls, cotton batting, and small stuffed animals. Also place in the tub one item that is not soft, such as a square of sandpaper or a rock. A youngster closes his eyes and reaches into the tub. He feels all the items and finds the one item that is not soft. Then he pulls the item out of the tub and opens his eyes. After confirming that it isn't soft, he places it back in the tub and repeats the activity!

Jane Vogt and Jackie Miller
Cleveland Child Care
Cleveland, OH

Alphabet Soup
Literacy Center

Transform your water table into a big bowl of alphabet soup! Make pairs of craft foam letter cutouts. Then float the letters in your water table. Provide a large plastic mixing spoon. A youngster stirs the soup with the spoon. Then he chooses a letter, finds its twin, and places the letters in a container. He continues in the same way with each remaining pair of letters in the water table.

Denise Cook
Children's Courtyard
Grapevine, TX

Forming Features
Play Dough Center

Glue a green stem to each of several orange pumpkin cutouts. Then laminate the pumpkins and place them at a center along with a variety of cookie cutters and a supply of black play dough. A student presses the play dough into a thin layer. Then she cuts shapes from the play dough and places them on the pumpkins to make faces. Just look at all those fascinating features!

Sue Yakscoe
Sterling Annex Preschool
Sterling, VA

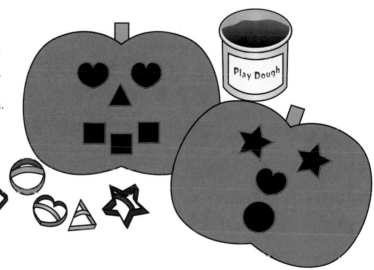

Sew Your Crops
Fine-Motor Center

Make several fall fruit and vegetable cutouts from tagboard. Punch holes around each cutout. Cut several lengths of yarn and dip an end of each length into glue to keep the ends from fraying. When the glue is dry, tape the remaining end of each length to the back of a different cutout. Then place the cutouts at a center. A student chooses a cutout and laces the yarn through the holes.

Karen Eiben
The Learning House Preschool
La Salle, IL

Learning Centers

Popcorn and Cranberries
Fine-Motor Area

Cut from craft foam a supply of extra large popcorn and cranberry cutouts. Punch a hole in the center of each cutout. Then tie a separate cutout to an end of each of several lengths of yarn. Dip the remaining end of each length in glue to keep the yarn from fraying. When the glue is dry, place the yarn lengths and remaining cutouts in a center. A child strings cranberries and popcorn onto a length of yarn to resemble holiday garland. Hey, that's an AB pattern!

Hot or Cold?
Science Center

Tissue boxes make the perfect bears for this sorting activity. Decorate an empty tissue box to resemble a brown bear and a second box to resemble a polar bear. Place the bears at your center along with several picture cards representing hot objects and cold objects. A child chooses a picture card. He places the card in the brown bear's mouth if the picture shows a hot object and in the polar bear's mouth if it shows a cold object. Then he repeats the process with each remaining card.

Amber Baker
Learn a Lot Christian Preschool
Mooresville, IN

Pretty Poinsettias
Art Center

Place at your art center red cellophane squares, gold glitter, a container of glue with paintbrushes, and a class supply of poinsettia patterns. A child brushes glue on a poinsettia pattern and then places cellophane squares over the glue. To make the center of the flower, he adds more glue and a sprinkling of gold glitter. Cut out the poinsettias. Then, if desired, display the finished flowers in a cluster on green bulletin board paper. How lovely!

Betsy Ruggiano
Featherbed Lane School
Clark, NJ

Up the Evergreen!
Literacy Center

With a little bit of imagination, the classic story *Chicka Chicka Boom Boom* by Bill Martin Jr. and John Archambault can be perfect for the holidays! Mount a large evergreen tree cutout on a wall near your literacy center. Provide a variety of letter cutouts at a table along with a supply of craft items and glue. A child chooses a letter, traces it with her finger, and says its name (provide assistance with letter names if needed). Then she decorates the letter as desired. After the glue is dry, she tapes her colorful letter ornament to the holiday tree. When the tree is decorated, reread *Chicka Chicka Boom Boom,* replacing the phrase "coconut tree" with "holiday tree."

Carole Watkins
Holy Family Child Care Center
Crown Point, IN

Sparkly Snowfolk
Play Dough Center

Mix fine glitter with a supply of white play dough. Then place the sparkly dough at a center along with orange pipe cleaner pieces (noses), fabric scraps (scarves), and small black craft foam circles (features and buttons). A youngster makes a snowpal out of play dough and then embellishes him as desired.

Sandy Barker
South Washington County ECFE
Cottage Grove, MN

Brilliant Patterns
Math Center

Place black construction paper strips and colorful light-bulb cutouts at a table along with a supply of glue sticks. Have a youngster place bulbs on a strip to make a pattern. When he's pleased with the arrangement, encourage him to glue the bulbs in place. Allow time for the glue to dry. Then staple the strip to fit the child's head. These vivid crowns are sure to be a hit for the holidays!

Linda Peterson
Southwest Christian School
Fort Worth, TX

Brush, Brush, Brush!
Fine-Motor Center

Have little ones brush some less-than-clean teeth in this engaging center. After all, February is Children's Dental Health Month! Laminate large tooth cutouts; then scribble on each one with a dry-erase marker. Place the teeth at a center along with a supply of toothbrushes. A child chooses a tooth and then uses a toothbrush to remove the black marks. Now it's nice and clean!

Brenda Watkins
Sugar Bears
Henderson, NC

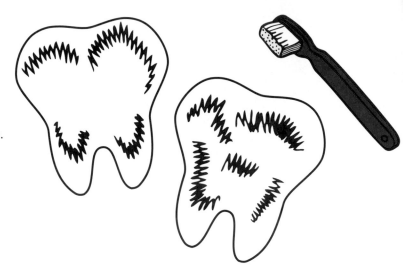

A Sweet Match!
Literacy Center

Label pairs of large colorful heart cutouts with simple matching words, as shown, so they resemble conversation hearts candy. A student chooses a heart, finds the heart with the matching word, and then places the cutouts together. She continues in the same way with each remaining pair.

adapted from an idea by Virginia Sorrells
Peachtree Corners Baptist Preschool
Norcross, GA

St. Patrick's Day Surprise!
Water Table

Everything is green on St. Patrick's Day—even the water in your water table! Use food coloring to whip up a batch of yellow and blue ice cubes. Just before center time, place several ice cubes in your water table. Provide access to mixing spoons. Children can stir the water as the ice cubes dissolve and watch the water change from clear to green. That's so festive!

Casey O'Donnell
Newtonville, MA

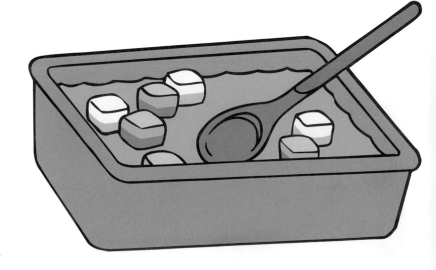

100

Rhyming Bees
Literacy Center

Color a copy of the bee cards and flower-center patterns on page 105; then cut them out. Glue each flower center to the middle of a construction paper flower cutout as shown. Then place the props at a center. A child chooses a bee and names the picture on its wing. He decides whether the name rhymes with the word *fan* or the word *whale*. Next, he places the bee near the corresponding flower. He continues in the same way with each remaining bee.

Kathryn Davenport
Partin Elementary
Oviedo, FL

Plant Parts
Science Center

Youngsters investigate real flowers at this center! Purchase an inexpensive flowering plant. Remove it from its container and place it in a tub. Then put the plant at a center along with a magnifying glass. Invite youngsters to use the magnifying glass to inspect the blooms, leaves, stems, and roots of the plant. After each child has had an opportunity to observe the plant, encourage youngsters to help you repot it.

Lisa Stewart
Mt. Pisgah Weekday School
Greensboro, NC

Powder Clouds
Art Center

Place at your art table a supply of cotton balls, a shallow container of baby powder, dark blue construction paper, scissors, and glue sticks. A child visits the center and swirls the glue stick over a sheet of paper. He dips a cotton ball into the powder and then pats it on the glue. Bits of the cotton ball as well as the powder stick to the glue, and the result is a lovely wispy cloud! If desired, encourage youngsters to cut out their clouds. Then add the clouds to a springtime display!

Renee Bakken
Olmsted County Head Start
Rochester, MN

Learning Centers

A Great Big Bloom
Fine-Motor Center

Cut a jumbo flower shape from bulletin board paper. Attach the flower to a tabletop and provide access to scissors, glue sticks, and a variety of gardening catalogs. Invite students to cut flower pictures from the catalogs and glue them to the giant flower to make a beautiful blooming collage!

Beth Baranowski
Roselle Park, NJ

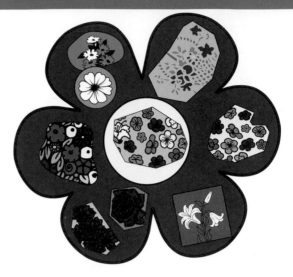

Counting on Fries
Math Center

Seal several business envelopes and then cut each one in half, as shown, to resemble french fry containers (or ask a local fast-food restaurant to donate several unused french fry containers). Label each container with a different number. Cut yellow sponges into strips to make a supply of pretend french fries. Then place the containers and fries in your math center. A child identifies each number, counts the matching number of fries, and then places them in the container. Five fries, comin' right up!

Jay P. Thomas
Pembroke Elementary
Virginia Beach, VA

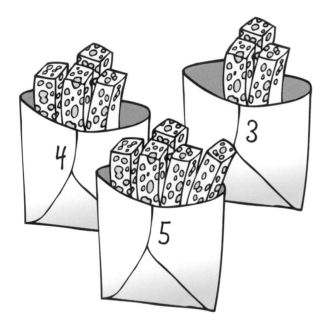

All About Mom
Writing Center

Youngsters make a memorable keepsake at this supervised center. Invite a child to your writing table and have him dictate responses to complete a questionnaire similar to the one shown. Have the child glue the questionnaire to the bottom half of a 12" x 18" sheet of construction paper. Encourage the child to draw a picture of his mom above the questionnaire. You may wish to laminate these adorable Mother's Day presents before sending them home for moms to enjoy.

Tracy Henderson
Brook Hollow Weekday Program
Nashville, TN

Jared

My Mom
My mom is _30_ years old.
My mom is the prettiest when _she goes to church_.
My mom likes to make _chocolate chip cookies_.
My mom always says, "_Use a tissue._"
My mom is funny when she _wears curlers in her hair_.

Night Lights
Math Center

This night sky is filled with great numbers of fireflies! Use a white crayon (or correction pen) to write the numerals 1 through 5 on a length of black paper. Cut out three yellow construction paper copies of the firefly patterns on page 106; then place the fireflies in a container. Put the container and prepared paper at a center. A child visits the center and places the appropriate number of fireflies on each numeral.

A Clean Scene
Water Table

Youngsters clean up this water table so it's a pleasing home for fish. Place in your water table colorful craft foam fish as well as items such as plastic bottles, pieces of bubble wrap, and other plastic litter. Provide access to a bucket and a small fishing or butterfly net. A youngster scoops up a variety of items from the water. She removes all the litter and places it in the bucket. Then she releases the fish back into the water. She continues in the same way until all the litter has been removed.

adapted from an idea by Kimberly Walsh
Toledo, OH

Fourth of July Mixture
Sensory Center

To make colored rice, place a supply of rice in a large resealable plastic bag; then add several drops of food coloring and a small amount of rubbing alcohol. Seal the bag and squeeze the mixture until the color is evenly distributed. Make a red and blue batch of rice in this manner, and then allow the rice to dry on waxed paper. Place the rice in a tub along with star-shaped confetti. Provide access to several cups, scoops, and containers. Then allow youngsters to investigate this patriotic rice.

Karen Pummill
Wee Care Enrichment Center
Cherokee Village, AR

Learning Centers

Blowing Bubbles
Science Center

Replace ordinary bubble wands with kitchen utensils for some fun bubble-blowing experimentation! Stock your science area with a shallow pan of bubble solution and a variety of slotted utensils, such as those shown. A youngster visits the center and explores making bubbles with the different utensils.

Leslea Howell
Tickle My Toes Day Care
Bettendorf, IA

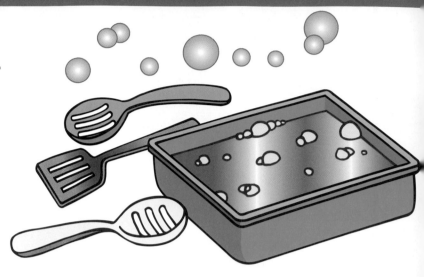

Bye-Bye Bugs
Art Center

Place several paper towels in a shallow tray. Then saturate the towels with tempera paint. Place the tray at a center along with crayons, an unused flyswatter, and a class supply of 12" x 18" construction paper. A youngster draws several bugs on a sheet of paper. She presses the flyswatter on the paint-soaked paper towels and then makes a print on top of one of her bugs. She continues in the same way with each remaining bug.

Michelle LeMaster-Johnson
St. Paul's School of Early Learning
Muskego, WI

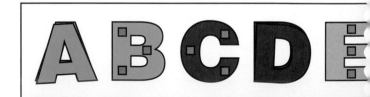

Diggin' for Letters
Literacy Center

Stash some letters in your sand table for a center that's a real treasure! To prepare, make two sets of letter cutouts. Glue one set of letters to a length of paper as shown; then attach the hook side of a Velcro fastener to each letter. Display the paper near your sand table. Attach the corresponding loop sides of Velcro fasteners to each letter in the remaining set. Bury the loose letter cutouts in your sand table. A youngster removes a letter from the sand and then attaches it to the matching letter on the display. He continues in the same way with other letters he finds in the sand.

Beth Edwards, Wintergreen Primary School
Greenville, NC

Firefly Patterns

Use with "Night Lights" on page 103 and "Flashing Fireflies" on page 306.

OUR READERS WRITE

Our Readers Write

Name Tracing Cards

I help my preschoolers learn to write their names with this easy idea! I use a dark marker to print each child's name on a separate index card. I place Sticky-Tac temporary adhesive on the back of each card. Then I attach the cards to a wall. When a child needs to label a paper or project with her name, she finds her card, puts it under her paper, and then traces the letters!

Lucia Westgate, Blissfield Preschool Cooperative Nursery, Blissfield, MI

Wearable Letters

To keep the letter of the week in front of my students' eyes, I wear it on my clothing! I cut out the letter from colorful felt. Then I spray the back of the letter with temporary adhesive and place it on my clothing. When I'm ready to remove the letter, it peels right off. These letters can be used again and again by simply spraying on another layer of adhesive.

Cindy Wetzig, Bethany Lutheran Preschool, Fairview Heights, IL

Handsome Prints!

Red! Red! What a wonderful hue!
Here are my colorful handprints for you!

To reinforce each color in my color unit, I have my youngsters make these handy take-home projects. For each child, I label a piece of paper with the poem shown, substituting the color currently being studied. Then I have each youngster make handprints on the paper in the corresponding color of tempera paint. When the paint is dry, I send the projects home with the students!

Jen Wilson, Wonder Years Child Care, Jersey Shore, PA

Boo-Boo Baggie

With this idea, my youngsters have clean, reusable ice packs to soothe bumps and scrapes! I cut kitchen sponges into small rectangles. Then I wet each rectangle, place it in a resealable plastic bag, and put it in the freezer. When a youngster needs an ice pack, I give her one of the bags. When she's finished, I can either remove the sponge and place it in a new bag to reuse later, or I can toss out the entire ice pack. It's so handy!

Nancy Goldberg, B'nai Israel Schilit Nursery School, Rockville, MD

Comfort Bear

I make the transition from home to school easier for my little ones with the help of a comfort bear. Before school begins, I send home a bear cutout with a note asking each family to personalize the bear with their preschooler's help. For example, they might color the bear, glue photographs to it, or give it a lipstick kiss. Then each child brings his bear to school with him on the first day so that he has a special reminder of his family!

Stefanie Harden, Trinity Lutheran Day School, Wichita Falls, TX

Fabulous Fabric Paint!

Instead of using nametags to label students' seats, I use fabric paint to write each child's name directly on the tabletop. The paint lasts a long time and comes off easily with a straightedge paint scraper!

J. Cook, Madison Primary Preschool, Middletown, OH

Ever-Changing Tree

This tree is a popular display in my classroom all year long! I cut a large tree from bulletin board paper and post it on a wall (or, if appropriate, paint a tree directly on the wall). My youngsters help me decorate the tree for seasons and holidays. Depending on the time of year, we might have fall leaves, bats, turkeys, or blossoms on our tree. My preschoolers just love it!

Melisa Horsfield, Bright Beginnings Preschool, Fort Payne, AL

Postcards for Preschoolers

When I go on vacation during the summer months, I send a postcard to each student in my upcoming preschool class. The students enjoy finding out what I'm doing on my summer vacation, and they feel as if they already know me when it's time for school to begin!

Jan Reed, Christopher Robin Preschool, Glendive, MT

Watch Me Grow!

September 7, 2005
3 feet 4 inches

May 30, 2006
3 feet 6 inches

Watch Me Grow!

With a small amount of preparation now, I have a head start on my preschool keepsakes for the end of the year! During the first week of school, I take a picture of each child in my class and then record the date and the student's height on the back of the photo. I repeat the process at the end of the year. To put a keepsake together, I write on a sheet of construction paper the title shown and the recorded information; then I attach the photos. This keepsake is always popular!

Lois Bellhorn, Flickinger Elementary, Utica, MI

Our Readers Write

Holiday Crayons

I make art time special with crayons in holiday-related shapes! I remove the wrappers from old crayons and place them in a disposable aluminum pan. Then I heat the pan in a 250 degree oven. When the crayons are melted, I remove the pan from the oven and pour the wax into holiday candy molds. When the wax is hard, I simply pop out the shapes!

Janet Knox, Preschool Pals, Crown Point, IN

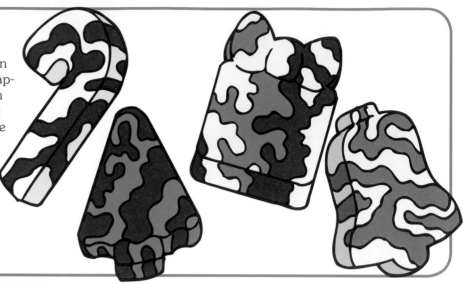

Easy Name Labels

For easy labeling of art projects and other student work, I personalize each pocket in a plastic shoe organizer with a different child's name and picture. Then I place a supply of name slips in each corresponding pocket. A child simply removes a slip and tapes it to her project!

Marsha Feffer, Bentley School—Salem Early Childhood Center, Salem, MA

Who Pudding

As a follow-up to a reading of Dr. Seuss' story *How the Grinch Stole Christmas!* I have youngsters make Who Pudding! I add the pudding mix and milk to a bowl according to package directions. My students take turns stirring the mixture until the pudding is thick. Then each child adds a sprinkle of special Who Seasonings (colored sprinkles). They enjoy their snack as we revisit the story!

Melissa Goodrich, Northwest Daycare Center, South Bend, IN

A Gift for Everyone!

Rather than give me personal gifts for the holidays, I request that parents send a gift that can be used by the entire class, such as a book or stickers. My students and I are so excited to unwrap and use these special gifts!

Heidi Peck, First United Methodist Preschool and Daycare, Cedartown, GA

Snowman in the Classroom!

My little ones have a lot of frosty fun with this little snowman! I fill a small, a medium, and a large balloon with water; then I place them in the freezer. When the water is frozen, I remove the balloons and use a sprinkling of salt to fuse the balls together to resemble a snowman. I use cotton batting to prop up the snowman in a plastic container. Students dress him up with felt scraps and old accessories until he melts away!

Jennifer Avegno, Carousel Preschool, Cypress, CA

Snacktime Manners

Each day during snacktime, I ask each child whether he would like to have a serving of the particular snack for the day. He responds by saying, "No, thank you" or "Yes, please." When children are comfortable answering the question, I throw in some questions guaranteed to produce giggles, such as "Would you like some purple pizza?" or "Would you like to have some dinosaur stew?" Little ones love the silly questions and continue to practice using polite words!

Linda Ludlow, Bethesda Christian Schools, Brownsburg, IN

Donation Tree

I let my preschoolers' parents know what's needed for upcoming projects with a donation tree! I label each of several index cards with items I need and the date they're needed by. I insert each one into a photo tree and then display the tree in the classroom. A parent can remove a card and then bring in the item by the designated date.

Heather Parker, Our Guardian Angel Home Daycare, Monroe, MI

Paint Pops

To make paint pops, I squirt tempera paint into the sections of an ice cube tray. I cover the tray with aluminum foil and poke a craft stick through the foil and into each cup. Then I place the tray in the freezer. After the paint pops freeze, I remove them from the tray and my little ones use them to paint. The colors are bright and oh so cool!

Svetlana Borukhova, Herbert G. Birch Western Queens ECC, New York City, NY

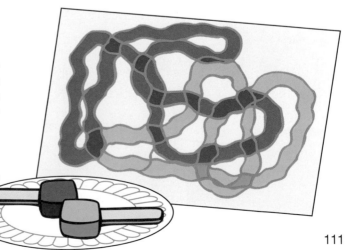

111

Our Readers Write

Acts of Kindness

Before Valentine's Day, I have my students discuss ways that people can be kind to each other. Then I send home with each child a resealable plastic bag containing four heart cutouts and a parent note similar to the one shown. When the hearts are returned to school, I display them on a bulletin board with youngsters' handprints. This popular display has always been a big hit!

Debra Moses, Abundant Ark Children's Center, Houston, TX

Love Those Books!

When I give parents monthly book-order forms, I also provide a list of books previously read in our classroom that are being offered on the form. Parents appreciate the help in choosing quality literature and youngsters love to have their favorite storytime selections at home!

Andrea Henderson, Jefferson Brethren Preschool, Goshen, IN

Simple Lacing Cards

I transform seasonal cardboard decorations into lacing cards! I simply laminate the decoration and then use a large hole puncher to make holes around the edge. I tie a shoelace to a hole on each lacing card and then place the cards in my lacing center. My students love them!

Tammy Pol, Children's Castle Childcare LLC, Salt Lake City, UT

Peg-Puzzle Painting

I put incomplete peg puzzles to good use—as paint stampers! A youngster simply holds onto the peg and then dips the piece into a shallow pan of paint. Then he presses it onto his paper. They're easy and fun to use!

Melissa Rose, Early Childhood Alliance, Fort Wayne, IN

Class Book Covers

Gift bags make great covers for class books! I trim off the bottom and one side of a gift bag. After I fold in the remaining side, I reinforce it with tape. Then I label the front of the bag with the title of the class book. Finally, I use brads to attach the completed pages to the reinforced strip. The bag's handles make this class book easy to display and store!

Judy Knapp, Wilcox Primary, Twinsburg, OH

Weather Photos

I cut photographs from nature magazines that show various types of weather. Then I post the photos in our daily weather center and label each one. Weather seems very real to my youngsters when they view it this way. I've also labeled pictures of the seasons and added them to this display!

Sherrie Kautman, Handicare Inc., Coralville, IA

Brilliant Pasta

To dye pasta bright, beautiful colors, I use acrylic paint from the craft store! I squeeze about one-third of a small bottle of paint into a large resealable plastic bag. Then I pour in a supply of pasta. I squeeze and shake the bag until the paint coats all the pasta. Then I pour the pasta onto newspapers to dry. After a few minutes of drying time, I rub the pasta between my hands to make sure there aren't any pieces stuck together. This method works with regular acrylic paint as well as metallic, glitter, and neon varieties!

Jean Blosser, Joy Early Childhood Education Center, Glendale, AZ

Pot-o'-Gold Hunt

We celebrate St. Patrick's Day with a treasure hunt! For each child, I place a few chocolate coins in a small resealable plastic bag and then tie curling ribbon around the bag, as shown. Then I hide the resulting gold around the classroom. My little ones love to search the room and find their pieces of leprechaun gold!

Tammy LaMothe-Toland, Suffolk, VA

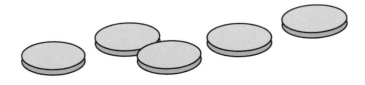

Special Seeds

To make this Mother's Day gift, I cut a supply of sealed business envelopes in half. Each child stamps decorations on his envelope half. Then he slips a package of seeds in the envelope and glues the poem shown to the front. I punch two holes in the envelope as shown; then I thread a ribbon through the holes and tie a bow. This adorable gift has always been a big hit!

Sharon Winter, Our Lady of Hope/St. Luke School, Baltimore, MD

These little seeds of love will grow

Stronger every day, you know.

So plant them in the ground this May.

And have a happy Mother's Day!

Individual Flannelboards

My youngsters had difficulty sharing the limited amount of space on our flannelboard. To solve this problem, I cut pieces of felt to fit in large box lids. I glued the felt in place and voilà! We had several personal, portable flannelboards!

Nan La Fitte, Wesley Academy, Houston, TX

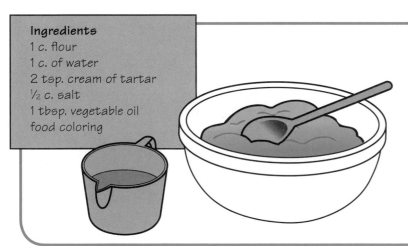

Ingredients
1 c. flour
1 c. of water
2 tsp. cream of tartar
½ c. salt
1 tbsp. vegetable oil
food coloring

Microwave Play Dough

I make all of my play dough in the microwave! Mix in a microwave-safe bowl the ingredients shown. Place the bowl in the microwave and cook the ingredients on high for three minutes, stopping to stir after each minute. Then turn the dough onto a floured surface and knead it until it's cool. Store the play dough in an airtight container.

Daisy Green, The Learning Center, Hagerstown, MD

An Artsy Display

For our student art show, I transform cardboard boxes into unique displays. I collect a variety of large cardboard boxes and then paint them black. Next, I stack the boxes at different angles, as shown, and attach student artwork to the sides. After the art show, it's easy to break down the boxes and store them for next year!

Jacqueline A. Higgins, Eastminster Presbyterian Pre-School, Indialantic, FL

Songs & Such

SONGS & SUCH

Eating Apples

When a crow is feeling peckish, nothing tastes better to it than five red apples! Lead students in performing this counting song five times, decreasing the number in the first line and the number of fingers held up by one for each repetition.

(sung to the tune of "Six Little Ducks")

[Five] red apples on a tree
Looked as juicy as could be.
A crow swooped down to get some lunch.

It ate one apple with a crunch, crunch, crunch!

Crunch, crunch, crunch, crunch, crunch, crunch,
It ate one apple with a crunch, crunch, crunch!

Hold up fingers.
Wiggle fingers.
*Move other hand in a
  swooping motion to
  resemble a beak.*
*Open and close the
  hand over one finger.*

*Fold over the finger to
  represent the missing
  apple.*

LeeAnn Collins
Sunshine House Preschool
Lansing, MI

Cleanup Time!

Cleanup time is a snap with this spiffy tune!

(sung to the tune of "Clementine")

Time to clean up. Time to clean up.
Clean the floors and tables too.
We know how to clean our classroom.
We're the preschool cleaning crew!

adapted from an idea by Tammy Block
Church on the Hill Christian Child Care Center
Norco, CA

Handsome Hands

Spotlight successful hand washing with this catchy ditty! Have youngsters pantomime turning on a sink and putting a dollop of soap on their hands; then lead them in performing the song.

(sung to the tune of "Are You Sleeping?")

Tops and bottoms, Tops and bottoms.	*Rub tops and palms of hands.*
In between, In between.	*Rub between fingers.*
All around your hands, All around your hands.	*Rub all over each hand and wrist.*
Now we're clean. Now we're clean.	*Hold up hands and wiggle fingers.*

Tina Rumburg
First Presbyterian
Gastonia, NC

The Name Chant

This action-packed chant helps little ones learn the names of their classmates! Begin leading youngsters in the chant, substituting a student's name when indicated. During the first and second lines, invite the student named to join you in performing the action described; then have his classmates join in for the remainder of the chant. Repeat the chant with different student names and actions (see the suggested actions below).

[Austin], [Austin], clap your hands!
[Austin], [Austin], clap your hands!
Everybody clap your hands.
Clap with [Austin]!

Suggested actions: *touch your nose, pat your head, touch your knees, nod your head, stomp your feet, wiggle your hands, turn around*

adapted from an idea by Amy Poole
Jack and Jill Early Learning Center
Norcross, GA

Get Out Fast!

Spotlight important fire safety information with this red-hot song! After all, October 9–15 is Fire Prevention Week! Lead youngsters in singing the song. Then sing other verses using the suggestions provided.

(sung to the tune of "This Little Light of Mine")

If there's a fire inside,
I'm gonna get out fast!
If there's a fire inside,
I'm gonna get out fast!
If there's a fire inside,
I'm gonna get out fast!
Get out fast, get out fast, get out fast!

Other suggestions:
If there's smoke inside, I will crawl outside.
If my clothes catch fire, I'll stop, drop, and roll.

Shelley Hoster
Jack and Jill Early Learning Center
Norcross, GA

Pumpkin Trees?

This giggle-inducing action rhyme is sure to become a classroom favorite! Lead students in reciting the rhyme, pausing briefly after the question in the fourth line for youngsters to share their responses.

It's harvesttime and what do I see?	*Put hand up to forehead. Look around.*
Pumpkins! Pumpkins in a tree!	*Point upward.*
In a tree? That can't be!	*Place hands on cheeks.*
Where, oh where, should pumpkins be?	*Throw hands outward.*
On the ground? Yes, on the ground!	*Point to the ground.*
That's where pumpkins should be found!	*Place hands on hips.*

Deirdre Banks
Growing Angels Center for Learning
Fort Meade, MD

Creepy Companions!

Your youngsters' classmates might look a little bit different during a Halloween celebration. So prepare your little ones for a slew of creepy companions with a "spook-tacular" song!

(sung to the tune of "Head and Shoulders")

Monsters, cats, and spiders too (Spiders too!)
Are walking all around with you. (Yes, with you!)
On this night, it is quite all right.
On Halloween it's what we do. (What we do!)

Linda Gordetsky
Palenville, NY

A Thankful Holiday

Children recognize the very first Thanksgiving Day with this splendid song selection!

(sung to the tune of "Sing a Song of Sixpence")

Each year in November we celebrate the time
When Native Americans sat down to dine
With pilgrims who had traveled from far, far away.
And that's the reason why we celebrate Thanksgiving Day!

SONGS & SUCH

Are We Ready?

Here's a song that helps little ones remember how to dress for outdoor winter play! Lead students in singing the song below as they pantomime putting on each piece of clothing. At the conclusion of the last verse, have youngsters replace the word *no* with *yes*.

(sung to the tune of "Skip to My Lou")

[Pick up your snow pants; pull them on.]
[Pick up your snow pants; pull them on.]
[Pick up your snow pants; pull them on.]
Are we ready to go? No!

Continue with the following: *Next are your tall boots, left and right. Next is the warm coat; zip it up. Next is the fuzzy hat, on your head. Last are the mittens; now we're done.*

Jodie Holman
Little Blessings Nursery School
Madison, WI

The Washing Machine

This action poem is full of good clean fun!

I could be a washing machine.	*Twist body from side to side.*
I could be a washing machine,	*Continue twisting.*
Getting all your clothing clean.	*Continue twisting.*
I could be a washing machine.	*Continue twisting.*
Simply put in lots of shirts.	*Pretend to pick up shirts.*
Add pants and sweaters too.	*Pretend to pick up pants and sweaters.*
But if you have some stinky socks.	*Hold nose.*
There's nothing I can do!	*Hold nose and shake head.*

adapted from an idea by Cris Edwards
Sprouts Child Development Center
Sarasota, FL

A Cheery Chant

This call and response chant answers a few pressing questions about a certain jolly man!

Teacher: Who makes toys for Santa's shelves?
Children: It's Santa's, Santa's, Santa's elves!

Teacher: What makes Santa look so cute?
Children: It's Santa's, Santa's, Santa's suit!

Teacher: What speeds Santa on his way?
Children: It's Santa's, Santa's, Santa's sleigh!

Teacher: Who guides Santa without fear?
Children: It's Santa's, Santa's, Santa's deer!

Ann Fisher
Toledo, OH

The New Year's Bell

Ring in the new year with this festive little song! If desired, have a volunteer ring a bell or shake a jingle bell bracelet throughout the performance.

(sung to the tune of "Twinkle, Twinkle, Little Star")

Ringing, ringing New Year's bell,
You are happy, I can tell.
Wishing all a good new year
Filled with kindness, filled with cheer.
Ringing, ringing New Year's bell,
You are happy, I can tell.

SONGS & SUCH

Groundhog Day

Commemorate this unique holiday with a cute little song!

(sung to the tune of "Do Your Ears Hang Low?")

Well, it's Groundhog Day.
See him pop out of his hole.
See him look with fright
To the left and to the right.
If he doesn't run away,
You know spring is on its way.
Yes, it's Groundhog Day!

Heather Lickliter
Athens, GA

A Springtime Rhyme

The snow is melting and the grass is beginning to grow. Celebrate signs of spring with this adorable action rhyme!

The flowers start to bloom.	*Move arms to resemble opening petals.*
The grass begins to grow.	*Wiggle fingers near the floor.*
The warm rays of the sun	*Hold arms above head to resemble the sun.*
Have melted all the snow.	*Move arms back and forth parallel to floor.*
The birds look for worms	*Look at the floor as if searching.*
And they begin to sing.	*Flap arms as if they are wings.*
You'll know when these things happen	*Shake index finger.*
Then it must be spring!	*Throw arms outward as if to say "Hooray!"*

Deborah Garmon
Groton, CT

A Little Valentine

This Valentine's Day ditty is sure to delight your little ones! Lead students in singing the song. After the spoken line, have one of your youngsters name who they would give the valentine to. Repeat the song several times, having a different student answer the question each time.

(sung to the tune of "Baby Bumblebee")

I'm bringing home a little valentine.
It says, "I love you. Please won't you be mine?"
I'm bringing home a little valentine.
Who should I give it to? (spoken)

Karen Amatrudo
The Learning Village
Madison, CT

I love you. Please won't you be mine?

Five Wee Leprechauns

Spread St. Patrick's Day cheer with this counting chant! Make five green leprechaun cutouts. Ready the leprechauns for flannelboard use and then place them in a row on your flannelboard. Lead students in reciting the rhyme, removing each leprechaun when indicated.

Five wee leprechauns were sitting by my door.
One danced away and then there were four.
Four wee leprechauns were giggling with glee.
One left to check his gold and then there were three.
Three wee leprechauns, just a busy few.
One hid in a shamrock patch and then there were two.
Two wee leprechauns were having lots of fun.
One climbed up the rainbow and then there was one.
One wee leprechaun left to explore.
Now how many leprechauns are sitting by my door?

Elizabeth Brandel
Little Acorns Preschool
Milwaukie, OR

SONGS & SUCH

A Great Year

This song is a fun way to wrap up the school year! It also makes a nice addition to an end-of-the-year program.

(sung to the tune of "I've Been Working on the Railroad")

I've been having fun in preschool,
Learning all year long.
I can tell you all about it.
Just listen to this song.

We've been learning shapes and colors,
Letters and numbers too.
I've learned how to share with others.
Now our year is through.

Aimee Gross
Living Word Christian Academy
West Haven, CT

Summertime!

Sun, pool parties, and backyard playtime—summertime is one terrific season! Have students celebrate summer with this bouncy little tune.

(sung to the tune of "Jingle Bells")

Summertime, summertime—
It is so much fun!
Playing in our backyard
In the summer sun.
Splash with friends in the pool.
We have such a blast!
It's too bad that summertime
Has to go so fast!

Deborah Garmon
Groton, CT

SCIENCE EXPLORATIONS

Science

Same and Different

Cultivate little ones' abilities to observe and compare with this apple investigation.

by Lucia Kemp Henry, Fallon, NV

STEP 1

Place each apple in a separate lunch bag. Gather a small group of students and display the bags. Ask students to guess the contents of the bags, leading them to conclude that it's difficult to identify an object without using the senses of sight and touch.

STEP 2

Open one of the bags, remove the apple, and allow youngsters to observe it. Encourage them to describe the apple without touching it.

STEP 5

Place the apples side by side. Have students describe some ways the apples are the same as well as some ways they are different, prompting youngsters to discuss shape, texture, color, and size.

STEP 6

Finally, ask students to predict whether the insides of the apples will look the same. After listening to their predictions, slice the apples into halves and have youngsters describe what they see and discuss whether their predictions were correct.

Explorations

To explore the similarities and differences between two apples, you will need the following:

small red apple
large green apple
two brown paper lunch bags

STEP 3

It feels smooth.

Invite each child to touch the apple and describe how it feels.

STEP 4

Have youngsters explore the remaining apple in a similar way, repeating Steps 2 and 3.

Did You Know?

Around 2,500 different kinds of apples are grown in the United States alone! Thousands of additional varieties are grown throughout the world.

What Now?

Place one red, one green, and one yellow apple at a center. Encourage youngsters to use their senses of sight and touch to describe and compare the apples.

Science

Investigating Thumbprints

Little ones are sure to give a big thumbs-up for this fascinating exploration of thumbprints!

by Suzanne Moore, Tucson, AZ

STEP 1

It's smooth!

Gather a group of youngsters. Encourage each student to observe the pad of her thumb and describe what she sees.

STEP 2

There are little bumps!

Give each child a hand lens. Have her observe her thumb through the hand lens. Once again, have youngsters describe what they see.

STEP 5

?

Have each child predict whether her thumbprint will look exactly like her classmates' prints.

STEP 6

Encourage youngsters to compare their prints to their classmates' prints. Are they the same or different? Explain that everyone's fingerprints are different and that's just one of the things that makes an individual unique!

Explorations

To investigate thumbprints, you will need the following:
hand lenses
black ink pad
index card for each child

STEP 3

Have each child press his thumb on the ink pad; then help him gently press his inked thumb on an index card.

STEP 4

I see a lot of lines!

Encourage each student to examine his thumbprint with the hand lens and describe what he sees.

Did You Know?

Monkeys have fingerprints too. In fact, some varletles of monkeys even have unique tail prints!

What Now?

Have students compare other kinds of prints, such as elbow prints, palm prints, or footprints!

Science

Amazing Evaporation!
Mittens can get very wet during wintertime play—but they don't stay that way! Use a slightly soggy mitten to help little ones explore evaporation.

by Lucia Kemp Henry, Fallon, NV

STEP 1

It's really soft!

Gather a small group of youngsters and present a mitten. Invite each child to touch the mitten and describe how it feels.

STEP 2

Show youngsters the container of crushed ice. Tell students that they are going to pretend the ice is snow. Then invite each child, in turn, to put on the mitten and touch the snow.

STEP 5

Next, have students watch as you hang the mitten in a warm, dry location. Allow the mitten to hang overnight.

STEP 6

Present the mitten the next day and encourage each child to touch it. Invite youngsters to guess where the water went, leading them to conclude that although we can't feel it, the water has left the mitten and is now in the air.

Explorations

To explore evaporation, you will need the following:
mitten
shallow container of crushed ice, slightly melted
clothespin

STEP 3

Now it's wet!

Once again, have each child touch the mitten and describe how it feels. Explain to youngsters that mittens get wet when people wear them while playing in the snow. If you live in an area where it snows, remind students of their own mittens after outdoor play.

STEP 4

Maybe we could squeeze it dry.

Have students predict ways to dry the mitten.

Did You Know?

There is about the same amount of water on our planet today as there was when dinosaurs were roaming the earth!

What Now?

After your study of evaporation, explore condensation with your little ones. Place ice and a colorful drink in a plastic cup. After several minutes, have students touch the outside of the cup. Where did the water come from?

Science

Mixing Up Colors
Little ones whip up secondary colors with this vivid investigation!

by Suzanne Moore, Tucson, AZ

STEP 1

That's blue!

Tint each of three containers of whipped topping a different primary color. Gather a small group of youngsters and present the whipped topping. Encourage students to identify the colors.

STEP 2

?

Place dollops of blue and yellow whipped topping in a bowl. Ask youngsters to predict what will happen when the two colors are mixed.

STEP 5

What will happen?

Repeat Steps 2 and 3 with yellow and red whipped topping and with blue and red whipped topping.

STEP 6

Give each child slices of fruit and dollops of green, purple, and orange whipped topping. Invite each child to dip her fruit into these tasty secondary colors and then nibble on her snack.

Explorations

To explore color mixing, you will need the following:
3 small containers of whipped topping
red, yellow, and blue food coloring (gel food coloring works best)
3 bowls
3 spoons
a small paper plate for each child
fruit slices for each child
home-school connection sheet on page 134 (optional)

STEP 3

Invite a child to stir the whipped topping as the remaining youngsters observe.

STEP 4

It's green!

When the colors are completely mixed, encourage children to identify the new secondary color.

Did You Know?

Some animals can't see certain colors. In fact, it's thought that dogs see the world in shades of just one color!

What Now?

Experiment with some chilly color mixing! Place water in the sections of an ice cube tray and then tint the water primary colors (yellow, blue, and red). Have each child choose two cubes in different colors and place them in a glass of clear soda. As the ice melts, the soda transforms into a secondary color!

Mixing Up Colors

We mixed  and .

It made  .

It tasted    .

Ask me to tell you more about our science investigation!

STORYTIME

Storytime

Pete's a Pizza

Written and illustrated by William Steig
It's raining and Pete is miserable because he can't go outside to play. How does his father cheer him up? Why, by turning him into a pizza, of course! This simple, yet imaginative, story is sure to delight young and old alike!

ideas contributed by Ada Goren, Winston-Salem, NC

I like to jump in puddles!

Before You Read

Build excitement for this storytime session with some rainy day discussion! Open up a colorful umbrella and tell youngsters what you like to do on a rainy day. Allow each child the opportunity to hold the umbrella and share what he likes to do on a rainy day. Then explain to youngsters that the story you're about to share is about a little boy who is sad because it's raining and he wants to go outside to play. Then tell students that he is so miserable, it prompts his father to do something very, very silly!

After You Read

With this giggle-inducing activity, little ones get an opportunity to be a pizza just like Pete! Encourage students to lie on the floor on their stomachs. Brush each child's back with a clean, dry paintbrush to represent brushing on the olive oil. Scatter red construction paper circles (pepperoni) and white paper scraps (cheese) over them. Then tell students you're sliding them into the oven. When you determine that the student pizzas are ready, exclaim how nice they look. Then encourage students to jump up just like Pete does. They're sure to love your expression of shock when you find out your pizzas are really preschoolers!

The Very Busy Spider

Written and illustrated by Eric Carle

An industrious spider spends her whole day spinning a web, ignoring a host of farm animals asking her to take part in their activities. She may not stop to join her barnyard buddies, but in the end she has been a helpful friend for catching a pesky fly!

ideas contributed by Ada Goren, Winston-Salem, NC

I walked to school with my mom!

Before You Read

What have your youngsters done today? No doubt they woke up, got dressed, had breakfast, and completed oodles of other tasks. Before reading the story, invite your students to share what they've done so far during their busy day. Then tell them that the story you're going to share is about a very busy critter who only does one task all day long!

After You Read

Make a textured spiderweb by drawing a web on a large sheet of paper and then tracing the lines with glue. After the glue dries, tape the paper to a tabletop. Invite a small group of youngsters to the table. Allow each child to touch the web and compare it to the textured web in the book. Then help each child make a rubbing of the web on a sheet of white construction paper. Help each student add brown construction paper strips to the rubbing to make a fence. Then encourage each child to draw a sleeping spider on her paper. That spider's been very busy!

Storytime

Corduroy

Written and Illustrated by Don Freeman

Corduroy, a cuddly stuffed bear, sits on a department store shelf day after day hoping someone will take him home. Despite his missing button, a nice little girl decides that he is the bear she's always wanted. Finally, Corduroy has the home—and the friend—he's been longing for!

ideas contributed by Suzanne Moore, Tucson, AZ

Before You Read

Introduce this adorable story with a quick button search! Before youngsters enter the room, place a brightly colored jumbo button within view of your circle-time area. Gather youngsters and tell them that you have lost a button. Describe what it looks like. Then have students scan the room from their seats. When they see the button, retrieve it and congratulate them on their keen observation skills. Then explain that the book selection for storytime is about a teddy bear who also happens to be looking for a button!

Corduroy climbs down!

After You Read

Corduroy climbs *down* from the shelf, he rides *up* the escalator, and he topples *off* the bed! This little bear sure knows his positional words! Have each child transform a bear cutout into a stick puppet similar to the one shown. During a retelling of the story, invite youngsters to use their puppets to imitate the teddy bear's movements.

Gingerbread Baby

Written and Illustrated by Jan Brett

When the Gingerbread Baby escapes from Matti's oven, he is chased around the countryside by a variety of people and animals. Meanwhile, Matti remains at home cooking up a way to catch this mischievous cookie!

ideas contributed by Suzanne Moore, Tucson, AZ

What's in the bag? Let's take a look. A [spoon] is a clue about our book!

Gingerbread Mix

Before You Read

Serve up clues about the story with a sack full of mystery items! Place in a paper sack the following clues about the story: a mixing spoon and bowl, a box of gingerbread mix (or a sack of sugar), and a gingerbread man cookie cutter. Recite the rhyme shown, removing the spoon from the sack after the second line. Then invite youngsters to guess what the story might be about based on this clue. Continue in the same way for each remaining clue. Once all the items have been revealed, present the book with great fanfare. Then invite youngsters to settle in for a tale about a gingerbread cookie on the run!

After You Read

With this sweet activity, little ones create a house for the Gingerbread Baby just like Matti does! Help each youngster cut out a construction paper copy of the house pattern on page 147; then have her decorate it with craft supplies to resemble a gingerbread house. Staple the house atop a sheet of construction paper, as shown, to make a flap. Next, instruct her to draw a picture of the Gingerbread Baby under the flap. Invite little ones to retell the story and flip open their houses to reveal the conclusion!

Storytime

Rain

Written by Robert Kalan
Illustrated by Donald Crews

As a storm approaches, white clouds and a blue sky are replaced by gray clouds and a gray sky. Then, suddenly, there's lots and lots of rain! It falls on the red car, the orange flowers, and many other objects in this vivid rain-drenched landscape.

ideas contributed by Roxanne LaBell Dearman
Western NC Early Intervention Program for Children
Who Are Deaf or Hard of Hearing
Charlotte, NC

Before You Read

Before reading the book, engage students in this whole-group game! Give a raindrop cutout to a child and ask her to place it somewhere in the classroom where it can easily be seen. Have students identify the object that the raindrop is sitting on and the object's color. For example, they might say, "There's rain on the green carpet." Continue in the same way for several rounds, inviting a different child to place the raindrop each time. Then explain that the storytime selection for the day is about many colorful objects that get covered with rain!

There's rain on the purple chair!

Anna

Rain on <u>my blue house</u>.

After You Read

This artsy writing project is reminiscent of the book's striking pictures! In advance, program a sheet of paper with the word *Rain* repeated to resemble the rain in the book. Make blue construction paper copies of the sheet; then cut the copies into strips. To begin, give each child a sheet of construction paper labeled with the prompt shown. Help her determine something rain might fall on and the object's color. Then write her words to complete the prompt. Have her draw a picture of the object above the words. Finally, encourage her to glue strips of rain to the paper.

Sylvester and the Magic Pebble

Written and Illustrated by William Steig

When Sylvester the donkey finds a magic pebble, he transforms himself into a rock to escape from a ferocious lion. No doubt he didn't think ahead and wonder how he would transform from a rock back into Sylvester!

Before You Read

To prepare for this prereading activity, paint a stone red and then allow the paint to dry. Present the stone to your little ones. Then explain that the story you're about to read is about a donkey who finds a special red pebble that makes wishes come true. Invite each student to hold the stone and predict what Sylvester might wish for. After each child has an opportunity to share, collect the stone for safe-keeping. Then have little ones settle in for this fanciful read-aloud!

The donkey would wish for a new toy!

What I Would Wish For

a new bike	Josh
a cookie	Ian
a little brother	Ling
pink shoes	Myricle
a truck	D'Juan
pretty dolls	Tory

After You Read

Trim a piece of bulletin board paper to resemble a large rock. Glue a small circle of red paper to the rock to resemble the magic pebble. Then write the heading shown and attach the rock to your classroom wall. Invite a student to the display and ask her what she might wish for if she had a magic pebble. Write her words and her name on the rock. Then continue in the same way with each remaining youngster. Share students' wishes during a future circle-time gathering.

Storytime

Have You Seen My Duckling?

Written and Illustrated by Nancy Tafuri
When a playful duckling swims away from its family, Mother Duck and her remaining ducklings scour the pond questioning its inhabitants. Where is the missing duckling? It's cleverly nestled in the background in every scene!

ideas contributed by Roxanne LaBell Dearman
Western NC Early Intervention Program for Children
Who Are Deaf or Hard of Hearing
Charlotte, NC

Before You Read

Before sharing the story, cut out a yellow construction paper copy of the duckling pattern on page 148. Then attach the duckling to a wall or display in your classroom. Ask students if they've seen your duckling, encouraging them to scan the classroom for the lost critter. React with great excitement and joy when youngsters share the duckling's location. Next, explain that the storytime selection is about a duck that's also looking for a lost duckling. Finally, have little ones settle in for a read-aloud of the story.

There's your duckling!

After You Read

Cut a pond shape from blue bulletin board paper and place it in your circle-time area. Have each child color and cut out a personalized duckling pattern (see the pattern on page 148). Next, place all the ducklings on the pond. Gather youngsters around the pond and ask, "Have you seen [child's name]'s duckling?" Then invite the student to find her duckling. Continue in the same manner until each youngster has found her duckling.

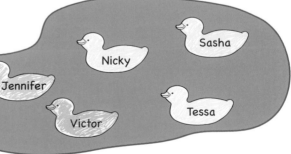

Inch by Inch

Written and Illustrated by Leo Lionni

A clever inchworm keeps itself safe from a hungry robin by doing what it does best—measuring! The robin is so impressed with the inchworm's ability that it takes the critter to measure some feathered friends. But can the inchworm continue to save itself from becoming a tasty snack?

ideas contributed by Roxanne LaBell Dearman
Western NC Early Intervention Program for Children
Who Are Deaf or Hard of Hearing
Charlotte, NC

Before You Read

Show youngsters just how long an inch is with this prereading activity. Give each child a one-inch strip of green tagboard to resemble an inchworm. Ask students to observe their inchworms; then ask how a creature this tiny could get away from a hungry bird. After students share their thoughts, collect the inchworms and put them aside for the activity below. Then invite youngsters to listen to the story and find out how this inchworm protects itself from a hungry bird!

After You Read

Your little ones can measure birds too! Put the inchworms used in the activity above in a container. Place the container at a center along with several colorful bird cutouts (see the pattern on page 148). Show students how to place the inchworms end to end to measure a bird. Finally, invite youngsters to the center and encourage them to explore measurement by placing worms on the birds on their own.

Storytime

Chicka Chicka Boom Boom

Written by Bill Martin Jr. and John Archambault
Illustrated by Lois Ehlert

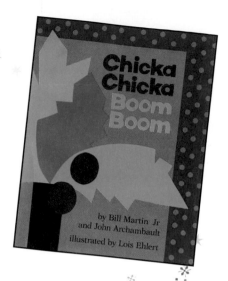

Skit skat skoodle doot, flip flop flee—you've got to read this book about a coconut tree! A group of mischievous lowercase letters race to the top of a coconut tree. But will there be enough room? This engaging rhythmic adventure is sure to enthrall your little ones.

ideas contributed by Ada Goren, Winston-Salem, NC

Before You Read

Present an adhesive bandage to your youngsters. Ask them to explain what bandages are used for and then share experiences they've had using them. After they share their stories, explain that the book you're about to read has several characters that topple out of a tree and one of them has to use a bandage. Then have little ones listen to a read-aloud of this classic story, encouraging youngsters to watch for the bandage among the pile of letters.

After You Read

Have students sit in a circle on the floor. Review the illustration that shows all the letters in a pile after they've fallen out of the tree. Then place a pile of letter cutouts in the middle of the circle to resemble those in the book. Lead students in reciting the rhyme shown. Then encourage a child to pick up a letter and help him identify its name. Repeat the process several times, reciting the rhyme and calling on a different child each time.

Chicka chicka boom boom
Flip, flop, flee!
What letter fell
From the coconut tree?

Swimmy

Written and Illustrated by Leo Lionni

How will a school of fish frolic in the sea when a big hungry tuna is lurking about? A little fish named Swimmy has the answer! This timeless tale of teamwork will enthrall your youngsters from beginning to end!

Before You Read

Lead into the story with a demonstration of teamwork! Before children arrive for the day, scatter several blocks (or other toys) around the room. To begin, gather youngsters in your large-group area. Begin picking up the blocks; then stop and explain that it will take a long time if you continue by yourself. Invite the students to help you. Once the blocks are back where they belong, explain that when people work together they can often do things faster and more easily than if one person were to try to complete a task by herself. Then tell youngsters that the book you're about to share is about a school of fish that work together so they can swim safely.

After You Read

Remind youngsters of Swimmy's splendid idea with this simple snack! Draw a fish shape on a paper plate for each child. Give each student a plate and have her arrange orange fish-shaped crackers within the fish outline. Encourage her to add a fish-shaped cracker in a different color to make the fish's eye. Then invite her to nibble on her treat. Look—it's Swimmy!

Jana Sanderson
Rainbow School
Stockton, CA

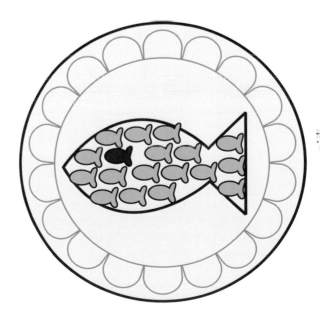

Storytime

Chrysanthemum

Written and Illustrated by Kevin Henkes

Chrysanthemum, a little mouse, adores her lovely name. But when she goes to school her classmates make fun of her, saying that her name is too long and flowery. Then one day a very special teacher helps the children see that the name Chrysanthemum *is absolutely perfect!*

ideas contributed by Janet R. Boyce, Cokato, MN

My name is Conner!

Before You Read

Set the stage for this storytime selection with a quick name introduction! To begin, explain to youngsters that names are very special and that each student should be proud of his name. Then say, "My name is [your name]." Encourage students to say hello and then repeat your name. Next, prompt a child to say his name in the same way and encourage students to say hello and repeat the child's name. Continue in the same way for each child in the class. Then explain that the story you're about to read is about a little mouse with a very unique name!

After You Read

Youngsters are sure to bloom before your eyes with this flowery follow-up! Give each child in a small group a white construction paper circle. Provide access to yellow and orange ink pads. Then have each student make fingerprints on her circle to transform it into a flower. Invite each child to glue her flower to a green construction paper stem. Then have her glue green construction paper leaves to the stem. Explain that the flower resembles a chrysanthemum, the kind of flower that the mouse in the story is named after. Write each child's name on her flower. Then attach it to a bulletin board titled "Absolutely Perfect Names."

TEC41022

Duckling Pattern
Use with "Before You Read" and "After You Read" on page 142.

TEC41024

Bird Pattern
Use with "After You Read" on page 143.

TEC41024

Book Units

The Napping House

Written by Audrey Wood
Illustrated by Don Wood

On a dreary day, a granny, a child, and three cuddly critters take a nap. But during all the dreaming and dozing, a tiny flea creeps up on the unsuspecting nappers. No doubt this wakeful flea will put a halt to everyone's peaceful slumber!

THE NAPPING HOUSE
by AUDREY WOOD
Illustrated by DON WOOD

ideas contributed by Roxanne LaBell Dearman
Western NC Early Intervention Program for Children
Who Are Deaf or Hard of Hearing
Charlotte, NC

Who Naps?

Making a personal connection
Lots of people and animals nap! Before reading the story, have students share the names of people and animals that take naps; write each name on a sheet of chart paper under the heading shown. Your little ones may be surprised at the large number of nappers! Next, explain that the book you're about to read is about an entire household that takes a nap at the same time!

Who Naps?
Shana
Aunt Gracie
Shawn
John's cat, Fluffy
Kim's hamsters
Bears at the zoo
Lee's dad
Babies
Dogs
Uncle John
Danny

Missing Nappers
Identifying characters in a story
With this whole-group activity, youngsters use flannelboard props to review the characters in the story! Color and cut out a copy of the patterns on pages 152 and 153. Ready the cutouts for flannelboard use. To begin, place the bed on your flannelboard. Then enlist youngsters' help in recalling the characters from the story and placing them above the bed in the correct order.

Next, have youngsters hold their hands over their eyes as you remove a character from the board. Have students remove their hands and identify the missing character. When they guess correctly, reveal the character and place it back on the board. Continue in the same way with other characters.

Slumber Music
Reviewing story events through song

This toe-tapping ditty is a fun way to review story events!
Lead students in singing the song below as you refer to each corresponding illustration in the book.

(sung to the tune of "The Farmer in the Dell")

The granny sleeps on the bed.
The granny sleeps on the bed.
She sleeps away the rainy day.
The granny sleeps on the bed.

Continue with the following verses: *the child sleeps on the granny, the dog sleeps on the child, the cat sleeps on the dog, the mouse sleeps on the cat.* Then sing the following stanza and additional verses:

The flea wakes up the mouse.
The flea wakes up the mouse.
It gets a scare, jumps in the air.
The flea wakes up the mouse.

Continue with the following verses: *the mouse wakes up the cat, the cat wakes up the dog, the dog wakes up the child, the child wakes up the granny.*

The Napping School
Creating a story innovation

This class book is sure to be a hit with your little ones! Help each child write his name on a copy of the prompt shown. Have him glue his prompt to the bottom of a 9" x 12" sheet of construction paper. Next, instruct each student to draw a picture of himself during rest time at your school. Bind all of the completed papers together with a cover titled as shown. Then read students this very entertaining bedtime story!

Billy sleeps during rest time
In the napping school,
Where everyone is sleeping.

Character Patterns

Use with "Missing Nappers" on page 150.

TEC41022

TEC41022

TEC41022

TEC41022

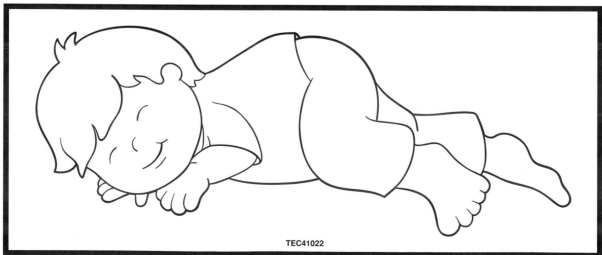

TEC41022

TEC41022

TEC41022

Jamberry

Written and Illustrated by Bruce Degen

Follow a lovable bear and his boy companion through their adventures in an imaginary berry-filled land! Captivating rhymes and detailed illustrations are sure to leave youngsters hungry for repeated readings of this sweet story.

ideas by Lucia Kemp Henry, Fallon, NV

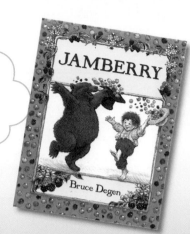

Bunches of Berries!
Building prior knowledge

Before sharing this read-aloud, familiarize youngsters with some "berry" sweet fruits. Color and cut out a copy of the berry patterns on page 156. Place the berries along the left-hand side of a pocket chart. Make a name card for each berry. To begin, prompt students to name each berry. Then enlist their help in placing each name card next to its corresponding cutout. After reading each card aloud, ask students to share observations about the words, leading them to notice how all of the names end with the word *berry*. Finally, explain to students that the story you are about to read is about a fantastical land filled with oodles of berries!

	strawberry
	blueberry
	blackberry
	raspberry

A Merry Berry Poem
Developing number recognition

The bear and boy encounter so many berries that it would be difficult to count them all. Counting the berries in this flannelboard activity, however, is as easy as pie! Make ten blueberry cutouts from blue construction paper using the pattern on page 156. Label each berry with a different number from 1 to 10; then ready the cutouts for flannelboard use. Lead little ones in reciting the rhyme shown, displaying each berry on the flannelboard when indicated. When youngsters are comfortable with the rhyme, place the materials at a center for independent practice.

One berry, two berry, tasting a blueberry.
Three berry, four berry, munching some more berry.
Five berry, six berry, Popsicle licks berry.
Seven berry, eight berry, pie on my plate berry.
Nine berry, ten berry, filled up again berry!

A Hat Full of Berries
Repeating rhyming pairs

Instead of gathering blueberries in a pail, the bear uses his hat! Your little berry pickers follow the bear's lead during this circle-time activity. Give each youngster a blue pom-pom to represent a blueberry. Hand a hat to a student and recite a pair of rhyming words from the story (see the suggestions provided). Have her repeat the words as she drops her blueberry into the hat. Continue in this manner for each remaining child.

Suggestions:
bramble/jamble
mountain/fountain
strawberry/pawberry
raspberry/jazzberry,
lamb/jam
boomberry/zoomberry

In Berryland, __Abby__ saw a __strawberry snail__.

In Berryland
Dictating information to complete a sentence

Strawberry lambs and raspberry rabbits! What other interesting creatures might live in Berryland? For each student, program a sheet of paper with the prompt shown. After a review of the illustrations, invite little ones to suggest imaginary animals or objects that they might see on a visit to Berryland. Give each child a copy of the programmed paper and a berry cutout (see the patterns on page 156). Have her color her cutout and glue it to her paper. Then encourage her to add details to create an imaginary animal or object. Finally, write each child's dictated words to complete the sentence.

Comparing Jam
Sorting

Cut enough slices of bread into quarters to provide two pieces for each child. Have each youngster use a plastic knife to spread blackberry jam on one piece of bread and strawberry jam on his second piece of bread. Invite him to eat his snack. Next, give each youngster a personalized bread cutout (see the patterns on page 157) and have him color it to match the jam he liked better. Instruct him to glue his cutout to a large paper plate. Then lead students in sorting the plates by color to determine how many students preferred each jam flavor.

Tom

155

Berry Patterns

Use with "Bunches of Berries!" and "A Merry Berry Poem" on page 154 and "In Berryland" on page 155.

blackberry

raspberry

blueberry

strawberry

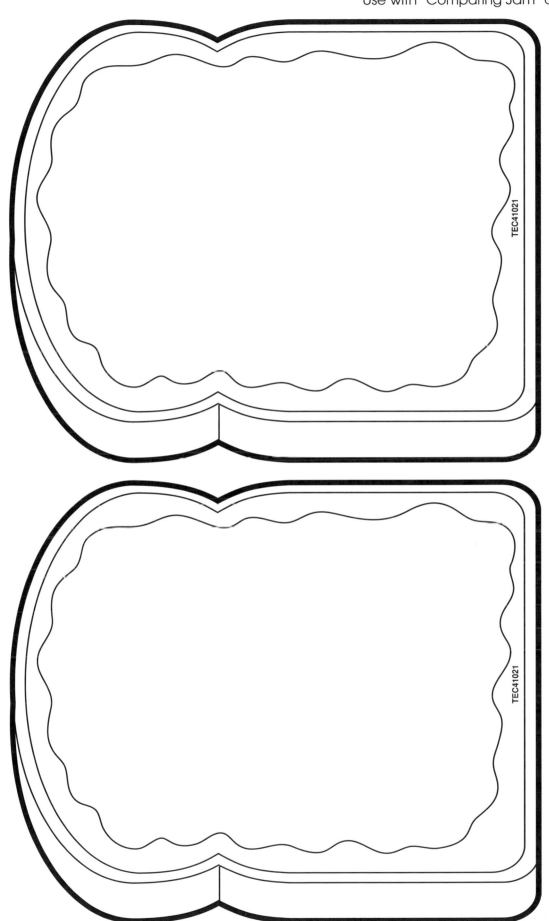

TEC41021

TEC41021

Mouse Paint

Written and Illustrated by Ellen Stoll Walsh

Three white mice standing on a white piece of paper are nearly invisible to a lurking cat. But when the mice discover jars of red, yellow, and blue paint, they partake in some risky color mixing! No doubt these color-conscious rodents will remember that the cat is still hovering nearby.

ideas contributed by Roxanne LaBell Dearman
Western NC Early Intervention Program for Children Who Are Deaf or Hard of Hearing
Charlotte, NC

Almost Invisible!
Building prior knowledge

Introduce youngsters to the concept of camouflage with this engaging prereading activity! Cut out a copy of the mouse pattern on page 160, making sure to completely trim off the bold outer line. Tape the mouse to a sheet of white construction paper and then display the paper near your large-group area. To begin, express dismay at how difficult it is to see the white mouse on white paper. Encourage youngsters to suggest ways they could make the mouse show up more, such as coloring him red or placing him on a blue sheet of paper. Then explain that your storytime selection for the day is about three white mice that hide from a cat on a sheet of white paper.

Dance, Dance, Dance!
Expressing oneself through art

The brightly colored mice are shocked when their dancing feet mix up puddles of secondary colors. No doubt your little ones will want to try some mixing fun as well! For each child, place dollops of red, yellow, and blue paint on a 12" x 18" sheet of white construction paper. Then give each youngster three cotton balls to resemble mice. Play a recording of upbeat music and have little ones dance their mice through the paint. That little mouse made the color green!

Mixing Colors

Developing color recognition

Little ones brush up on color recognition with this nifty rhyme. Use the pattern on page 160 to make a mouse cutout in each of the following colors: blue, yellow, and red. Make a matching puddle cutout for each mouse. Next, attach the red mouse and blue puddle to your board as shown. Lead students in reciting the rhyme below. Then invite them to guess the color that results from mixing red and blue paint, reviewing the book's illustrations if needed. Continue in the same way with other combinations of mice and puddles, replacing the color word in the first line of the rhyme each time.

Dance little [red] mouse; stomp your feet.
Wiggle your tail as you feel the beat.
Then look down; don't be afraid
To find out what new color you've made!

The blue mouse is hiding on the blue bookcase.

Hide-and-Seek

Developing connections between spoken and written words

Where should a little mouse hide from a hungry cat? Why, on something the same color as its fur, of course! Have each child color and cut out a copy of the mouse pattern on page 160. Next, help each youngster think of a good hiding place for the mouse. For example, a blue mouse could hide very nicely on a blue bookcase. Have the child observe as you write a sentence on a matching strip of paper to explain where the mouse is hiding. Then help the child attach the mouse to the location indicated. Look at all the mice hiding in the classroom!

159

Preschool Painters

Listening for the beginning sound /p/

No painting smocks are needed for this unique whole-group activity! Give each child a clean paintbrush and a copy of page 161. Encourage students to say the word *paint* several times, leading them to notice that the word begins with the /p/ sound. Then have students locate the picture of the pig and say its name, emphasizing the /p/ sound. Guide students to conclude that the word *paint* and the word *pig* both begin with the /p/ sound. Then encourage students to brush their paintbrushes over the pig while repeating the /p/ sound a few times. Repeat the process with each picture on the page. If desired, encourage each youngster to take his paper home to color with his family.

Name MiKayla

Listen for directions.

Painting Pictures

Beginning sound /p/

Mouse Pattern

Use with "Almost Invisible!" on page 158 and "Mixing Colors" and "Hide-and-Seek" on page 159.

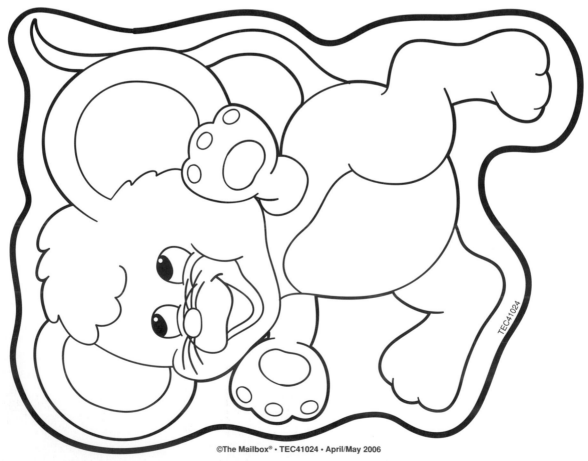

TEC41024

160

Name_____ Beginning sound /p/

Painting Pictures

Listen for directions.

Fish Eyes:
A Book You Can Count On

Written and illustrated by Lois Ehlert

A little black fish explores a sea of colorful friends in this counting extravaganza! The clever cutout eyes of the fish he meets and the subtle addition skills incorporated in the story make this book appealing to all. So dive right in; the water is fine!

ideas contributed by Suzanne Moore, Tucson, AZ

Movin' to the Motion
Building prior knowledge

Fish in the story flip, dart, and jump and so can your youngsters with this engaging prereading activity! To begin, explain that fish move in many different ways. Tell students that some fish dart, moving suddenly and quickly. Then encourage children to move about the room like darting fish. Have little ones suggest other ways fish might move, encouraging them to demonstrate each movement. Then lead students in performing the song shown before they settle in for a read-aloud of the story.

(sung to the tune of "Head and Shoulders")

I can move just like a fish. (See me jump!)
I can move just like a fish. (See me dive!)
Jumping up and diving down,
I can move just like a fish. (Swish! Swish!)

Fish With Flair
Dictating information to complete a sentence

The book's narrator wishes she could be a fish and then imagines what other fish she might see. With this idea, your little ones use their imaginations in a similar way. To prepare, make a class supply of fish cutouts. Program for each child a sentence strip with the prompt shown. Encourage each youngster to decorate his fish with craft items. Next, ask him to describe his finished fish. As he does, write his response on a strip to complete the prompt. Finally, display the fish and corresponding strips on a wall with the title "If I Were a Fish."

I'd see <u>fish with sparkly stripes.</u>

One Fish, Two Fish
Counting to 10
These fish frolic in a beautiful blue sea just as the fish in the book do! Cover a tabletop with blue plastic wrap to resemble water. Glue green strips of crepe paper down the middle of the water to represent seaweed. Make ten colorful fish cutouts. Then place the cutouts to one side of the seaweed. To play, a child visits the table and counts aloud as he "jumps" each fish to the other side of the seaweed.

Match and Munch
Matching items one-to-one
The colorful eye cutouts in this book are sure to intrigue your little ones. After youngsters have had an opportunity to investigate the cutouts, invite them to this sweet math center! Make ten construction paper fish cutouts. Then hole-punch an eye for each fish. Place the fish at a center along with a cup of colorful loop cereal. When a child visits the center, have her put one cereal piece on each fish eye. Then give her a fresh cup of cereal to snack on!

Plus Me!
Dramatizing the story
The little black fish adds himself to the number of fish on various pages. With this idea, youngsters add you to a group! Have a child stand and pretend to be a fish. Lead youngsters in reciting the first four lines of the chant below as the volunteer moves her arms as if they were fins. During the final line of the chant, stand next to the child and move your arms in a similar way. Then help the children count both you and the volunteer to make a total of two fish. Have the youngster sit down. Then repeat the process, inviting two new students to pretend to be fish and changing the number in the rhyme appropriately.

Teacher: How many fish are swimming in the sea?
Children: [One] little fish is/are swimming in the sea.
Teacher: [One] fish?
Children: Yes, [one!]
Teacher: [One] fish plus me!

If You Take a Mouse to School

Written by Laura Numeroff
Illustrated by Felicia Bond

"If you take a mouse to school, he'll ask you for your lunchbox." Thus begins an energetic romp that takes a mouse and his boy companion through a fun-filled school day. At the end of the day, the mouse realizes that he's left the lunchbox behind. That's when this adorable tale comes full circle in a supremely satisfying conclusion!

ideas by Ada Goren, Winston-Salem, NC

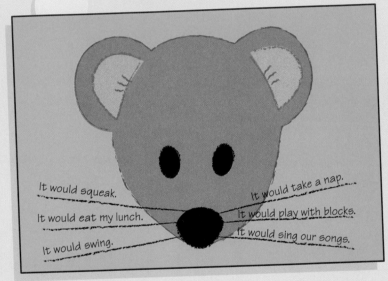

It would squeak.
It would eat my lunch.
It would swing.
It would take a nap.
It would play with blocks.
It would sing our songs.

A Very Special Visitor
Predicting story events

What would a mouse do if it were to visit your classroom? Your youngsters are sure to have a few ideas! Trim a piece of paper to resemble a mouse head. Draw facial features on the mouse. Then attach it to a sheet of colorful paper. Draw whiskers on the mouse Then post the paper in your large-group area. To begin, have youngsters look at the cover of the book and describe what they see. After you read aloud the title, invite students to predict what a mouse would do if it were to visit your school. Write children's responses on the mouse's whiskers. Next, read the book aloud. Then revisit the list and have students determine whether any of their predictions were similar to the events in the story.

School Day Sequencing
Sequencing story events

Science experiments, building with blocks, and bookmaking—this mouse's day is jam-packed with events! Invite students to sequence those events during a second reading of the story. Color a copy of the sequencing cards on page 166 and laminate them for durability. Place Sticky-Tac adhesive on the back of each card (or attach a small piece of tape to the top of each card) and arrange them on a tabletop in a random fashion. Begin reading the story. As each pictured event occurs, have a volunteer find the corresponding card on the tabletop and place it on the board to show the sequence of events. That's one busy little critter!

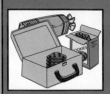

Super Science!
Observing a demonstration

During science time, the mouse creates great globs of oozing purple lava! You can let youngsters in on the mouse's secret recipe with this riveting demonstration. Display the picture that shows the mouse and his science experiment and have little ones describe what they see. Then tell them that you're going to perform a similar experiment. Pour one-fourth cup of white vinegar into a clear plastic cup; then use food coloring to tint the vinegar purple. Next, have students watch carefully as you sprinkle some baking soda into the purple liquid. Encourage students to describe the resulting reaction. So that's how the mouse makes that lava!

An Awesome Abode
Responding to literature through play

The mouse builds a house out of blocks and then fashions furniture from clay. No doubt your preschoolers will be inspired to make a cozy mouse house too! Place at a center several mouse cutouts, a supply of building blocks, and colorful play dough. A visiting student builds a house and pieces of furniture using the blocks and play dough. Then he places a mouse cutout in its cozy new home. That's a house fit for a mouse!

Munchies From Mouse
Using positional words

The mouse put his lunchbox in a safe place—and then he forgot it! Maybe he left a lunchbox in your classroom too! Place in a lunchbox a resealable bag filled with cookies and a note similar to the one shown. Then hide the lunchbox in your classroom. Tell youngsters that the mouse came to visit and left his lunchbox somewhere in the room. Invite students to guess where the lunchbox might be located, encouraging them to use positional words in their responses. When youngsters guess the correct location, show them the box, read the note, and then share the mouse's snack. Chocolate chip cookies must be the mouse's favorite treat!

Dear Boys and Girls,
I left this snack for you!

Love,
Mouse

Sequencing Cards
Use with "School Day Sequencing" on page 164.

©The Mailbox® · TEC41020 · Aug./Sept. 2005

CENTER UNITS

Gobblin' Good Centers!

Stuffed with learning fun, this collection of convenient centers is an engaging way to spotlight that oh-so-unique bird—the turkey!

ideas contributed by Jana Sanderson, Rainbow School, Stockton, CA

Science Center
The Best Nest

Youngsters may be surprised to find out that wild turkeys use leaves to build nests on the ground! To have youngsters make their own wild turkey nests, place at a center white egg cutouts, brown leaf cutouts, glue, and a class supply of 9" x 12" construction paper sheets. Also provide access to brown watercolor paints and a toothbrush. A youngster visits the center and glues several leaves to a sheet of paper to resemble a nest. He glues eggs to the nest. Then he taps a paint-covered toothbrush over the eggs to give them their distinctive brown speckles.

Water Table
Bird Bath

Use the pattern on page 171 to make several craft foam turkey cutouts. Place the cutouts in your water table along with several turkey basters. Then have students give their fine-motor skills a workout as they baste the turkeys!

Literacy Center
Turkeys in the Straw

Use the pattern on page 171 to make a supply of turkey cutouts. Label half of the cutouts with a chosen letter and the remaining half with a different letter. Nestle the cutouts in a container of brown paper shreds (straw). Color and cut out two copies of the barn pattern on page 171; then glue each one to a different piece of poster board. Label each poster board piece with a different letter to match the turkey cutouts. Then place the container and poster board pieces at a center. A child reaches into the straw and finds a turkey. Then she places it in the corresponding farmyard. She continues in the same way with each remaining turkey in the straw.

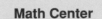

Math Center
Acorns, Bugs, and Berries!

Youngsters practice sorting skills while learning a thing or two about a typical wild turkey diet! Make three copies of the food patterns on page 172. Color and laminate the patterns; then cut them out. Glue one of each type of pattern to a separate container. Then scatter the remaining patterns around a traffic-free area of the floor. Place the containers nearby. Explain to youngsters that wild turkeys will eat nuts, berries, and insects. Students visit the center and pretend to be wild turkeys looking for food. They pick up each type of food found and then sort it into the correct basket.

Snack Center
Turkey Taco Salad

Everyone helps make this healthy snack! A child visits the center and uses a butter knife to cut several lettuce leaves and a slice of lunch meat into small strips. He places his prepared ingredients in a large bowl along with a sprinkle of cheese. After each child has had a chance to visit the center and add to the salad, embellish it with nacho chip feathers. Tape a turkey body cutout to the bowl as shown. (If desired, use an enlarged copy of the turkey body pattern below.) For snacktime, give each child a small serving of salad and several chips. If desired, provide salsa or dressing as a salad topper.

Fine-Motor Area
Clip-On Feathers!

To prepare the center, make two copies of the turkey body below. Color and then cut out the patterns. Also cut a paper plate in half. (You may wish to choose a colorful paper plate like the one shown.) Then glue each turkey to a plate half. When the glue is dry, place the plates at a center along with a collection of colorful plastic clothespins. Have each youngster clip clothespins to each turkey to give it a lovely array of feathers.

Eileen Mattas, Little Learners Preschool, Glenview, IL

Turkey Body Patterns

Use with "Leafy Turkey" on page 35 and "Turkey Taco Salad" and "Clip-On Feathers!" on this page.

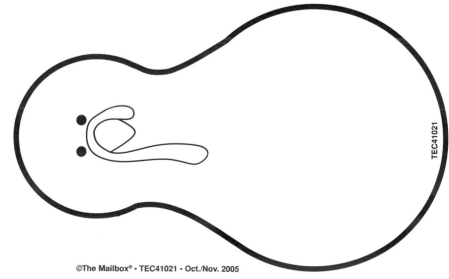

TEC41021

Turkey Profile Pattern
Use with "Bird Bath" on page 168 and
"Turkeys in the Straw" on page 169.

TEC41021

Barn Pattern
Use with "Turkeys in the
Straw" on page 169.

TEC41021

Wild Turkey Food Patterns

Use with "Acorns, Bugs, and Berries!" on page 169.

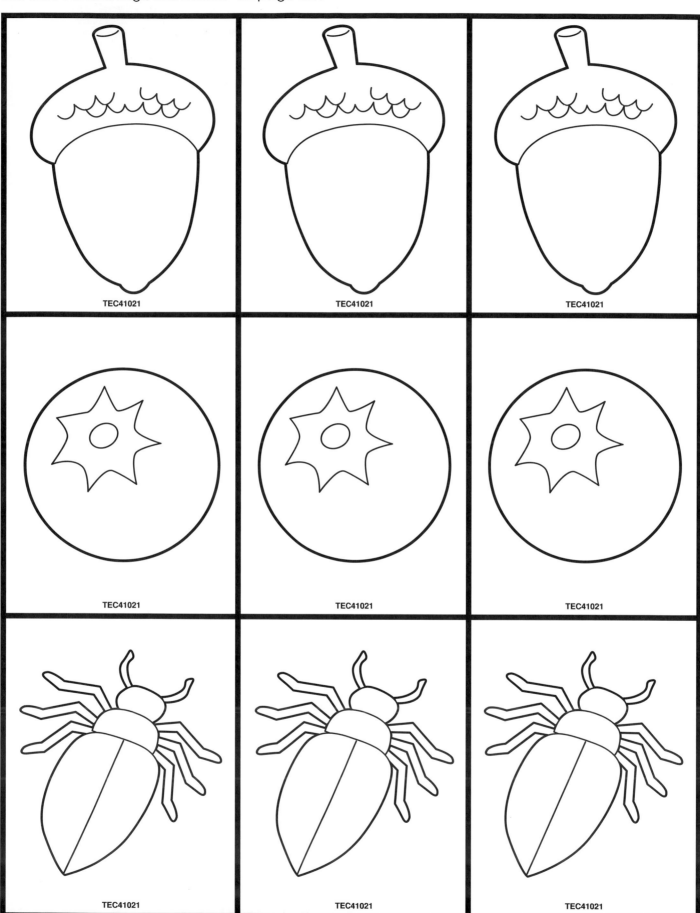

TEC41021

TEC41021

TEC41021

TEC41021

TEC41021

TEC41021

TEC41021

TEC41021

TEC41021

All Aboard for Centers!

Delight your little train enthusiasts with centers they'll choo-choo-choose time and time again!

ideas contributed by Angie Kutzer, Garrett Elementary, Mebane, NC

Literacy Center
The Letter Express
Sorting letters from other symbols

Cut out a construction paper copy of the engine pattern on page 176 and several colorful copies of the boxcar pattern on page 177. Label the engine "The Letter Express." Label each car with either a letter or a different symbol, such as a shape or number. Place the engine and cars at a center. A child builds a train, choosing only the boxcars labeled with letters to place behind the engine.

Fine-Motor Center
Making Tracks!
Developing fine-motor skills

With this imaginative center, youngsters build railroad tracks and furnish the surrounding area with some eye-catching scenery! Tape a length of green bulletin board paper to a tabletop. Draw railroad tracks on the paper. Then place glue at the table along with a supply of craft sticks. Have students glue craft sticks to the tracks to resemble the rails and ties. After all the tracks have been laid and the glue is dry, provide access to paper, glue, markers, and small boxes. Then invite students to use the supplies to make trees, stores, houses, and bushes to add to the scene. This area is booming since the railroad came to town!

173

Writing Center
Railroad Crossing!
Developing prewriting skills

Make a railroad crossing sign, similar to the one shown, with dashed lines to indicate the sign's details. Then make a yellow construction paper copy of the sign for each child. Explain that the sign warns people to be careful because there is a railroad crossing ahead. To use the center, a youngster chooses a sign and traces the dashed lines with a black marker. Then he mounts the sign on a paint-stirring stick.

Phyllis Prestridge
First United Methodist Church Early Learning Center
Amory, MS

Sensory Center
The Texture Train
Exploring texture

Gather a variety of textured materials, such as sandpaper, cellophane, bubble wrap, corrugated cardboard, and craft feathers. Cut any large materials into smaller pieces; then place all the materials in a container. Put the container at a table along with glue and a class supply of colorful construction paper boxcars (see the pattern on page 177). Have each youngster choose a boxcar and then glue a variety of textured items to it. When the glue is dry, display the projects at student eye level behind an engine cutout (see the pattern on page 176). Then encourage students to gently run their hands along the train to feel the different textures!

Math Center
Puff! Puff!
Making sets

Use the pattern on page 176 to make five colorful engine cutouts. Label each cutout with a different number from 1 to 5 and the corresponding number of dots. Place the cutouts in a center along with a supply of cotton balls. A youngster counts the dots on an engine. Then he counts out the corresponding number of cotton balls and places them above the engine's smokestack to resemble puffs of smoke. Toot! Toot!

Block Center
Building a Train
Exploring transportation through pretend play
Cut out several construction paper copies of the train engine and boxcar patterns on pages 176 and 177. (Reduce the patterns, if needed, to fit on building blocks.) Laminate the cutouts for durability; then mount each one on a different building block. Place the blocks at your block center. Youngsters can use the blocks to build trains in many different lengths!

Snack Center
Chew, Chew, Chew!
Following directions
This caboose is on the loose and it's headed straight for your little one's snack center! Explain that a caboose is a train car usually found at the end of a train. Then have a child spread red-tinted frosting on a graham cracker square to make the body of a caboose. Instruct him to place two Mini Oreo cookies below the graham cracker to resemble wheels. Finally, have him munch on his tasty treat as you read aloud a train-themed book, such as Donald Crew's *Freight Train*.

Games Center
Load It Up!
Matching colors
These boxcars are loaded with a wide variety of colorful items! Use the engine and boxcar patterns on pages 176 and 177 to make a colorful train similar to the one shown. Place the train in a center along with a pillowcase full of small items in matching colors. Two students visit the center. One child closes his eyes, reaches into the bag, and removes an item. Then he identifies its color and places it on the matching boxcar. The students continue in the same way, taking turns, until all the freight has been loaded onto the train!

Engine Pattern

Use with "The Letter Express" on page 173, "The Texture Train" and "Puff! Puff!" on page 174, and "Building a Train" and "Load It Up!" on page 175.

TEC41022

Boxcar Pattern
Use with "The Letter Express" on page 173, "The Texture Train" on page 174,
and "Building a Train" and "Load It Up!" on page 175.

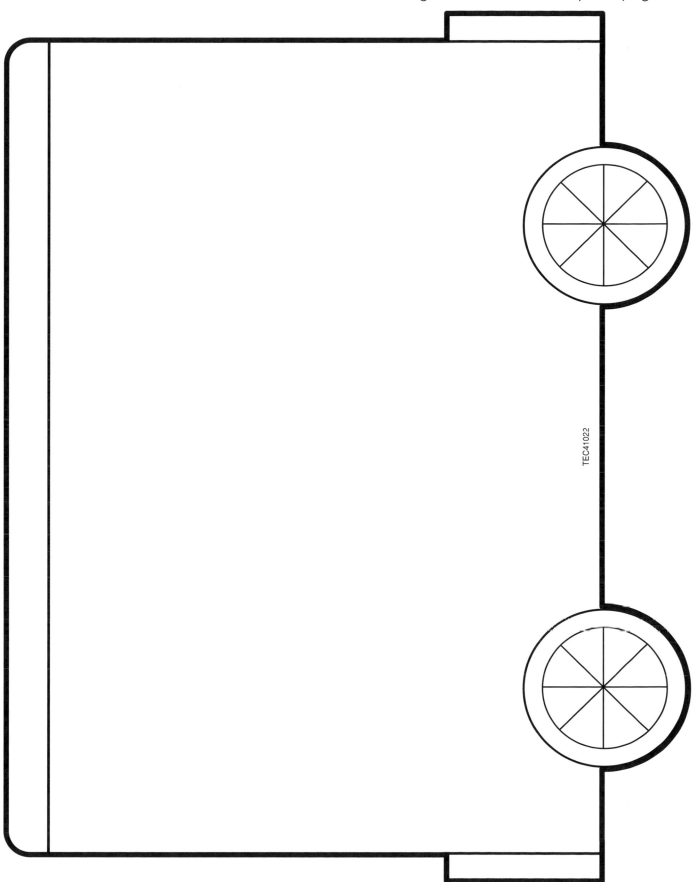

TEC41022

A Rainbow

Brighten up your classroom with this colorful collection of center ideas that are sure to please!

ideas contributed by Ada Goren, Winston-Salem, NC

Math Center

Color Search
Matching colors

Each youngster contributes to this vivid tabletop rainbow! Tape colorful strips of bulletin board paper to a tabletop to resemble a rainbow. Place scissors, glue, and a supply of magazine pages (or grocery store circulars) at the table. A youngster looks through the pages to find pictures that match the colors of the strips. When she finds a picture, she cuts it out, identifies the color, and then glues it in place. Beautiful!

Literacy Center

Rainbow Rubbings
Identifying letters

Write the word *rainbow* in black marker on several tagboard strips. Then trace the letters with thick lines of white glue. When the glue is dry, tape the strips to a tabletop. Stock the center with unwrapped crayons, tape, and a supply of white copy paper. A visiting child feels the letters and names any he recognizes. Then he tapes a sheet of paper on top of the strip (provide help with taping as needed). Finally, he rubs a variety of colorful crayons over the paper.

Writing Center

Color Favorites
Connecting spoken language with written words
Make a class supply of the poem pattern on page 181. Place the poems at a center along with 12" x 18" sheets of construction paper, crayons, and glue. Arrange for an adult to assist youngsters at this center. When a child visits the center, the adult reads the poem aloud and writes the youngster's dictated responses on the lines. Then the student glues her poem to the bottom half of a sheet of construction paper and draws corresponding pictures above the poem as shown.

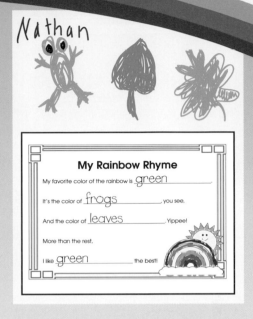

My Rainbow Rhyme

My favorite color of the rainbow is green.

It's the color of frogs, you see,

And the color of leaves. Yippee!

More than the rest,

I like green the best!

Snack Center

Cup of Colors
Following directions
This fruity snack serves up a rainbow of colors! Place at a center separate bowls of strawberry slices, mandarin orange sections, pineapple pieces, green grape halves, blueberries, and purple-tinted whipped topping. A child places a tablespoon of each fruit in a clear plastic cup and then tops it with a scoop of whipped topping. What a tasty rainbow!

Sensory Center

Scoop and Search
Using the sense of touch to explore objects
Fluffy clouds are hidden in this rainbow of rice! To prepare, mix a small amount of rubbing alcohol and food coloring in a large resealable plastic bag. Then add rice and shake the bag until it is thoroughly coated. Pour the rice on paper towels to dry. Prepare several additional colorful batches of rice in the same manner. Pour the prepared rice in a large plastic tub and mix in several cotton ball clouds. Place near the tub several sieves with large holes. A child chooses a sieve and then uses it to scoop up some of the mixture. As the rice funnels through the sieve, it leaves behind the fluffy clouds!

adapted from an idea by Teresa Gmerek
Glendale Head Start
Flinton, PA

Colorful Collage Headband
Using a variety of media

Youngsters showcase their favorite colors with this vibrant headband. Place at a center a supply of colorful construction paper strips labeled with color words as shown. Also provide access to glue and a variety of craft materials, such as tissue paper, sticky dots, gift ribbon, and craft feathers. A child chooses a strip and then glues materials of the same color to the strip. When the glue is dry, size the strip to fit the child's head. These creative headbands are the tops!

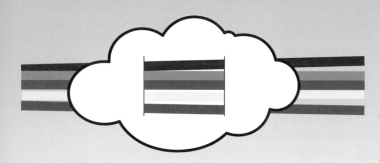

Fine-Motor Area

Cloud Weaving
Developing fine-motor skills

This simple weaving project is a visual delight! For each child, make two parallel cuts in a large cloud cutout as shown. Place the clouds and a large supply of colorful construction paper strips at a center. A child weaves as many strips through the cloud as desired. Then he glues the strips in place (provide assistance with gluing as needed).

Gross-Motor Area

Toss the Rainbow
Developing gross-motor skills

To make a rainbow tossing toy, poke a hole through the lid of a film canister. Thread colorful lengths of curling ribbon through the hole. Then knot the ribbons together under the lid and snap it on the canister. Attach two large cloud cutouts to your floor, making sure they are several feet apart. Place the canister on a cloud. A pair of students visits the center, and each child stands behind a different cloud. One child tosses the rainbow toward his partner's cloud. The other youngster retrieves the rainbow and tosses it back toward the other cloud. Students continue tossing the rainbow as time allows.

My Rainbow Rhyme

My favorite color of the rainbow is _____ .

It's the color of _____ , you see,

And the color of _____ . Yippee!

More than the rest,

I like _____ the best!

©The Mailbox® • TEC41024 • April/May 2006

Note to the teacher: Use with "Color Favorites" on page 179.

Send In the

Floppy shoes? Red noses? Big silly hats? The clowns must be in town! Engage little ones in this collection of clown-themed centers, and you're sure to see miles of smiles!

ideas contributed by Roxanne LaBell Dearman
Western NC Early Intervention Program for Children Who Are Deaf or Hard of Hearing
Charlotte, NC

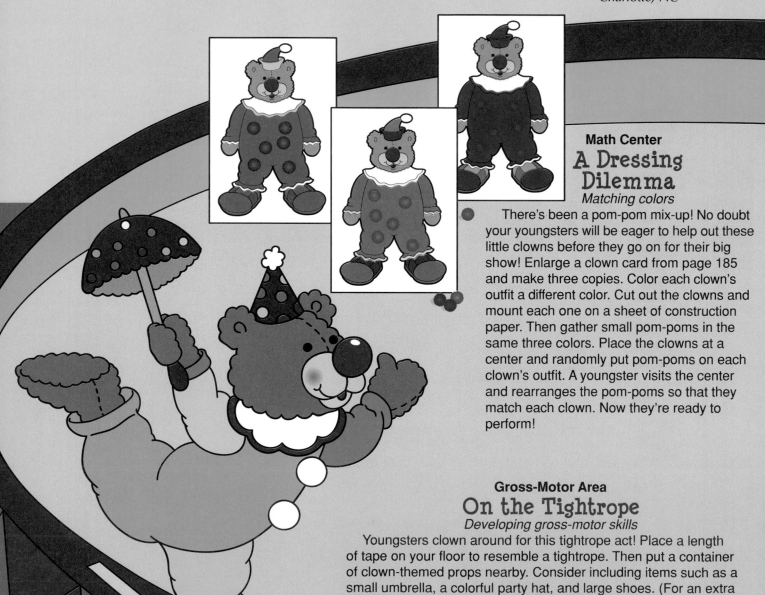

Math Center

A Dressing Dilemma
Matching colors

There's been a pom-pom mix-up! No doubt your youngsters will be eager to help out these little clowns before they go on for their big show! Enlarge a clown card from page 185 and make three copies. Color each clown's outfit a different color. Cut out the clowns and mount each one on a sheet of construction paper. Then gather small pom-poms in the same three colors. Place the clowns at a center and randomly put pom-poms on each clown's outfit. A youngster visits the center and rearranges the pom-poms so that they match each clown. Now they're ready to perform!

Gross-Motor Area

On the Tightrope
Developing gross-motor skills

Youngsters clown around for this tightrope act! Place a length of tape on your floor to resemble a tightrope. Then put a container of clown-themed props nearby. Consider including items such as a small umbrella, a colorful party hat, and large shoes. (For an extra clownish touch, spray-paint the shoes red.) A youngster chooses any desired accessories to use for her tightrope performance. Then she carefully walks across the tightrope.

Clown Centers!

Fine-Motor Area
A Good Hair Day!
Developing fine-motor skills

Clowns need to have bright, colorful hair—and this clown is no exception! Draw a large clown face and collar, similar to the one shown, on a piece of bulletin board paper. Tape the paper to a table. Then place on the table a container of construction paper scraps along with scissors and glue. Each youngster cuts several pieces of construction paper and then glues them to the clown's head. Wow! Look at all that hair!

Snack Center
Crunchy Clown Hats
Following directions

This splendid treat is supersimple! A child visits the snack table and places loop cereal on a colorful clown hat cutout similar to the one shown. When a desired effect is achieved, he nibbles on his tasty decorations!

Block Center
Fantastic Formations
Developing spatial skills

When you attach clowns to your building blocks, youngsters can arrange them to show spectacular clown gymnastics! Make several colorful copies of the clown cards on page 185. Cut out each card and laminate it for durability. Then tape each card to a separate block and place the blocks at a center. Students visit the center to build formations with these cute clowns!

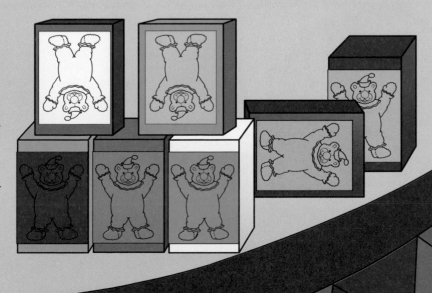

183

Games Center
Nose Throws
Developing turn-taking skills

To prepare this center, draw on a piece of bulletin board paper a large clown face without a nose. Place the clown on the floor in a traffic-free area of your room. Attach a length of tape to the floor a few feet from the clown. Then put a large red craft foam circle (nose) next to the tape line. Two children visit the center. One child stands on the tape line and picks up the nose. Then he tosses the nose toward the clown. The student retrieves the nose and gives it to his partner. Then the partner repeats the process. The students continue in the same way, taking turns, until each child has had several opportunities to toss the nose on the clown.

Literacy Center
A Clown Car
Identifying the letter C

How many clowns can your little ones fit on this car? Quite a few! Color a copy of the car pattern on page 186. Glue the car to the top half of a sheet of construction paper as shown. Write the letter *C* below the car. Make several copies of the clown cards on page 185 in a variety of colors. Cut out the cards. Then label several clowns with the letter *C* and each of the remaining clowns with other letters. Place all of the items at a center. A child finds all the clowns labeled with the letter *C* and places them on the car. Will they all fit? Sure!

Clown Cards

Use with "A Dressing Dilemma" on page 182, "Fantastic Formations" on page 183, and "A Clown Car" on page 184.

TEC41023

TEC41023

TEC41023

TEC41023

Clown Car Pattern

Use with "A Clown Car" on page 184.

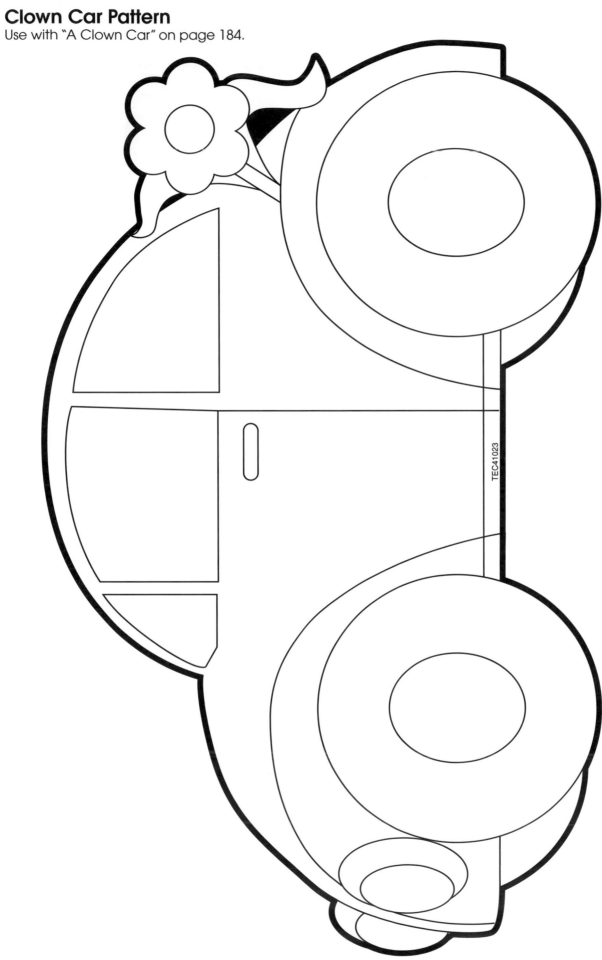

Wild About Watermelon Centers

What cool summer treat can't be beat? Why, watermelon, of course! Bring this popular summertime theme to your classroom with refreshing center ideas!

ideas by Ada Goren, Winston-Salem, NC

Literacy Center
W Is for Watermelon
Identifying the letter W

These fingerprint seeds help little ones remember the shape of the letter *W!* Make a class supply of red or pink watermelon slice cutouts. Use a pencil to lightly write the letter *W* on each slice. Then put the slices at a table along with a black ink pad, green tissue paper squares, and a container of glue with a paintbrush. A youngster chooses a slice and then identifies the letter (with help, as needed). She presses her index finger into the ink pad and then makes fingerprints along the *W* to resemble seeds. Finally, she brushes glue on the outer edge of the slice and then presses crumpled tissue paper squares in the glue to resemble the rind.

Math Center
Marvelous Melon Slices
Sorting

Watermelon slices help sorting skills take shape at this math center. Color and cut out three copies of the patterns on page 190. Then attach a different pattern to each of three paper plates. Set the plates and the remaining slices at a center. A child sorts each watermelon slice onto the corresponding plate. What a fun way to ripen students' sorting skills!

Fine-Motor Center
Lace a Slice
Developing fine-motor skills
Little fingers get a wonderful workout lacing these watermelon slices. Make several tagboard watermelon slices. Draw black seeds on each slice; then laminate the slices for durability. Next, hole-punch each slice as shown. Tie one end of a length of green yarn to a hole in each cutout. Wrap the remaining ends with masking tape for easy lacing. A visiting child threads the yarn length through the holes to create the rind.

Art Center
Three-Dimensional Melons
Expressing oneself through arts and crafts
These unique projects are sure to remind youngsters of real watermelons! Place at a table a class supply of lunch-size paper bags and a container of newspapers strips. Have a child stuff a bag with newspaper strips. Help her fold over the open end of the bag and tape both ends with masking tape as shown so the bag resembles a watermelon. Then have each child paint her watermelon green. After the paint dries, invite her to add lighter green details as shown. If desired, use the completed projects with the dramatic-play center below.

Dramatic-Play Center
Welcome to the Patch!
Participating in imaginary play
Spread a green blanket on the floor and place on top of the blanket the watermelons from "Three-Dimensional Melons" above (or green watermelon cutouts). Consider adding items such as a scale, a pretend cash register, and some big baskets. Little ones use desired props to pick and purchase melons. There are plenty of pleasing melons in this patch!

Play Dough Center
Sweet-Smelling Slices
Exploring the sense of smell

Whip up two batches of your favorite play dough recipe; then tint one batch red and one batch green. Add a package of sugar-free watermelon-flavored gelatin to each batch. Place the play dough at a center stocked with plastic knives, paper plates, and black craft foam pieces to resemble seeds. Little ones roll and cut watermelons and watermelon slices from the scented dough.

Writing Center
A Slice of Writing
Making a connection between spoken and written words

Make a copy of page 191 for each child. Place the copies at a table, along with a black marker and green and pink crayons. Arrange for an adult to be stationed at the center. Help each youngster think of two words that describe watermelon. Then use the black marker to write her chosen words on a slice. Next, read the completed rhyme aloud to the child and then encourage her to decorate the slice with crayons. If desired, cut out the slices and attach them to a red and white checkered background for a delicious display!

By the chunk or by the slice,
Watermelon is quite nice.
It is **yummy** **pink**
and sweet.
What a tasty summer treat!

Sensory Center
Searching for Seeds
Matching numbers

Send your little ones on a hunt for watermelon seeds! Place pink or red paper shreds in a large plastic tub. Make ten large black construction paper seeds; then use a white correction pen (or gel pen) to number the seeds from 1 to 10. Nestle the seeds in the shreds. Label a sentence strip with numbers from 1 to 10 and place it beside the tub. A child finds a seed, identifies the number, and then places it below the corresponding number on the sentence strip. She repeats the process for each seed in the tub.

189

Watermelon Slice Patterns

Use with "Marvelous Melon Slices" on page 187.

TEC41025

TEC41025

TEC41025

TEC41025

TEC41025

TEC41025

By the chunk or by the slice,
Watermelon is quite nice.

It is _____, _____ and sweet.

What a tasty summer treat!

TEC41025

©The Mailbox® • TEC41025 • June/July 2006

Note to the teacher: Use with "A Slice of Writing" on page 189.

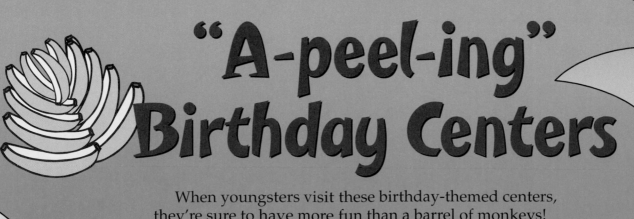

"A-peel-ing" Birthday Centers

When youngsters visit these birthday-themed centers,
they're sure to have more fun than a barrel of monkeys!

ideas contributed by Ada Goren, Winston-Salem, NC

Literacy Center
Whose Cake?
Recognizing one's name

Students feel like top bananas when they personalize and decorate this oversize cake! Gather three pieces of construction paper in different sizes and tape them together to resemble a tiered cake. Write "Happy Birthday" on the cake. If desired, laminate the cake for durability. Then place it at a center along with student name cards and a container of colorful cutouts, such as those shown. A youngster visits the center, finds his name card, and places it on the cake. Then he places cutouts on the cake to decorate it as desired. After admiring his work, he removes the name card and cutouts to ready the cake for the next youngster. This dinosaur-themed cake is the best!

Happy Birthday

Simeon

Fine-Motor Area
Wrap and Ribbon Snip
Developing fine-motor skills

Gift wrap and ribbon remnants are put to good use at this cutting center! Collect scraps of birthday-themed gift wrap and colorful ribbon. Place the scraps in a large plastic tub and then place the tub at the center along with a supply of children's scissors. A visiting student gives her cutting skills a workout by snipping the pieces of gift wrap and ribbon into smaller pieces over the tub. Snip, snip, snip!

Puzzle Center
Plenty of Plates
Developing spatial skills

Serve up spatial skills with sturdy puzzles made from decorative birthday plates! Obtain several decorative plates with different themes. (You may wish to send a note home with youngsters asking parents to send in decorative plates left over from previous birthday celebrations.) After you've gathered several different plates, puzzle-cut each one into two or three pieces. Place the pieces for each puzzle in separate resealable plastic bags and place the bags at a center. A child chooses a bag, removes the pieces, and then reassembles the plate. When he's finished, he puts the pieces back in the bag and chooses a new puzzle.

Art Center
Balloon Prints
Expressing oneself through art

Flour-filled balloons make wildly unique print-making materials! Place the open end of a balloon around the bottom of a funnel. Partially fill the balloon with flour. Then remove the funnel and tie a knot in the end of the balloon. Fill other balloons with flour in a similar way. Place each balloon at your art center next to a shallow tray of tempera paint. Have an adult helper stationed at the art center. A youngster visits the center, presses a balloon into the paint, and then makes several prints on a sheet of colorful paper. He repeats the process with other balloons and colors of paint. When his project is dry, he draws strings on the balloons and glues pieces of colorful confetti to the paper. What fun!

Reading Area
It's a Reading Party!
Demonstrating an interest in books
Little ones will go bananas for this festive reading area! Wrap a box and its removable lid with colorful gift wrap. Attach a large decorative bow to the lid. After placing a selection of birthday-themed books in the box, put the box in your reading area. Further decorate the area with colorful streamers and birthday banners. A visiting child chooses a book from the box and then settles in for a good read!

The Birthday Bananas

Snack Center
Crunch and Munch Candles
Following directions
These tasty candle look-alikes are sure to spark youngsters' imaginations! A child places five Ritz Sticks crackers (candles) on a plate. He makes cheese flames by tearing a slice of sandwich cheese into small pieces and placing a piece above each candle. Then he digs in to this fun snack! Yum!

Math Center
How Old?
Matching numerals
Preschoolers love to identify how old they are. That's why excitement is in the bag with this numeral-matching activity! Label each of three decorative bags with a different numeral and corresponding number of dots, making sure that each student's age is represented. (A greater number of bags can be used if needed.) Make several numeral cards to match each bag. Place all the items at a center. A child chooses the bag that represents his age and sets the other bags aside. He spreads out all of the cards. Then he finds the cards with the matching numeral and places them in the bag.

Games Center
Top It With a Bow!
Matching colors

Get youngsters into the swing of matching colors! Gather six bows in different colors. Cut a construction paper rectangle (gift) to match each bow. Glue a construction paper square to each side of an empty tissue box to make a die that represents the six colors. Place the die, bows, and gifts at a center. A visiting student rolls the die and names the color. Then she places the corresponding bow on top of the matching gift. The child continues in the same way until each bow is placed on a gift. Great!

Name **Jay**   Writing
What's Inside?
Listen for directions.

What is in this box?
What could it be?
If I took the paper off,
What would I see?

I think there is a toy
car in the box.

Writing Center
It's a Mystery!

Connecting spoken language with written words
What's in the mystery box? Encourage little ones to share their ideas at this teacher-directed center! Place a present, such as a special snack, in a box; then wrap the box and top it with a bow. Make a copy of page 196 for each child. To begin, invite a youngster to join you with the present at a table. Help the child write his name on his sheet. Then read the poem. Encourage the child to guess what the present might be. Write his words in the space provided; then invite him to color the sheet. After each child has had an opportunity to share his ideas, gather youngsters and open the gift! How delightful—it's a snack for everyone to share!

195

What's Inside?

Listen for directions.

What is in this box?

What could it be?

If I took the paper off,

What would I see?

_____

_____

LITERACY UNITS

A "Purr-fect" Time for Rhyme!

Youngsters can sink their paws into these engaging activities, which are perfectly groomed to help them gain an understanding of rhyme!

ideas contributed by Angie Kutzer, Garrett Elementary, Mebane, NC

From Lap to Lap

Bat, hat, mat, sat—there sure are a lot of words that rhyme with *cat!* That's why they're the focus of this nifty whole-group activity! Obtain a small cat stuffed animal or a cat cutout. Gather youngsters in a circle. Chant, "Cat, mat," encouraging students to join you as they pass the cat around the circle. Then say a different rhyme for students to chant, such as "Cat, hat." Continue this rhyming game as long as desired, with students passing the cat from lap to lap all the while. Rhyming words are fun to say!

Cat, mat.

Kitty Characteristics

Rhyming words abound in this cute-as-a-button action rhyme! Lead youngsters in performing the rhyme shown, stressing the rhyming word at the end of each line. After repeated performances, drop out before the end of each line and encourage the students to supply the rhyming word.

What do kittens like to do?

They like to nap	*Pretend to sleep.*
On someone's lap.	*Pat your lap.*
They sharpen claws	*Hold up both hands as if they have claws.*
On their front paws.	*Pretend to sharpen claws.*
They like to stalk	*Crouch down like a kitten.*
Where people walk.	*Pretend to stalk.*
They pounce on feet,	*Pounce!*
Then look so sweet.	*Smile sweetly.*

198

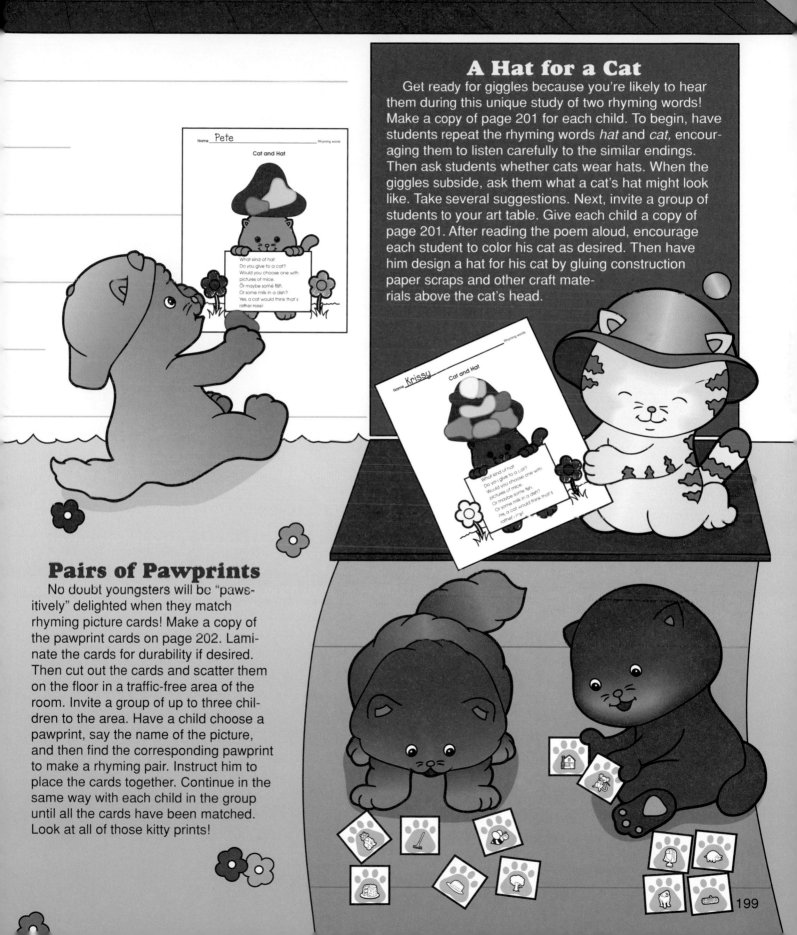

A Hat for a Cat

Get ready for giggles because you're likely to hear them during this unique study of two rhyming words! Make a copy of page 201 for each child. To begin, have students repeat the rhyming words *hat* and *cat*, encouraging them to listen carefully to the similar endings. Then ask students whether cats wear hats. When the giggles subside, ask them what a cat's hat might look like. Take several suggestions. Next, invite a group of students to your art table. Give each child a copy of page 201. After reading the poem aloud, encourage each student to color his cat as desired. Then have him design a hat for his cat by gluing construction paper scraps and other craft materials above the cat's head.

Pairs of Pawprints

No doubt youngsters will be "paws-itively" delighted when they match rhyming picture cards! Make a copy of the pawprint cards on page 202. Laminate the cards for durability if desired. Then cut out the cards and scatter them on the floor in a traffic-free area of the room. Invite a group of up to three children to the area. Have a child choose a pawprint, say the name of the picture, and then find the corresponding pawprint to make a rhyming pair. Instruct him to place the cards together. Continue in the same way with each child in the group until all the cards have been matched. Look at all of those kitty prints!

Where Are the Whiskers?

Rhyming words are the cat's meow with this flannelboard activity! Make a cat head cutout from felt. Use a black permanent marker to draw facial features on the cat; then cut six thin strips of black felt to resemble whiskers. Place the cat head cutout on your flannelboard.

To begin, gather youngsters around the flannelboard. Say a pair of words (use one of the suggested pairs shown if desired). Help youngsters identify whether the words rhyme. After arriving at the correct answer, invite a child to add a whisker to the cat cutout. Continue in the same way until the cat has six whiskers. What an adorable kitty!

Suggested pairs of words: *cat/sat, purr/fur, pet/meow, fish/wish, paw/claw, mice/dog*

Purr and fur rhyme!

Finicky Felines

Finicky kittens only have an appetite for fish that show rhyming pairs! Make a blue construction paper copy of the fish cards on page 203. Laminate the cards if desired; then cut them out. Locate a plastic bowl to represent a cat's dish. To begin, explain to a small group of children that they are going to pretend to be kittens. Then tell them that they want to have fish for dinner, but they are very picky and will only eat pairs of fish that have rhyming pictures. Place in front of the youngsters three fish, two of which are a rhyming pair. Prompt the students to say the name of the picture on each fish; then help them find the picture whose name does not rhyme with the others. Have the students place the rhyming fish in the food dish. Place the other fish in a separate pile. Continue in the same way for the remaining fish. Time for dinner!

Cat and Hat

What kind of hat
Do you give to a cat?
Would you choose one with
pictures of mice
Or maybe some fish
Or some milk in a dish?
Yes, a cat would think that's
rather nice!

Pawprint Cards

Use with "Pairs of Pawprints" on page 199.

©The Mailbox® • TEC41020 • Aug./Sept. 2005

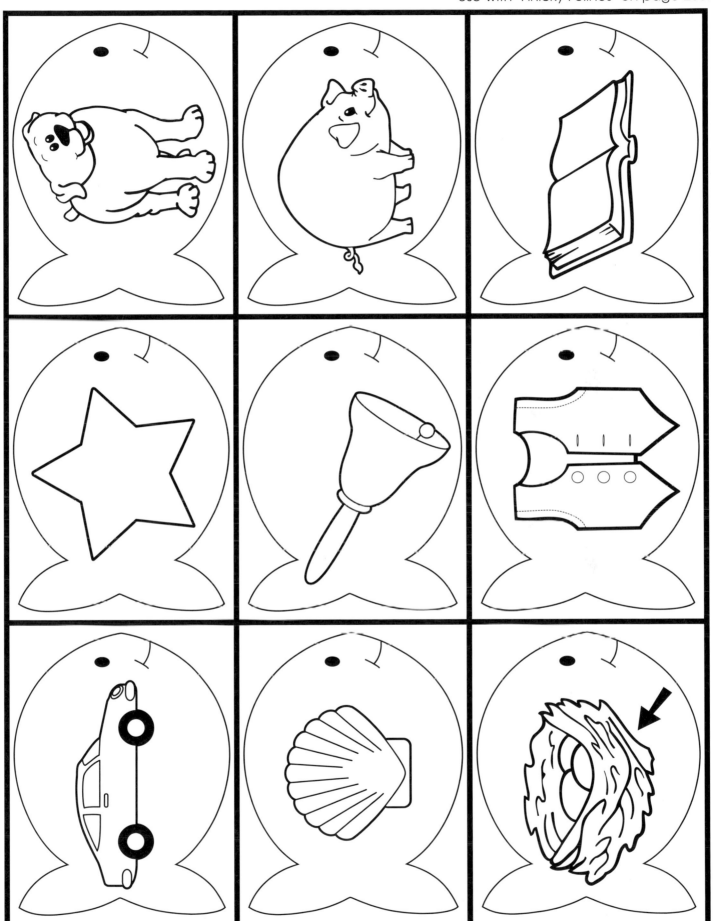

A Sequencing Smorgasbord

What is on the menu? A tantalizing serving of sequencing activities, sure to be generous on learning fun!

ideas contributed by Roxanne LaBell Dearman
Western NC Early Intervention Program for Children Who Are
Deaf or Hard of Hearing, Charlotte, NC

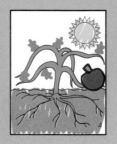

Make It Again!

Youngsters make a tasty snack and then use the same order of events to make a pretend version in your dramatic-play area! Invite a small group of students to a table. Have each child spread frosting on a graham cracker and then shake sprinkles on top of the frosting. As the children eat their snacks, review the order in which they made them. Next, place in your dramatic-play area duplicates of the items used to make the snack, replacing the crackers with squares of cardboard and making sure the frosting container and shaker are empty and clean. Then encourage students to visit the center and pretend to make the snacks, using the same sequence of events they learned during snacktime!

Pumpkin Progression

Share a story about the life cycle of a pumpkin, such as Jeanne Titherington's *Pumpkin Pumpkin.* Then gather a small group of youngsters and give each child a copy of the life cycle pages on page 206. Guide each student to complete the pages using the directions shown. Invite him to further embellish each scene with crayons. Then help him cut out the pages. After he arranges the pages in order, help him transfer them to a 6" x 18" piece of construction paper and then glue them in place.

Directions:
Page 1: Make a brown fingerprint to resemble a seed.
Page 2: Draw small leaves on the vine.
Page 3: Draw large leaves on the vine. Glue a piece of yellow tissue paper to the vine to resemble a blossom.
Page 4: Draw large leaves on the vine and attach a pumpkin sticker (or glue a pumpkin cutout) to the vine.

Bedtime Story

Bath time, snacktime, storytime—each child completes her own unique ritual before going to bed. Invite little ones to sequence these bedtime events with this unique idea! Give each child a copy of pages 207 and 208. Encourage each student to draw a picture of herself on the bed. Then have her embellish the bed and cards as desired. Prompt each student to select three of the items pictured that she does during her own bedtime ritual. Then help her cut out the cards and arrange them on the bed in the order in which she completes them. Finally, invite her to glue the cards in place.

What Comes Next?

Motor skills get a workout when little ones pantomime different steps in several familiar activities! Encourage youngsters to pantomime sitting down at a dinner table and picking up a spoon as you narrate the actions. Then prompt students to pantomime the next logical step in the sequence—eating dinner! Repeat the process with each suggestion below.

Suggested activities:
Put on your paint smock. Dip your paintbrush in the paint. Paint a picture.
Turn on the water. Put soap on your hands. Wash your hands.
Climb up the slide. Sit down at the top. Slide down the slide.
Put toothpaste on your toothbrush. Turn on the water. Brush your teeth.

An Orderly Day

Color and cut out a copy of the picture cards on page 209. Then attach each card to a different block. At the beginning of a school day, gather youngsters in your large-group area. Sequence the blocks to show the order of activities for the current day; then discuss each one. When the activities represented on the blocks have been completed, gather youngsters again and mix up the blocks. Then have the students help you place them back in the correct order. No doubt this fun sequencing activity will become a permanent part of your daily schedule!

Sarah Berger
Fountain/Warren Head Start
Covington, IN

Pumpkin Life Cycle Pages
Use with "Pumpkin Progression" on page 204.

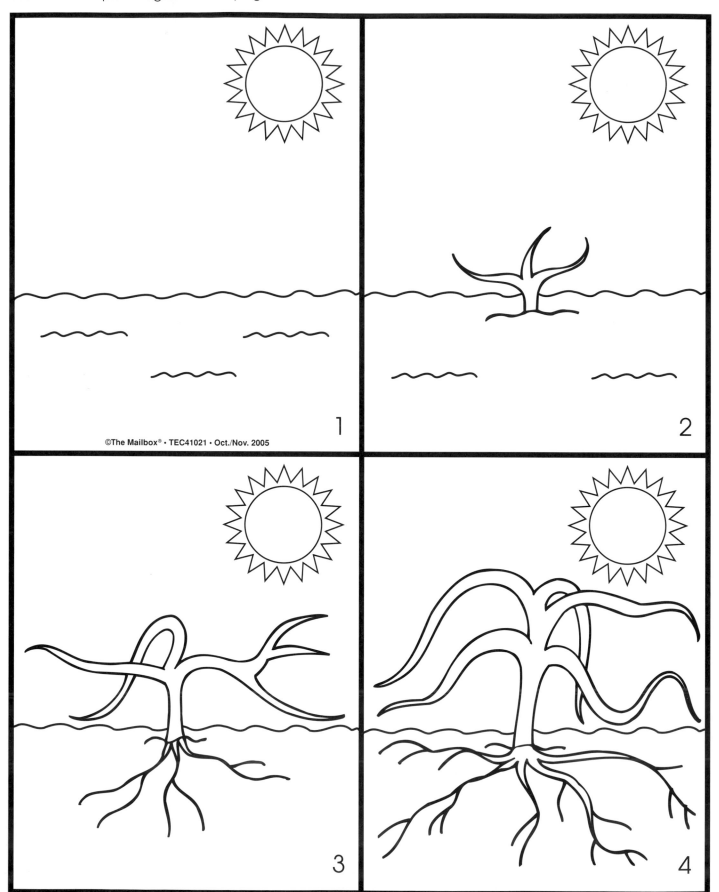

©The Mailbox® • TEC41021 • Oct./Nov. 2005

1

2

3

4

Name

It's Bedtime!

Note to the teacher: Use with "Bedtime Story" on page 205.

Bedtime Picture Cards

Use with "Bedtime Story" on page 205.

Brush your teeth.

Read a story.

Eat a snack.

Put on pajamas.

Turn off the light.

Take a bath.

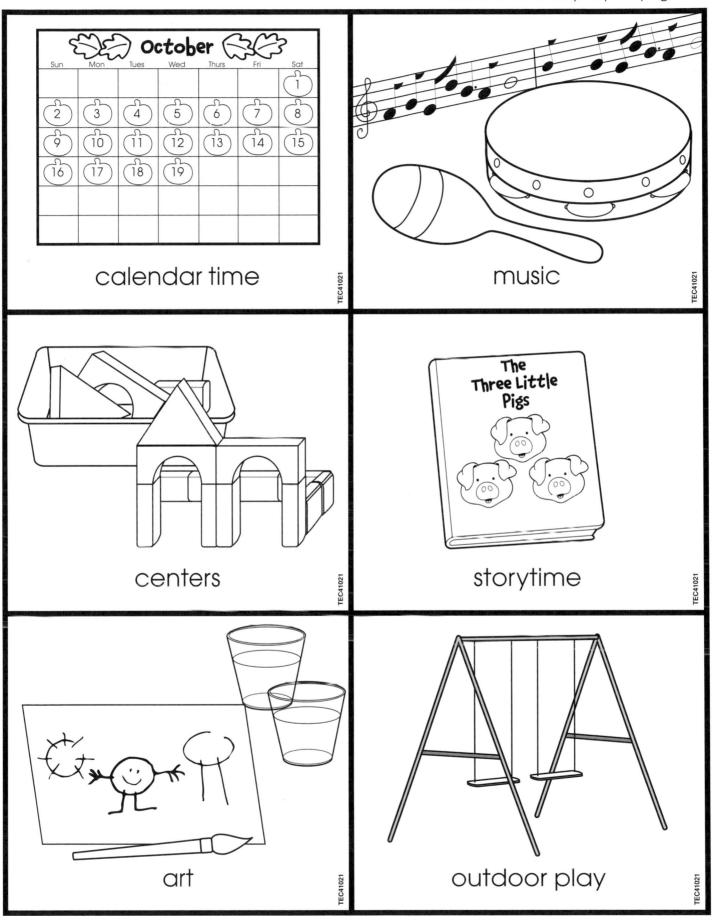

calendar time

music

centers

storytime

art

outdoor play

Fun With Beginning Sounds!

Are these little elves building toys or making shoes? Nope!
They're here to show this merry collection of explorations—
specially selected to help increase your little ones' awareness
of beginning sounds!

ideas contributed by Ada Goren, Winston-Salem, NC

All Wrapped Up!

Build excitement for sound explorations with a wrapped gift! Gift-wrap a box and its corresponding lid separately. Top the lid with a bow. Put in the box three items whose names begin with the same sound; then replace the lid. After presenting the gift to youngsters, remove the lid with great fanfare. Then hold up each item and have students repeat its name. Encourage children to recite the names of the items several times, leading them to notice that they move their mouths in the same way to form the beginning of each word. Then integrate the items into students' center time or playtime for the day.

Matthew begins
like moon!

SANTA'S LIST

Alex

Treena

Kim

Matthew

On the List

Little ones are sure to be tickled when they notice that their names begin with the same sound as other words! Post a length of red paper titled "Santa's List" near your circle-time area. To begin, present a student's name card and have youngsters say the name. Set the card aside and hold up two picture cards, one with a picture whose name begins with the same sound as the student's name. Have youngsters say the name of each picture. Then prompt them to identify the picture whose name has the same beginning sound as their classmate's name. After they identify the correct picture, have the student tape his name to Santa's list!

Cookies or Cake?

Serve up sound awareness with a center just perfect for the holidays! Place at a center a variety of baking-themed dramatic-play items. To begin, lead youngsters in reciting the rhyme shown several times. Guide students to notice that the words *cookies* and *cake* both begin with the same sound. Then invite little ones to recite the rhyme each time they visit the baking center to whip up imaginary cookies and cake!

Santa's Sacks

Color and cut out a copy of the picture cards on page 213; then ready them for flannelboard use. Make two felt sack cutouts. (If desired, add details to the sacks with a permanent marker.) Place the sacks on your flannelboard. Then place a picture of the cat on one sack and the picture of the boat on the second sack. Have students name the pictures on the sacks. Then show them a different picture card and help them decide whether the picture's name begins like *cat* or like *boat*. Invite a child to place the card on the corresponding sack. Continue in the same way with each remaining card. These sacks are full of gifts!

Many Mini Marshmallows

Your little elves savor the /m/ sound with this craft based on a favorite wintertime warm-up! For each child, make a white construction paper mug cutout. Have each student use a brown marker to color the inside of the mug to resemble hot cocoa. Then invite him to use crayons to color the outside of the mug as desired. Have youngsters say, "many mini marshmallows," drawing out the /m/ sound in each word. Help students notice that each word begins with /m/. Then instruct each youngster to dip his finger in a shallow pan of white paint and press it repeatedly on the hot cocoa to resemble mini marshmallows. As he adds the marshmallows, encourage him to repeat "many mini marshmallows." It's fun to say /m/!

I made a wuzzle!

Wonderful Wordplay!

When you pretend to be an elf for this whole-group activity, your little ones will giggle with glee! To begin, explain that you are an elf and you have made some toys. (To give yourself an elfish appearance, you may wish to don a construction paper headband embellished with elf ears.) Prompt students to recite the chant provided. Then hold up a toy and say its name, replacing the beginning sound in the word. For example, you might hold up a puzzle and say, "I made a 'wuzzle'!" No doubt students will immediately correct your mistake. Then repeat the process with other toys.

Little elf, little elf, what kind of toy
Did you make for a girl or a boy?

TEC41022

TEC41022

TEC41022

TEC41022

TEC41022

TEC41022

TEC41022

TEC41022

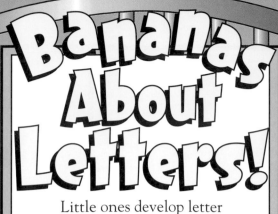

Bananas About Letters!

Little ones develop letter recognition skills with these exciting learning opportunities—and that's no monkey business!

ideas contributed by Angie Kutzer, Mebane, NC

Monkey See, Monkey Do!

This circle-time game is more fun than a barrel of monkeys! Make a class supply of the monkey pattern on page 217. (You may need to add an extra copy for yourself to make an even number.) Label pairs of monkeys with matching letters; then cut out the monkeys and give one to each child. After reciting the chant shown, have each student hold up his letter and then find the classmate that has the matching letter. Help each pair identify its letter. Then collect the monkeys for another round!

Monkey see, monkey do.
Who has a letter just like you?

Bunches of Bananas

Youngsters put these bananas back in a bunch! Make 12 yellow construction paper copies of the banana pattern on page 217. Label each set of four bananas with a different letter and then cut out the bananas. Place the bananas at a center. A student visits the center and matches the bananas to make three different bunches. Then he identifies the letters on each bunch.

Fruity Letters

To prepare for this fine-motor center, whip up your favorite recipe of play dough and mix in several drops of yellow food coloring and artificial banana flavoring. Make large laminated letter cards, such as those shown, and place them at a table along with the play dough. A youngster chooses a letter card and identifies the letter (with help, as needed). Then she rolls pieces of play dough and places them over the letter. It's an *S*!

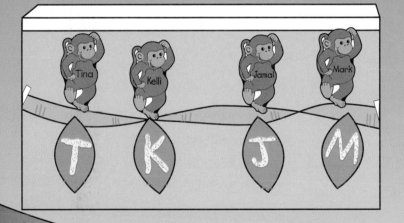

Initials Are Divine!

Youngsters focus on first initials for this leafy idea! Mount green crepe paper on a wall to resemble a vine. For each child, display a personalized monkey cutout (see the pattern on page 217) above the vine. To begin, give each child a leaf cutout programmed with his first initial. Help him identify the letter. Then encourage him to squeeze glue along the letter and sprinkle glitter over the glue. When the glue is dry, help each child find his name on the display and then mount his leaf near his monkey.

Slip 'n' Slide

Slip letter recognition into center time with this fun gross-motor activity. Make several yellow construction paper copies of the banana peel on page 218. Label each one with a different letter. Then cut them out and use Cont-Tact paper to attach them to your floor in a random arrangement. Invite youngsters to carefully walk through the area, identifying familiar letters they see and taking care not to step on the slippery peels. If a child steps on a peel, encourage some pretend slipping and sliding before he continues with the activity.

Go Bananas!

Here's a small-group game sure to get lots of giggles! Transform a square tissue box into a die similar to the one shown, labeling five sides with different letters and attaching a banana peel cutout to the sixth side. (If desired, use a reduced copy of the banana peel on page 218.) Cut out five copies of the monkey pattern on page 217 and label each monkey with a matching letter from the die. To begin, invite up to five youngsters to join you and encourage a child to roll the die. If it shows a letter, have all the children identify the letter; then encourage the child who rolled to find the matching monkey and set it aside. If it shows the banana peel, encourage all the youngsters to say, "Go bananas!" and make silly faces. Continue in the same way until all of the monkeys have been chosen.

One Little Monkey

Your little monkeys are sure to enjoy this whole-group rhyme and activity! Invite a child to pretend to be a monkey and have her sit in a tall chair to represent a tree. Tell the remaining students that they will pretend to be alligators. Give the monkey a letter card and have students identify the letter. Then lead them in reciting the rhyme shown, encouraging the monkey to drop the card at the end of the third line and having the alligators move their arms to resemble jaws during the fourth line. Have an alligator pick up the letter and give it to you for safekeeping. Continue in the same way with different letters and student volunteers.

One little monkey, sitting in a tree,
Feeding all the alligators ABCs.
Here's a yummy [_G_], just as tasty as can be!
SNAP!
"Whew!" said the monkey. "I'm glad that wasn't me!"

SNAP!

G

Monkey Pattern
Use with "Monkey See, Monkey Do!" on page 214, "Initials Are Divine!" on page 215, and "Go Bananas!" on page 216.

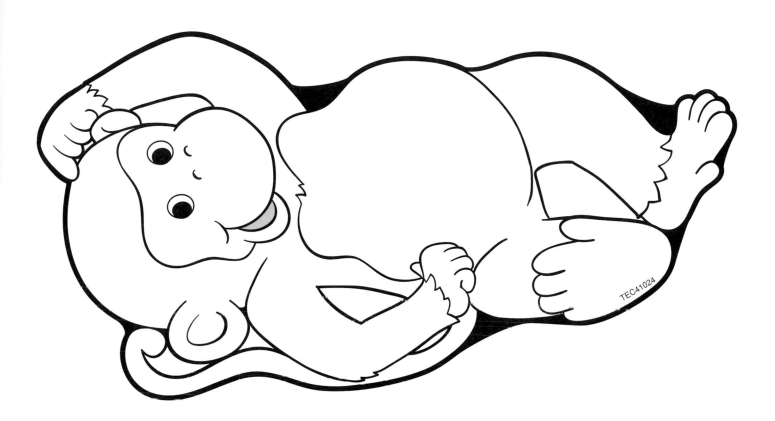

TEC41024

Banana Pattern
Use with "Bunches of Bananas" on page 214.

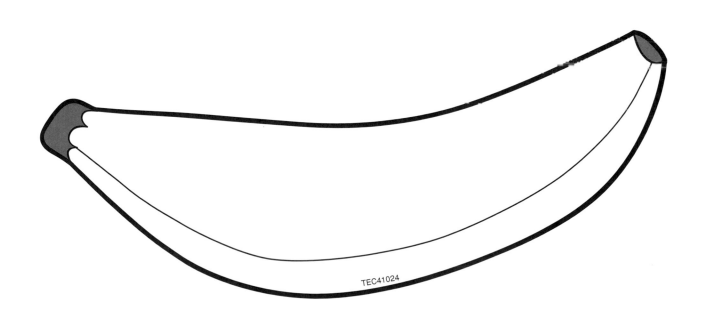

TEC41024

Banana Peel Pattern

Use with "Slip 'n' Slide" on page 215 and "Go Bananas!" on page 216.

TEC41024

Literacy in the Forecast

These fun weather-themed ideas are sprinkled with literacy concepts. Now that's sure to cause a flurry of excitement!

ideas contributed by Lucia Kemp Henry, Fallon, NV

Sing a Song of Weather!

Following text from left to right

This catchy little song highlights many different kinds of weather. Write the provided song on chart paper, omitting the underlined word. Laminate the paper and post it at student eye level in your large-group area. Then tape a weather-related cutout to a jumbo craft stick to make a pointer. To begin, gather youngsters around the chart paper. Have a student name a type of weather. Use a wipe-off marker to write the word in the space on the chart. Then help a child use the pointer to follow the words as you lead students in singing the song. After erasing the featured weather word, continue in the same way with other weather words.

(sung to the tune of "She'll Be Comin' Round the Mountain")

Oh, what kind of weather will we see today?

Oh, what kind of weather will we see today?

Yes, no matter what the season,

Weather changes—that's the reason

Why we could see [windy] weather here today!

Snowflake Letters

Developing letter recognition

You'll see a blizzard of activity around this snowy center! Write a desired letter on a sheet of copy paper. Then make a blue construction paper copy for each child. Place the letters at a center along with a shallow pan of white tempera paint and several empty thread spools. A youngster visits the center and takes a paper. She says the name of the letter. Then she presses the end of a spool into the paint and makes snowflake prints on the letter. That's simply splendid!

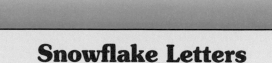

219

Writing About Weather

Developing prewriting skills

Set up a writing center with a weather theme! Suspend blue crepe paper streamers from the ceiling to resemble a rain shower. Place a table under the streamers. Then put large cloud cut-outs, pencils, and crayons at the table. Finally, post labeled pictures of various kinds of weather for youngsters to use as a reference. Invite youngsters to visit the center and write on the clouds.

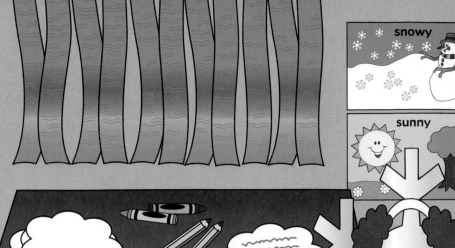

Blowing in the Wind

Rhyming

What did the wind blow in? A bunch of objects with rhyming names, that's what! Cut out a colorful copy of the cards on page 222. To begin, read aloud the popular story *The Wind Blew* by Patricia Hutchins. Then scatter the picture cards faceup around a small area on the floor. Gather youngsters around the pictures and express shock and dismay at the unusual objects the wind blew in! Have students name the object on each card. Then help them arrange the cards in pairs to show the rhymes. The wind blew in a cat and a hat!

R Is for Rain!

Reinforcing beginning sound /r/

Make a blue construction paper copy of the raindrop cards on page 223. Laminate the cards for durability. Then cut them apart and nestle them in a container full of cotton batting (clouds). Gather youngsters around and explain that the word *rain* begins with /r/. Then invite a child to pull a raindrop out of the cloud. Have the child identify the picture on the raindrop. Then invite the students to repeat the name, emphasizing the /r/ sound at the beginning of the word. Continue in the same way with the remaining picture cards, calling on a different child each time.

Splashy, Drizzly, and Misty

Exploring words that have similar meanings

Drizzly, misty, drippy—there are so many words that can describe a rainy day! Invite students to investigate a few of these exciting words with a splashy song! Write on separate index cards each of the following words: *rainy, drizzly, drippy,* and *misty.* Hold up the card labeled with the word *rainy* and encourage students to say the word. Then lead them in singing the song shown. Next, tell students that there are other words that can be used to describe a rainy day. Hold up a different word card and prompt youngsters to say the word. Then lead little ones in repeating the song, replacing the word *rainy* with the new word. Repeat the process for each remaining word card.

(sung to the tune of "A Tisket, a Tasket")

It's [rainy], it's [rainy],
It's damp and wet and [rainy].
We love a day that's soft and gray, and all the world is [rainy].

Kera

Thunder is very loud. Sometimes it makes me scared.

So Stormy!

Writing

How do your little ones feel about thunderstorms? Find out with this artsy writing activity! To begin, invite each child to express how she feels about storms as you write her words on a gray cloud cutout. Next, have the student glue her cloud to the top of a 12" x 18" sheet of construction paper. Then encourage her to dip a plastic dish scrubber into a shallow pan of blue tempera paint and then brush the scrubber down the paper several times to make rain. Finally, invite her to dip a finger in yellow tempera paint and add a lightning bolt to her project.

Rhyming Picture Cards

Use with "Blowing in the Wind" on page 220.

Learning Letters and Sounds

Little ones are sure to come out of their shells for these simple ideas that encourage them to make connections between letters and their sounds!

Snail Trails

This small-group activity has an adorable snail guide! Color and cut out a copy of the snail cards on page 227. Choose a letter familiar to your youngsters; then write the letter on each of four sheets of tagboard. Next, trace each letter with white glue. When the glue is dry, gather a group of up to four youngsters and give each child a snail and a letter. Explain that the snail has made a trail that looks like a letter. Help students identify the letter and say its sound. Then have each child move her snail along the trail as she repeats the letter's sound.

Roxanne LaBell Dearman
Western NC Early Intervention Program for
    Children Who are Deaf or Hard of Hearing
Charlotte, NC

The Letter-Pokey

Here's a twist on a familiar tune, which has little ones up and dancing with letters! Give half of your youngsters cards labeled with the letter *R*; then give the remaining half cards labeled with the letter *J*. (Or use different letters as desired.) Lead students with the letter *R* cards in performing the song shown. When the song is finished, help students identify the letter's sound. Then repeat the process with students who have the letter *J* cards, changing the song appropriately. For extra letter-sound reinforcement, have the two groups of students switch cards; then repeat the activity.

(sung to the tune of "The Hokey-Pokey")

You put your [R] in.
You take your [R] out.
You put your [R] in,
And you shake it all about.
You hold up letter [R] as you're dancing all around.
What is this letter's sound?

Deborah Garmon, Groton, CT

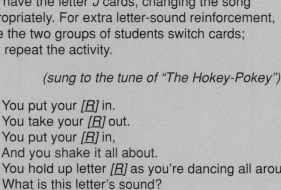

224

Smell a Sound

Reinforce letter sounds with a "scent-sational" small-group activity! Poke small holes in the lids of four film canisters. Gather coffee grounds, pieces of buttered popcorn, and slices of a lemon and ripe banana. Place each food item in a different canister. Then label each canister with the first letter of the item's name and replace the lids. Gather a small group of youngsters and explain that you have a mystery item that begins with the letter *B*. Have students review the sound of the letter *B*. After each child has had an opportunity to smell the corresponding canister, have youngsters suggest what the item might be. Congratulate them when they guess it's a banana. Then repeat the process with each remaining canister.

Roxanne LaBell Dearman

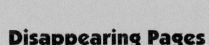

Disappearing Pages

This simple illusion will delight your little ones! Obtain a small photo album. Then insert a different letter card in each pocket in the first half of the album. Leave the second half of the album blank. Flip the album over so the last page is now the first page and present it to your youngsters. Reveal several of the blank pages as you explain that you filled the album with letters and now they're missing. Encourage youngsters to close their eyes and make a wish that the letters would reappear.

While their eyes are closed, flip the album so it's facing the correct direction. When students open their eyes, open the album and express relief that the letters have returned; then help students identify each letter and its sound. Youngsters are sure to ask for repeated reviews of this fantastic idea!

Shelley Hoster
Jack and Jill Early Learning Center
Norcross, GA

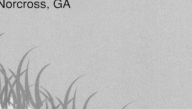

Sack-Lunch Sounds

Color and cut out a copy of the food cards on page 228. Ready the cards for flannelboard use and then place them on your flannelboard. Label one lunch-size paper sack with the letter *P* and a second sack with the letter *S*. Place the sacks near the flannelboard. To begin, have youngsters identify the letters and their sounds. Then encourage a child to choose one of the food items from the board and say its name. Prompt the child to decide whether the word begins with /p/ or with /s/. Then have her place the item in the corresponding bag. Continue in the same way with each item on the flannelboard. These lunches are all packed!

Adapted from an idea by Nancy Morgan
Care-A-Lot In-Home Daycare and Preschool
Bremerton, WA

Sound Swat

Place three letter cards on your floor (cards for the letters *F, M,* and *T,* for example); then gather a group of youngsters in front of the cards. Review the names of the letters and their sounds. Then give a youngster an unused flyswatter. Invite the youngster to swat the letter that makes the /f/ sound. Continue in the same way for several rounds, giving each youngster an opportunity to swat different letters.

Karen Eiben
The Learning House Preschool
La Salle, IL

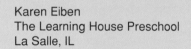

Letter on a Stick

Youngsters take ownership of letters and sounds with this whole-group activity. Glue each of several letter cards to a different craft stick to make stick puppets. Give each puppet to a different child. Encourage one of the youngsters to hold up his puppet for all to see. Help youngsters identify the letter. Then lead them in singing a version of the song below, inserting the appropriate student name, letter, and sound. Continue in the same way with each youngster in possession of a puppet.

(sung to the tune of "Mary Had a Little Lamb")

Anna's *B* says /b/, /b/, /b/,
/b/, /b/, /b/, /b/, /b/, /b/.
Anna's *B* says /b/, /b/, /b/.
The sound of *B* is /b/.

Christy McNeal
Hudson Elementary, Hudson, IA

226

Food Cards
Use with "Sack-Lunch Sounds" on page 226.

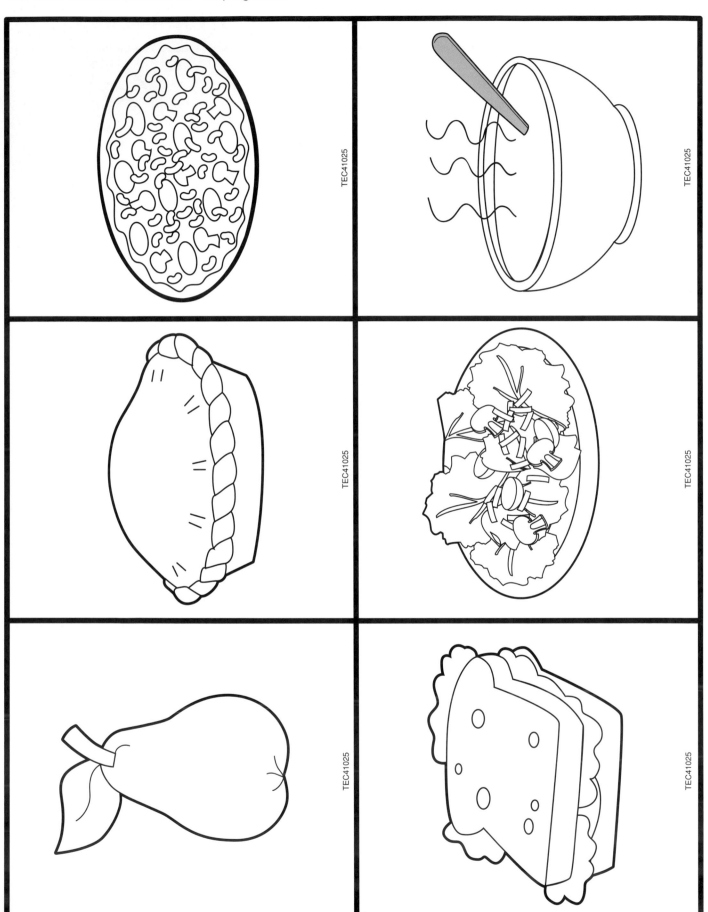

TEC41025

TEC41025

TEC41025

TEC41025

TEC41025

TEC41025

Math Units

Patterning
in Preschool

Join these prickly little hedgehogs for a heap of pleasing patterning practice!

ideas contributed by Angie Kutzer, Garrett Elementary, Mebane, NC

Rustle, swish, rustle, swish!

Leafy Loudness

What do youngsters hear when they run through a pile of leaves? Rustle, swish, crackle, crinkle! Why not use these fun leafy sounds for some fall-inspired patterning practice! Begin by chanting a simple AB sound pattern, such as rustle, swish, rustle, swish, encouraging youngsters to chime in when they're ready. Continue with other sound patterns, using the words mentioned above. When students are comfortable with this activity, encourage them to pretend to walk through piles of leaves as they recite the patterns.

Teeny, Tiny Patterns

These student-made patterning strips make simply smashing bracelets! Use decorative hole punches to make a supply of two different shapes. Sort the shapes into containers. Then place the containers at a table along with a supply of 1" x 9" construction paper strips and glue. Encourage each child to place six evenly spaced dots of glue on a strip. Have her place a cutout on each dot to make an AB pattern. When the glue is dry, staple the strip to make a bracelet.

Nancy Foss
Wee Care
Galion, OH

230

Totally Texturized!

Gather a variety of textured items, such as sandpaper, fake fur, corrugated cardboard, and aluminum foil. Cut the items into small squares. Glue some of the squares to sentence strips to make patterns. Then place the remaining squares in a container. Tape the strips to a tabletop and set the container nearby. A child feels each pattern; then he extends each pattern with the remaining squares. Rough, smooth, rough, smooth!

Nosy Hedgehogs

Make three construction paper copies of the hedgehog cards on page 233. Cut out the cards and laminate them for durability. Gather a supply of black and pink pom-poms and place them in separate containers. Then set the container and cards in a center. To begin, introduce youngsters to this unique little animal with a read-aloud such as *The Prickly Hedgehog* by Mark Ezra or *Hedgie's Surprise* by Jan Brett. Explain that hedgehogs' noses come in several different colors. Next, invite each child to visit the center and lay the cards in a row. Then have her place noses on the cards to make a pattern!

Snackin' on Patterns

Cereal isn't just for breakfast anymore—it's for patterning practice too! Give each child a napkin. Then place a small amount of two distinctly different kinds of cereal on each napkin. Also give each child a strip of paper sectioned into squares similar to the one shown. Encourage each child to place a piece of cereal in each square to make a simple pattern. Then have him munch on his treat.

Make It Bigger!

The result of this whole-group activity is an enormous floor pattern! Link together DUPLO blocks to make a pattern, making sure that the number of blocks is equal to the number of students in your class. Gather a 9" x 12" sheet of construction paper to match each block used. To begin, show youngsters the blocks and have them read the pattern by chanting the colors. Explain that they will make the same pattern they see on the blocks, but it's going to be so huge that it just might stretch all the way across the room! Give each child a sheet of construction paper. Then help students arrange their papers in a row on the floor to resemble the pattern of the blocks. Read the resulting pattern with your youngsters. It's the same, but bigger!

Parent Note
Send home at the completion of your patterning study.

Dear Family,
    We have been patterning in preschool! Help me use items we have at home to make patterns, such as forks and spoons, different kinds of crackers, or pencils and pens. There are so many possibilities!

Sincerely,

Your Preschooler

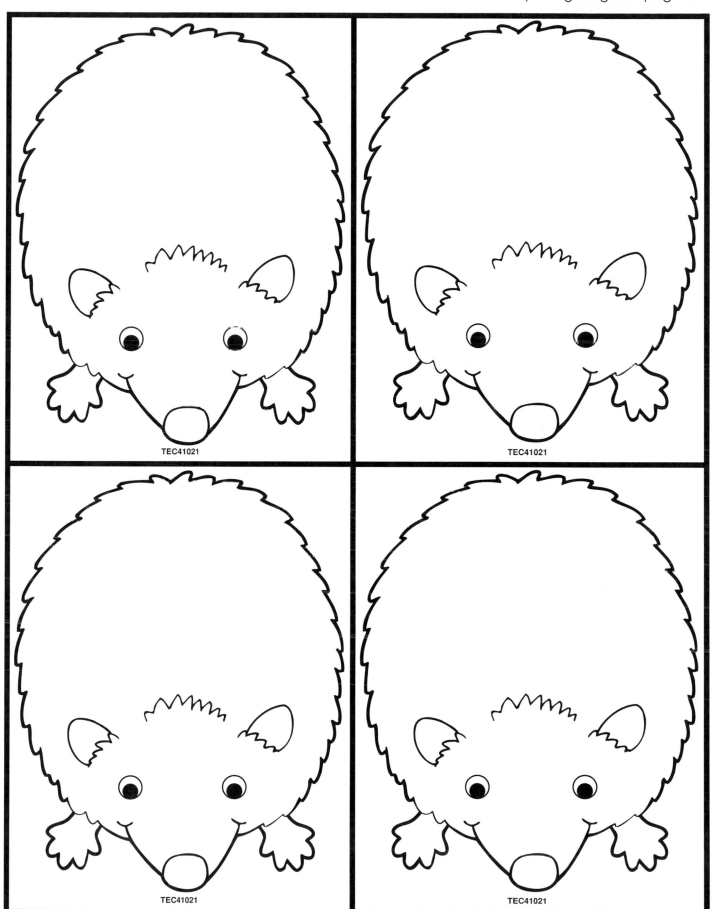

TEC41021

TEC41021

TEC41021

TEC41021

SHAPES ON PARADE

March little ones into shape exploration with this lively lineup of parade-inspired activities!

ideas contributed by Roxanne LaBell Dearman
Western NC Early Intervention Program for Children Who Are Deaf or Hard of Hearing
Charlotte, NC

GOTTA HAVE PEOPLE!
Identifying shapes

What is the main ingredient in any parade? People, people, and more people! Little ones make these unique people from basic shapes. To begin, read aloud the parade-themed book *Thump, Thump, Rat-a-Tat-Tat* by Gene Baer and encourage students to identify the different shapes in Lois Ehlert's engaging illustrations. Next, gather a small group of youngsters at a table and provide each child with a circle cutout and access to other die-cut shapes. Help the students identify the shapes. After each child draws facial features on his circle, encourage him to glue shapes together to make a person reminiscent of the shape people in the book. When the glue is dry, display the people on a wall in your classroom or hallway to resemble a parade!

A PLEASING PROCESSION
Exploring a shape through play

Vroom, vroom! Youngsters line up toy vehicles on this shapely parade route! Place lengths of tape on your floor to make a basic shape. Provide access to a selection of toy fire trucks, police cars, and other vehicles that might be found in a parade. A student visits the area. After she names the shape, she traces it with her hand. Then she lines up the toy vehicles along the parade route. If desired, repeat the activity with other basic shapes. Here comes the fire truck!

SHAPELY SNACKS
Recognizing shapes

Plenty of treats are available during a parade, and this booklet highlights a few shapely choices! Cut a circle, triangle, and square from a large sponge, making sure each shape fits on the corresponding booklet page (see page 236) as shown. Place the sponge shapes at your art center along with shallow pans of blue, brown, and pink tempera paint. Invite a child to the center. Name each shape and encourage the student to point to the corresponding sponge.

Next, give each child a copy of page 236 and help him write his name on the booklet cover. Guide him through the directions shown to complete each page. When the paint is dry, invite him to embellish the prints as desired. Then help him cut out his cover and pages and staple them together. Have each youngster take his finished booklet home to share with his family.

Directions:
Booklet page 1: Stamp a blue square below the popcorn to resemble a box.
Booklet page 2: Stamp a brown triangle on the plate to resemble a slice of pizza.
Booklet page 3: Stamp pink circles above the dish to resemble scoops of ice cream.

CLEANING CREW
Sorting by shape

After a parade passes through the streets, there's sure to be a lot of cleanup needed! Label each of three containers with one of the following shapes: a circle, a rectangle, and a square. Scatter pieces of clean litter around the room that correspond to the shapes, such as circular disposable drink lids, rectangular candy wrappers, and square napkins. Play a recording of marching music and encourage each child to find several pieces of litter and then sort each one into the basket labeled with the appropriate shape. What an efficient cleanup!

Shapely Snacks

by_____

popcorn

1

pizza

2

ice cream

3

Counting With Mice

Make math time merry with counting activities featuring this cozy gathering of mice.

ideas contributed by Lucia Kemp Henry, Fallon, NV

Blocks of Cheese!
Counting, one-to-one correspondence
Transform building blocks into blocks of cheese for hungry mice! Wrap each of five building blocks with yellow cellophane. Then use a permanent marker to draw holes on the cellophane to resemble Swiss cheese. Cut out a construction paper copy of the mouse patterns on page 240. Then fold and glue each cutout to make a three-dimensional manipulative as shown. Place the blocks of cheese and the manipulatives at a center. A youngster counts the five mice and the five blocks. Then he places one mouse on each block of cheese!

Cupboard Critters
Making a set of five
This cupboard has five little mousy guests! Have each youngster color and cut out a copy of the cupboard pattern on page 241. Help him glue the cupboard to the middle of a 9" x 12" sheet of construction paper as shown. Fold the ends of the sheet inward to make doors for the cupboard. Encourage each child to draw knobs on the doors. Next, open the doors. Prompt each child to press his finger into a shallow pan of tempera paint and count as he makes five fingerprints among the items in the cupboard. After the paint is dry, use a permanent fine-tip marker to embellish each print to resemble a mouse. Have each child open his cupboard and count the cute little mice. 1, 2, 3, 4, 5!

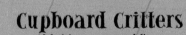

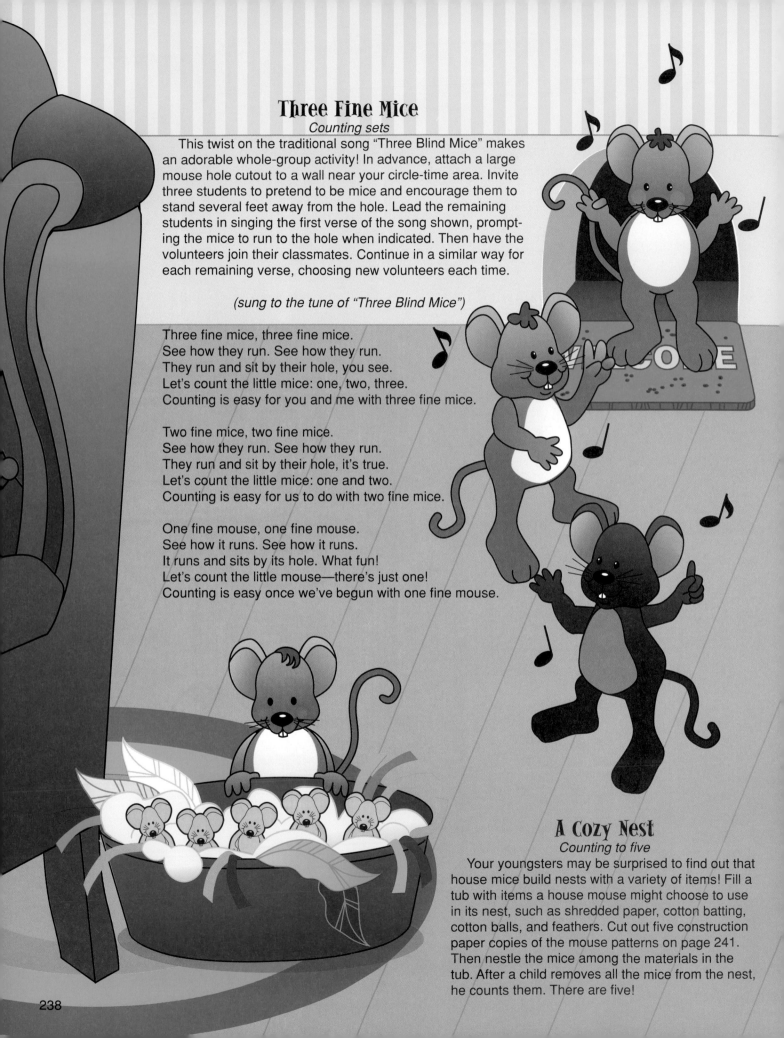

Three Fine Mice
Counting sets

This twist on the traditional song "Three Blind Mice" makes an adorable whole-group activity! In advance, attach a large mouse hole cutout to a wall near your circle-time area. Invite three students to pretend to be mice and encourage them to stand several feet away from the hole. Lead the remaining students in singing the first verse of the song shown, prompting the mice to run to the hole when indicated. Then have the volunteers join their classmates. Continue in a similar way for each remaining verse, choosing new volunteers each time.

(sung to the tune of "Three Blind Mice")

Three fine mice, three fine mice.
See how they run. See how they run.
They run and sit by their hole, you see.
Let's count the little mice: one, two, three.
Counting is easy for you and me with three fine mice.

Two fine mice, two fine mice.
See how they run. See how they run.
They run and sit by their hole, it's true.
Let's count the little mice: one and two.
Counting is easy for us to do with two fine mice.

One fine mouse, one fine mouse.
See how it runs. See how it runs.
It runs and sits by its hole. What fun!
Let's count the little mouse—there's just one!
Counting is easy once we've begun with one fine mouse.

A Cozy Nest
Counting to five

Your youngsters may be surprised to find out that house mice build nests with a variety of items! Fill a tub with items a house mouse might choose to use in its nest, such as shredded paper, cotton batting, cotton balls, and feathers. Cut out five construction paper copies of the mouse patterns on page 241. Then nestle the mice among the materials in the tub. After a child removes all the mice from the nest, he counts them. There are five!

In the Cookie Jar!

Naming "how many" concrete objects

How many mice are in the cookie jar? No doubt youngsters will be able to tell you without pausing to count! Conceal two large brown pom-poms in a cookie jar (or cookie tin) to represent mice. Gather a small group of students and quickly open and close the jar, allowing youngsters to view, but not count, the number of mice. Have students share how many mice are hiding in the jar. Then confirm the number by opening the jar and having youngsters count the mice. Repeat the process with groupings of up to three mice.

So Sneaky!

Developing a counting strategy

With this splendid action rhyme, youngsters learn that their fingers are handy manipulatives for counting to five!

One, two, three, four, five mice peek.
Cheese for lunch is what we seek!

Point to each finger on one hand.
Look from side to side.

One, two, three, four, five mice sneak.
Get that cheese now. Squeak, squeak, squeak!

Point to each finger on one hand.
Tiptoe in place.

One, two, three, four, five mice munch.
Cheese sure makes a tasty lunch!

Point to each finger on one hand.
Rub tummy.

Cheddar and Swiss

Comparing sets

Cut five pieces of orange felt to represent cheddar cheese and five pieces of yellow felt to represent Swiss cheese. Gather students in front of the flannelboard. Give each of four children a piece of cheddar cheese and each of five children a piece of Swiss cheese. Have the youngsters pretend to be mice as they scurry forward to place their cheese on the flannelboard. After the mice sit down, enlist students' help in sorting the cheese. Then have them count each group and determine whether there is more cheddar cheese or more Swiss cheese. Repeat the process using different amounts of each type of cheese.

Mouse Manipulative Patterns

Use with "Blocks of Cheese!" on page 237.

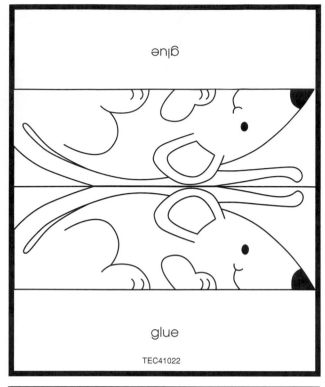

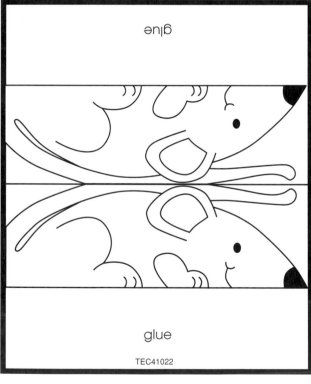

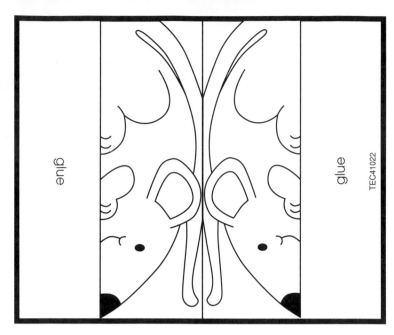

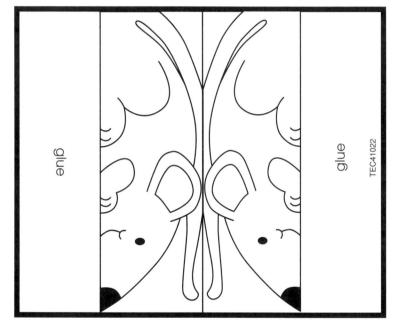

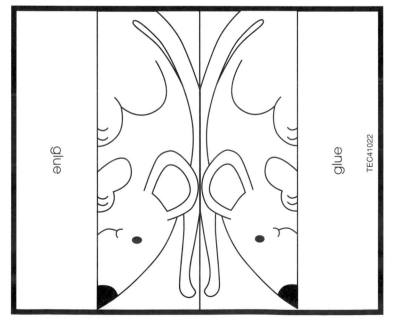

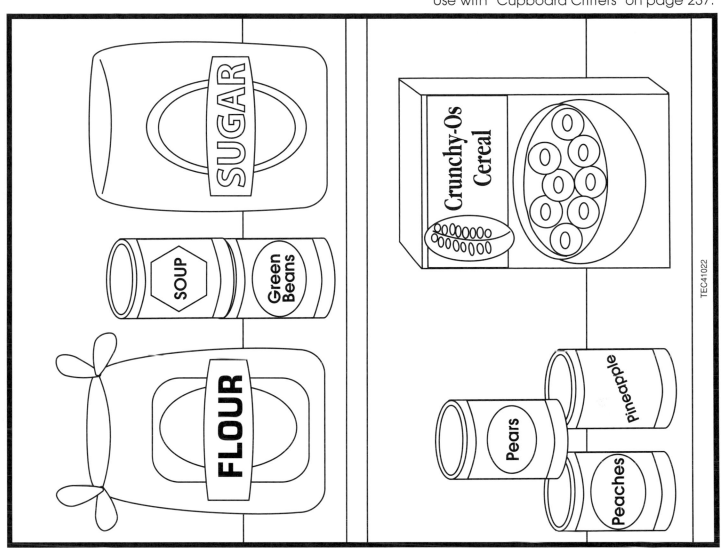

Exploring Measurement

These measurement ideas are inspired by the traditional tale *The Three Billy Goats Gruff*. So read your favorite version of the story to your youngsters and then dive into these nifty explorations. What a fun way to bridge the gap between storytime and math!

ideas contributed by Suzanne Moore, Tucson, AZ

Across the Bridge

With this pretend bridge, youngsters can compare the strides of a little goat, a medium goat, and a large goat. Place a strip of brown bulletin board paper on your floor to resemble a bridge. Then invite a child to pretend to be the littlest goat. Have him take baby steps across the bridge as you lead students in counting the number of steps. Then write the number on your board. Continue in the same way, having a second child take medium-size steps across the bridge and a third child take giant steps across the bridge. Next, help students compare the number of steps taken by the goats. That little goat had to take a lot of steps!

Green and Tasty

The three goats found loads of tender green grass on the other side of the bridge. No doubt youngsters will be reminded of the goats' marvelous meal with this comparison of length! Cut both long and short strips of green craft foam. Label a container with the word *long* and a second container with the word *short*. Draw a picture clue on each label as shown. Then scatter the grass on your floor and place the containers nearby. Youngsters visit the center and pretend to be goats as they pick up the blades of grass and sort them into the corresponding containers.

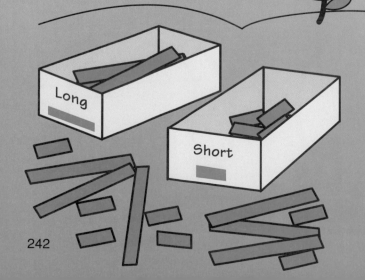

242

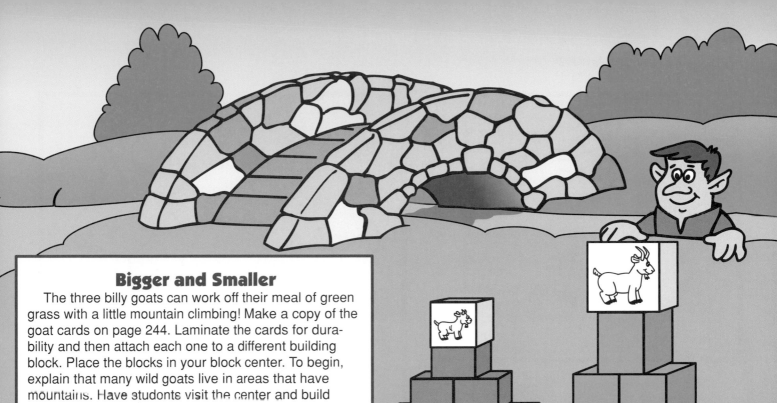

Bigger and Smaller

The three billy goats can work off their meal of green grass with a little mountain climbing! Make a copy of the goat cards on page 244. Laminate the cards for durability and then attach each one to a different building block. Place the blocks in your block center. To begin, explain that many wild goats live in areas that have mountains. Have students visit the center and build mountains for the goats to climb. While the students build, encourage them to use words to compare their mountains, such as *bigger, smaller, shorter,* and *taller.*

Water Under the Bridge

Youngsters explore capacity—and avoid a lurking troll—with this neat idea! Dye a supply of rice blue to represent water. (For dyeing instructions, go to "Lucky Leprechaun" on page 40.) Place the rice in a large plastic tub. Then nestle in the rice a colorful copy of the troll on page 245. Place the tub at a center along with a variety of plastic scoops and containers such as those shown. A student visits the center and scoops rice into the containers to explore capacity. He just might find a not-so-scary troll lurking in this river of rice!

A Happy Herd

Could the meadow feed more than just three billy goats? Certainly! With this activity, youngsters manipulate goats to cover the entire meadow. Make several copies of the large goat card on page 244. Cut a large rectangular piece of green bulletin board paper to resemble a meadow. Then place the meadow and the goat cards at a center. A youngster arranges the cards on the meadow until it's completely covered.

Goat Cards

Use with "Bigger and Smaller" and "A Happy Herd" on page 243.

TEC41023

TEC41023

TEC41023

Troll Pattern

Use with "Water Under the Bridge" on page 243.

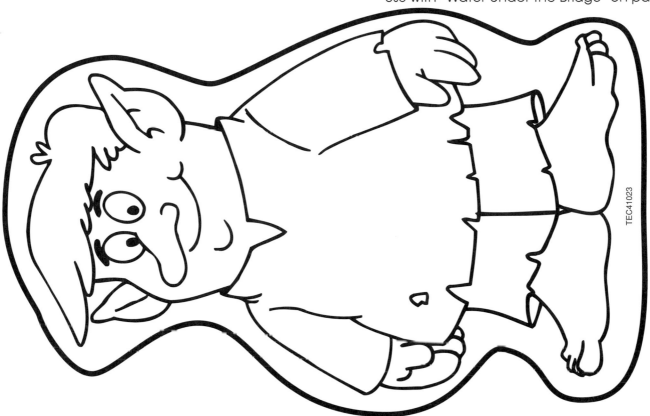

TEC41023

Parent Note

Send home at the completion of your measurement study.

Dear Family,
   We have been exploring measurement in our class. Help me explore measurement at home with one or more of the following ideas:

- Compare the lengths of different items, such as shoes or pencils.
- Measure ingredients to help make a snack or a meal.
- Compare the different heights of the people in our family.

Sincerely,
Your Preschooler

Recognizing Numbers!

Youngsters are sure to flock to these unique number recognition ideas all about that colorful rainforest bird: the toucan!

ideas contributed by Suzanne Moore, Tucson, AZ

Branching Out

How many toucans will perch on this branch? Your little ones find out with this whole-group number game! Cut out ten colorful copies of the toucan pattern on page 248. Cut a long branch shape from brown bulletin board paper. Then place the branch and the toucans on the floor in your circle-time area along with a stack of number cards with numerals from 1 to 10. To begin, lead youngsters in reciting the rhyme shown. Then have a child choose a card. After youngsters help him identify the numeral, encourage him to count out the corresponding number of toucans and then place them on the branch. Remove the toucans from the branch and repeat with the remaining number cards.

5

How many toucans will we see
Perched on the branch of the kapok tree?

Three

How Many Eggs?

To prepare for this small-group activity, cut a large hole in an oatmeal canister to resemble a hole in a tree trunk. (You may also wish to paint the canister brown.) Place shredded paper in the trunk to make a nest. Then mold white play dough into four balls to resemble eggs. Gather a small group of youngsters around the nest and explain that a female toucan builds a nest in a hollow tree and lays from two to four eggs. Have youngsters close their eyes as you place two, three, or four eggs in the nest. Then prompt students to open their eyes and say the number of eggs in the nest without counting. After confirming the number by counting, write the corresponding numeral on the board. Repeat the process several times.

Mmm, Berries!

What would a toucan like to eat? Berries are a favorite treat! Color and cut out a copy of the toucan pattern on page 248. Then ready the toucan for flannelboard use. Cut from felt ten round circles to resemble berries. Use a permanent marker to label each berry with a different numeral from 1 to 8. To begin, place the toucan on your flannelboard. Then recite the rhyme with your youngsters, placing the corresponding berries on the board in a row. Finally, ask youngsters questions about the berries, such as "Which berry shows the number 3?"

Toucan's hungry. What will he eat?
Berries are a favorite treat.
Feed him one, two, three, and four.
He's still hungry; give him more!
Feed him five, six, seven, eight.
No more berries on his plate!

Fly little flock. Fly high and low.
Fly really fast; then fly really slow.
Fly in a circle; then land on your feet.
Hop, hop, hop, and take a seat.

Flocks of Toucans

Gather a set of number cards with numerals from 4 to 10. Hold up a card and have students identify the numeral. Then invite the corresponding number of children to stand and pretend to be a flock of toucans. Lead the flock in performing the chant shown. Then repeat the process with the remaining cards.

Toucan Treats

Make a copy of the math mat on page 249 and label each toucan with a different numeral. Then give each student a copy of the programmed mat and a cup of colorful o-shaped cereal. Have each child identify the first number shown. Then have her count the corresponding number of cereal pieces and place them on the toucan's bill. Encourage her to repeat the process for each number on the page. Finally, invite her to nibble on the tasty toucan treats!

TEC41024

Note to the teacher: Use with "Toucan Treats" on page 247.

Get Ready for Graphing

From collecting data to making simple graphs, there are sure to be activities in this unit just perfect for your students' skill level. So pop on those sunglasses and slide into some flip-flops. It's time to get ready for graphing at the beach!

ideas contributed by Lucia Kemp Henry, Fallon, NV

Seashells in the Sand
Collecting data

Before youngsters dive into graphing activities, give them some practice collecting data. Make a class supply of colorful seashell cutouts. Laminate the cutouts; then scatter them about your classroom. Lead youngsters in singing the song shown. Then have them collect the seashells and place them in a container. When all the seashells have been found, gather youngsters in a circle and dump out the shells. Encourage students to make observations about the shells, noting their various colors and shapes. Finally, place the seashells in your sand table for youngsters to investigate independently.

(sung to the tune of "Take Me Out to the Ballgame")

Take me out to the ocean.
Take me out to the beach.
I see some seashells that look so grand.
I can see them all over the sand.
So let's make a seashell collection.
It's so easy to do.
You just pick up each one you find
Till you have a few!

Who's on the Beach?
Organizing data

To prepare for this large-group activity, use a length of tape to divide your pocket chart into two columns; then label the columns as shown. Cut out two colorful copies of the boy and girl cards on page 252. Place five towels on your floor to represent beach towels. Invite each of five youngsters to choose a towel to lie on and then pretend he's at the beach. (You may wish to provide children's sunglasses to enhance the role-playing.) Lead the remaining students in counting the number of boys and the number of girls at the beach. Then help a child use this information to place the corresponding number of boy and girl cards on the chart. Repeat the process several times with different numbers of boys and girls.

Splendid Starfish
Organizing data

To begin, have each child place a sheet of paper over a piece of sandpaper. Encourage her to rub an unwrapped crayon over the paper to make a sandy beach. Then have her attach five star stickers (starfish) on her beach, making sure to include at least three different colors. Encourage her to name the colors of starfish represented as you write the color words on her paper. Finally, have her count the number of starfish in each color; then help her write the corresponding number after each color word.

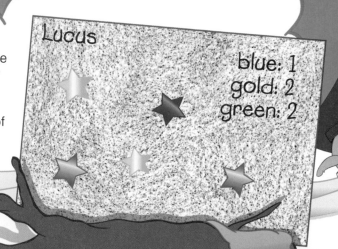

Lucus

blue: 1
gold: 2
green: 2

Dry Sand, Wet Sand
Organizing and interpreting data

Would your youngsters prefer to play with dry sand or wet sand? Place dry sand and moist sand in separate shallow tubs; then label the tubs accordingly. To begin, have each child make a name sign similar to the ones shown. Then invite each youngster to touch and manipulate the sand in each tub. When she decides which sand feels more appealing, she places her name sign in the corresponding tub. After all youngsters have had a turn, help them count the number of signs in each tub and compare them using words such as *less, more,* and *same.* Finally, remove the signs and replace them with some beach toys; then place the tubs at a center for independent exploration.

Pretty Pearls
Contributing to an object graph

To prepare for this activity, gather a supply of pompoms (pearls) in two different colors and place them in a container. Make a simple floor graph from bulletin board paper as shown. Then label the columns to represent the colors of the pearls. With great fanfare, show youngsters your fabulous collection of pearls. Then invite each child to take one from the container. Help each youngster place his pearl on the graph in the appropriate column. Ask students questions about their choices, such as, "Why did you choose to place your pearl in this column instead of the column where Anna placed her pearl?" Finally, help youngsters interpret the finished graph. Then invite each child to take his pearl home.

Boy and Girl Cards
Use with "Who's on the Beach?" on page 250.

TEC41025

TEC41025

TEC41025

TEC41025

THEMATIC UNITS

Making a Splash in Preschool!

Welcome youngsters to preschool with a refreshing wave of ocean-themed ideas!

ideas contributed by Jana Sanderson, Rainbow School, Stockton, CA

Preschool Superstars!

Miguel · Lee · Caroline · Tamika · Suna · Jackson · Katlin · Theo · Ashley · Benjamin

The Stars of Preschool!

Bulletin board

This underwater display spotlights all of your preschool stars! Use the pattern on page 257 to make a construction paper starfish cutout for each child. Personalize each starfish. Then have each youngster spread glue on his starfish, taking care to avoid getting glue on his name. Invite him to sprinkle wild rice over the glue. When the glue is dry, attach the starfish to a bulletin board with the title shown. If desired, add crepe paper seaweed, fish cutouts, and other ocean creatures to the scene.

Seashell Search

Getting acquainted activity

Digging in the sand is always fun. But it's even more fun when the sand contains personalized seashells! Copy the seashell patterns on page 258 onto colorful construction paper to make a class supply; then cut them out. Label each shell with a different child's name. Then laminate the shells and partially bury them in a shallow tub of sand. Choose a youngster and invite her to find a shell in the sand. Help her identify the name on the shell; then encourage her to give the shell to the corresponding student. Continue in the same way with each shell in the tub, calling on a different youngster each time.

Electra · Fishy · Scal

Go to the room at the end of the hall to meet Ms. Pellow, the school music teacher!

Message in a Bottle

School tour

Little ones investigate their new "sea-roundings" with the help of some floating messages! In advance, collect a supply of plastic water bottles and remove their labels. On each of several sheets of paper, write a message telling students to visit a different room, area, or staff member that needs to be introduced. Roll each message and tie a length of ribbon around it. Then insert each message into a bottle and replace the cap. Float the bottles in your water table. Have a child choose a bottle and give it to you. Read the message aloud. Then take students to visit the room, area, or person described. Repeat the process several times throughout the first few school days. What a fun way for youngsters to get acquainted with the school!

Aquatic Ambience

Room decoration

Here's an idea that will transform your room into a watery wonderland! Give each child a sheet of newsprint paper (or another large sheet of paper) and encourage her to use a spoon to dribble paint on her paper. Have her use a child-size paint roller to spread the paint over the paper. Then, after the paint is dry, fold the paper and cut out a simple fish shape, making sure to cut through both layers of paper. Staple the fish shapes together, leaving a small opening. Have the child stuff her fish with newspaper strips; then staple the opening closed. Invite her to add a sticky-dot eye to each side of the fish. Hang these three-dimensional fish from your ceiling along with strips of green crepe paper to resemble kelp.

Outstanding Octopuses

Nametags

These oh-so-cute octopuses make nifty nametags! Personalize a colorful copy of an octopus pattern (page 259) for each child. Cut out the octopuses. Then give each child an octopus and have him attach paper reinforcers to the arms to resemble suckers. Laminate the nametags for durability. Then use them to label cubbies or coatracks. Your youngsters are sure to receive armfuls of compliments about these cute octopuses!

Spiney

A Supersize Sandcastle

Action rhyme

When youngsters work together, they can build an imaginary sandcastle of enormous proportions! To begin, explain that to make a sandcastle, a person presses wet sand into a bucket, flips over the bucket, and then lets the molded sand slide out. Next, lead youngsters in performing the action rhyme below. Take a moment to admire each child's pretend sandcastle. Then tell students that one person can build a small sandcastle, but many people working together can build an enormous sandcastle! Begin reciting the rhyme again. When it's time for the students to flip over their pails, prompt them to add the imaginary sand to a large group sandcastle. Then admire the castle and comment on the wonderful creations they can make when they all work together!

Pat-a-cake, pat-a-cake,	Clap your hands.
Playing in the sand.	Continue clapping.
We're building up a castle	Continue clapping.
As fast as we can.	Continue clapping.
Scoop it and pat it,	Pretend to scoop and pat sand.
Then flip it—be quick!	Pretend to flip the bucket over.
Lift up the bucket.	Pretend to lift the bucket.
What a nifty trick!	Admire the pretend sandcastle.

All About Apples

If you blend your youngsters' favorite fall fruit with engaging learning opportunities, what will you get? This bushel of appetizing activities ripe for the picking!

ideas contributed by Lucia Kemp Henry, Fallon, NV

Apple Information
Tracking print from left to right

Little ones will be eager to share what they know about apples—and even more eager to track their printed knowledge with a cute little apple worm! Using the patterns on page 263, make a green construction paper worm and several red construction paper apples. Cut out the apples and glue them to a sheet of chart paper, placing one at the beginning of each line. Cut out the worm and glue it to a jumbo craft stick.

To begin, ask youngsters to share what they know about apples; write each piece of information next to a different apple cutout. Then introduce the worm cutout, explaining that the worm loves apples and is thrilled to read anything about them. Read each sentence aloud, beginning at the apple and using the worm to track the print from left to right. Invite students to practice tracking the print as you read. Then place the chart and worm in a center for youngsters to use independently!

Apples are crunchy.

Some apples are red.

They taste good.

I like apple pie.

There's an apple tree in our yard.

An "A-peel-ing" Crown
Copying a pattern

Give youngsters the royal treatment with this patterning activity! Using the pattern on page 263, make a supply of red and green construction paper apples. Glue the apples to a sentence strip in an AB pattern. Then place the strip, the remaining apple cutouts, and a supply of blank sentence strips at a table. Invite a group of youngsters to join you. Encourage each child to copy the pattern by placing apples on a sentence strip in the same arrangement. When the apples are arranged correctly, have her glue them down so that they stick out over the top edge of the strip. Allow time for the glue to dry. Then size the strip to fit the youngster's head. Voilà! It's a crown fit for a king or queen!

Plenty of Parts

Using vocabulary specific to a living thing

Watch vocabularies blossom when youngsters sing this catchy song about the different parts of an apple! Cut an apple in half, making sure that one half still has the stem attached. Lead youngsters in singing the song shown, pointing to the skin on an apple half when indicated. Repeat the song three more times, each time replacing the underlined portions with the next suggestion provided and pointing to the designated part.

(sung to the tune of "Did You Ever See a Lassie?")

Can you name the different parts of an apple, an apple?
Can you name the different parts of an apple for me?
Oh, [this is the skin].
Yes, [this is the skin].
Can you name the different parts of an apple for me?

Suggestions:
this is the stem
these are the seeds
this is the flesh

Inside and Outside

Making comparisons

This student-made poster helps youngsters get to know apples inside and out! Label a 9" x 12" sheet of construction paper with the words *inside* and *outside*. Place shallow pans of red and white tempera paint at a table and place an apple half next to each pan. Make available an additional apple half and a whole apple for youngsters to investigate. A child visits the table and examines the inside and outside of each apple. Then, using the apple halves, he makes a white apple print above the word *inside* and a red apple print above the word *outside*. He embellishes the prints with brown hole-punch dots (seeds) and stem and leaf cutouts. After the paint is dry, the child compares the inside and outside of an apple using the poster. "Tree-mendous"!

inside   outside

Apples on the Ground

Matching letters

Polish letter-matching skills with fallen apples! Make 14 red construction paper apples using the patterns on page 263. Program seven of the apples with an uppercase letter *a* and seven with a lowercase letter *a*. Glue one of each type of apple to a separate basket as shown. Place the baskets on the floor and scatter the apples around the baskets. A child picks up an apple, looks at the letter, and then places it in the corresponding basket. She continues in this manner until she's sorted all of the apples. Got 'em all!

Pie À La Mode

Practicing one-to-one correspondence

This activity serves up a generous helping of one-to-one correspondence! Cut a brown construction paper circle (apple pie) to match the size of an aluminum pie tin. After embellishing the pie as desired, cut the pie into six equal slices. Then put the slices in the pie tin. Place the tin at a table along with six paper plates and six balls of white play dough formed to resemble scoops of ice cream. Invite a child to place one pie slice on each plate. Then have him top each slice with one serving of ice cream. Mmm—pie!

A Peck of Pom-poms

Developing fine-motor skills

For this fine-motor extravaganza, kitchen tongs are tops! Make a large tree cutout. Place the tree at a center. Then place several large red pom-poms (apples) on the tree. Place a set of kitchen tongs and a basket near the tree. A child visits the area and uses the tongs to remove each apple and place it in the basket. After she picks all the apples, she uses her hands to place them back on the tree.

Apple and Worm Patterns

Use with "Apple Information" and "An 'A-peel-ing' Crown" on page 260 and
"Apples on the Ground" on page 262.

Plentiful Pumpkins!

Peruse this pumpkin patch and harvest a
bumper crop of learning opportunities. No
doubt the result will be oodles of cheery grins!

ideas contributed by Ada Goren, Winston-Salem, NC

What Is It?

Singing a song

Spotlight pumpkins with this divine little ditty! Make an orange
pumpkin cutout for each child plus one for yourself. Place the pumpkin
behind your back and sing to your youngsters the song shown, omitting the spoken line at the end. Have students guess the object that the
song describes. When they guess that the item is a pumpkin, reveal
the cutout. Next, give each child her own cutout and have her hide it
behind her back. Then lead students in singing the song, having them
add the final spoken line as they reveal their own hidden pumpkins!

Suzanne Moore, Irving, TX

(sung to the tune of "Six Little Ducks")

I'm very orange and I am round.
I grew from a seed down in the ground.
You can carve me a face or put me in a pie.
Now take a guess and tell me,
What am I? What am I? What am I?
Now take a guess and tell me, what am I?

(spoken) A pumpkin!

In Line on the Vine

Ordering numerals

Make five orange construction paper copies of the pumpkin pattern
on page 267. Label each pumpkin with a different numeral from 1 to
5 and the corresponding number of dots. Also label each of five index
cards in the same manner. Tape to a flat surface a length of green
yarn (vine) and green construction paper leaves. Then tape the index
cards in order along the vine. Place the prepared pumpkins nearby. A
child puts the matching pumpkin on top of each index card to arrange
the pumpkins from 1 to 5. For more advanced students, omit the index
cards from the activity.

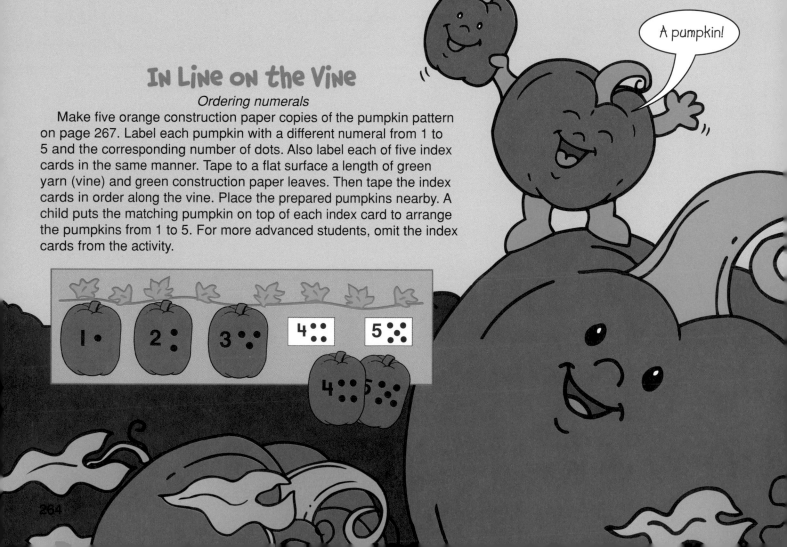

Orange, Round, and Gooey!

Using descriptive words

For each child, staple two orange construction paper pumpkins together (see the pattern on page 267). Personalize the top pumpkin in each set. To begin, display a pumpkin that has the top removed. Have students touch and describe the outside and then the inside of the pumpkin as you write their words on a sheet of chart paper. Next, give each child his prepared pumpkin cutouts. Have him glue pieces of yellow yarn and cleaned and dried pumpkin seeds to the bottom cutout to resemble the inside of the pumpkin. When the glue is dry, display the projects and the chart paper in your classroom.

Hilarie Hutt, Summit School, Summit, SD

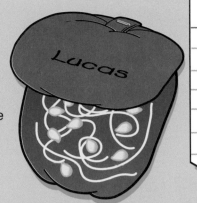

The outside is orange, smooth, round, and feels nice.

The inside is slimy, gooey, yellow, and icky.

Flannelboard Faces

Matching shapes

Youngsters transform a plain pumpkin into a jazzy jack-o'-lantern at this flannelboard center! Color and cut out a copy of the jack-o'-lantern cards on page 268. Then laminate them for durability. Cut from felt a large orange pumpkin and the following black shapes: three triangles, three circles, three squares, and a rectangle. Place the pumpkin on your flannelboard. Then set the cards and shapes nearby. A child chooses a card and then places shapes on the pumpkin to duplicate the face shown. After admiring her pumpkin, she removes the shapes. Then she continues in the same way with each remaining card.

A Prizewinning Patch
Developing fine-motor skills

Youngsters create a pleasing pumpkin patch mural with prints made from miniature pumpkins! Tape a length of bulletin board paper to a table. Cut a miniature pumpkin in half and place the halves, cut side down, in a shallow pan of orange tempera paint. Place the pan at the table. Next, invite one or two youngsters to the table and encourage them to make several prints on the paper. Repeat the process until each child in the room has had an opportunity to make prints. When the paint is dry, invite students to cut green construction paper leaves and then glue them to the paper. Embellish the patch with green curling ribbon to resemble vines. Then post this nifty mural on a wall in your classroom!

pie

Pass the Pumpkin
Listening for beginning sound /p/

Harvest phonemic awareness skills with this circle-time idea! Cut out a copy of the picture cards on page 269; then place them in a plastic trick-or-treat pumpkin. Gather students in a circle. Have youngsters pass the pumpkin around the circle as you lead them in singing the song shown. When the song is finished, locate the child holding the pumpkin and encourage him to remove a card. Have the student name the picture. Then instruct all the youngsters to say the name of the picture, emphasizing the /p/ sound at the beginning of the name. Continue in the same way for each card in the pumpkin.

(sung to the tune of "Clementine")

Pass the pumpkin, pass the pumpkin,
Pass the pumpkin round to me.
When it stops, I'll take out something
That begins with letter *P*!

TEC41021

Jack-o'-Lantern Cards

Use with "Flannelboard Faces" on page 265.

TEC41021

TEC41021

TEC41021

TEC41021

TEC41021

TEC41021

TEC41021

TEC41021

TEC41021

TEC41021

TEC41021

TEC41021

TEC41021

Bear Necessities

Here's a "bear-y" exciting selection of activities sure to get little ones interested in the wild world of bears!

ideas contributed by Suzanne Moore, Irving, TX

Good Eats!
Identifying needs of a living thing
Help youngsters recognize common foods in a bear's diet with this toe-tapping song and activity! Give each youngster a copy of page 273. Have children point to the bear. Explain that many bears eat a variety of things they can find in or near a forest, such as fish, berries, acorns, and honey. Instruct each child to point to each of these food items pictured on the page. Then lead students in singing the song, encouraging them to point to each type of food when appropriate. If desired, have each child color his page before taking it home to show to his family.

(sung to the tune of "My Bonnie Lies Over the Ocean")

Some bears eat the fish in the river.
Some bears like the berries so sweet.
Some bears eat the nuts from the forest.
Some bears think that honey's a treat.
Yummy honey, some bears think that honey's a special treat!
Yummy honey, and that's what some bears like to eat!

A Reading Den
Demonstrating an independent interest in books
Drape a dark blanket over a small table, leaving a wide opening as shown. Place silk or fabric leaves under and on top of the table to give the resulting den autumn appeal. Place a container of bear-themed books in the den. Add a bear stuffed animal if desired. Then invite youngsters to use this nice cozy reading area!

Who Has Your Fish?
Participating in a group activity

To prepare for this circle-time activity, make a fish cutout from tagboard. Invite a child to pretend to be a grizzly bear and have him sit with his back to the class. Give the fish to one of the students and have him conceal the fish by sitting on it. Then encourage youngsters to chant, "Grizzly bear, grizzly bear, who has your fish?" Encourage the grizzly bear to turn around and guess who has his fish, prompting him to use his classmates' names and allowing him several guesses. When the fish is found, have the child who was hiding the fish become the new grizzly bear!

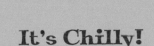

It's Chilly!
Investigating an animal's environment

Help little ones explore a polar bear's environment with this icy investigation! Make a class supply of polar bear cutouts using the pattern on page 274. Freeze a pan of water and place it at a table. Gather a small group of youngsters around the pan and give each child a polar bear. Explain that polar bears live where there is a lot of ice and snow. Invite each child to "walk" her polar bear across the ice. Next, give each youngster a 9" x 12" sheet of light blue construction paper. Encourage her to glue her polar bear to the paper. Then have her glue white craft items around the bear to represent ice and snow. Display the projects on a bulletin board titled "Polar Bears Live Where It's 'Bear-y' Cold!"

Berries for Brown Bear
Listening for the /b/ sound

Make a red construction paper copy of the berry cards on page 275. Then cut out the cards. Also make an enlarged brown construction paper copy of the brown bear pattern on page 274. Ready both the berries and bear for flannelboard use. Place the berries in a small container and place the bear on your flannelboard. To begin, choose a berry, making sure that youngsters do not see the picture on the card. Give the students a hint about the object pictured. For example, for the card that shows a bee you might say, "It begins with /b/ and likes to buzz around flowers." After youngsters guess the object, show them the card. Then invite a child to "feed" the berry to the bear by placing it on the flannelboard.

Mother Bear Says...
Following directions

How do bear cubs learn how to be bears? They copy the mother bear! Gather youngsters in your large-group area. Then tell the students that they are going to pretend to be bear cubs and they need to copy what you do so that they can learn important bear behaviors. Say, "Little cubs, climb a tree." Then pantomime climbing a tree and encourage the students to copy you. Continue in the same way with each of the suggested bear behaviors below.

Suggested bear behaviors: *stand on four legs, stand on two legs, sniff the air, catch a fish, go for a swim, dig a den, take a nap, roar, roll in the grass*

272

Name _____

"Bear-y" Good Food

Listen for directions.

©The Mailbox® • TEC41021 • Oct./Nov. 2005

Note to the teacher: Use with "Good Eats!" on page 270

Polar Bear Pattern

Use with "It's Chilly!" on page 271.

TEC41021

Brown Bear Pattern

Use with "Berries for Brown Bear" on page 272.

TEC41021

274

Gifts Galore!

Gift wrap, bows, and ribbons. It must be the season for gift giving! That makes it the perfect time to sprinkle these gift-themed activities throughout your youngsters' school day.

ideas contributed by Jana Sanderson,
Rainbow School, Stockton, CA

Add Some Ribbon!

Counting

Little ones use ribbon remnants to make snazzy presents. Make a bow cutout for each child (patterns on page 280). Label each bow with a desired number. To begin, gather a small group of children. Have each youngster glue his bow cutout to the top of a construction paper rectangle to resemble a gift. Help students identify the number. Next, provide access to a container of colorful fabric ribbon pieces. Encourage each child to count aloud as he removes the corresponding number of ribbon pieces from the container. Then have him glue the pieces to his gift!

What Could It Be?

Using descriptive words

Encourage each child to cut a picture from a magazine that shows an object a member of his family might like as a gift. Have him glue the picture to the inside of a sheet of folded construction paper. Then label the picture as shown. Next, write the name of the child and the recipient on a copy of the gift pattern from page 279. Help each child describe the picture without giving away its name. Write each child's words on the gift. Then help him cut out the gift and glue it to the outside of the folded paper. After the glue is dry, have students take their projects home. Youngsters will love it when the recipient uses the clues to guess what the present might be!

To: Dad
From: Joshua

Here are a few hints about your gift!
It is red. It has tires. It makes a noise like "vroom"!

It's a car!

Cooperative Collage

Developing fine-motor skills

Tape a length of bulletin board paper to a tabletop. Place at the table the following supplies: scissors, a container of gift wrap pieces, and glue. A youngster places glue on a small section of the bulletin board paper. Then he cuts or tears pieces of gift wrap and presses them onto the glue. Topped with a bow, this cooperative collage is sure to make a lovely wall mural!

Given With Love

Speaking to recite a rhyme

Youngsters celebrate the spirit of gift giving with this sweet little action rhyme!

Some gifts are big.	*Spread arms out wide.*
Some gifts are small.	*Move hands close together.*
Some gifts are short.	*Squat down with hands close to the floor.*
Some gifts are tall.	*Stand on tiptoe with hands high overhead.*
Big, small, short, tall—	*Repeat motions above.*
They're all given with love,	*Draw a heart in the air with both hands.*
And that's best of all!	*Clap on each of the last three words.*

Bags and Tags

Matching letters

Gather several small gift bags and label each bag with a different letter. For added flair, decorate each bag with cellophane or curling ribbon. Cut a number of construction paper gift tags equal to the number of bags. Label each tag with a matching letter; then punch a hole in each tag and thread a piece of pipe cleaner through the hole to make a hanger. (Tape any rough pipe cleaner ends to avoid scratches.) Place the bags and tags at a center. A child hangs each tag on the handle of the bag with the matching letter.

277

Thank you!

Pass the Present

Using polite words

Little ones practice saying thank you with this pleasing whole-group experience! Place in a box a gift for your students, such as a special book or tasty treat. Then wrap the box and top it with a bow. To begin, seat youngsters in a circle. Play a recording of festive music as youngsters pass the present around the circle. Then stop the music and locate the child holding the present. Prompt the child to politely say, "Thank you." Then praise the child for being so polite. After several rounds of the game, open the present and reveal the special gift. You're sure to hear a chorus of thank-yous!

A Glittery Gift

Strengthening home-school connections

Youngsters make these gorgeous gifts for their families! Help each child glue three skill sticks (or craft sticks) together, as shown, to make a snowflake. When the glue is dry, have her paint the snowflake with a mixture of white paint and glue. Encourage her to sprinkle glitter over the mixture. Allow time for the project to dry. Then attach a yarn hanger to the snowflake along with a colorful copy of the gift tag from page 279. Families are sure to treasure this glittery ornament.

Rachel Castro, Albuquerque, NM

My hands can paint.
My hands can glue
To make this special gift
Just perfect for you!

Small Bows, Big Bows!

Ordering by size

Collect four gift bows in different sizes. Place the bows at a table along with a shallow tray of tempera paint and a class supply of construction paper strips. Invite a youngster to the table and encourage him to choose a paper strip. Then have him press the smallest bow in the pan of paint and use it to make a print on the strip as shown. Have him continue in the same way with each bow from smallest to largest!

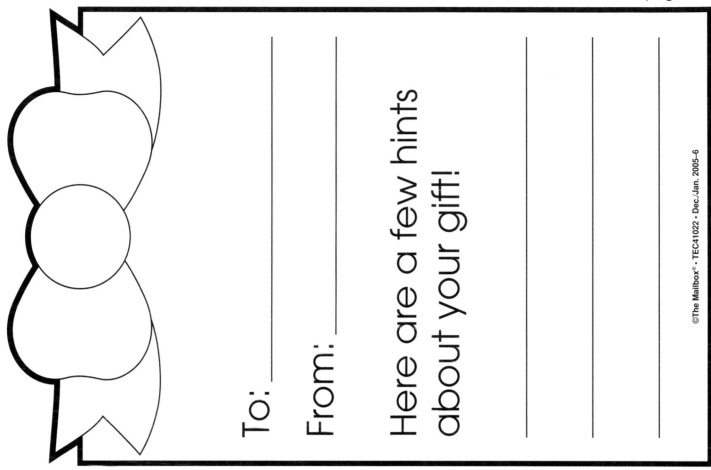

To: _____

From: _____

Here are a few hints about your gift!

©The Mailbox® • TEC41022 • Dec./Jan. 2005–6

Gift Tag Patterns
Use with "A Glittery Gift" on page 278.

My hands can paint.
My hands can glue
To make this special gift
Just perfect for you!

TEC41022

My hands can paint.
My hands can glue
To make this special gift
Just perfect for you!

TEC41022

My hands can glue
My hands can glue
To make this special gift
Just perfect for you!

TEC41022

Bow Patterns
Use with "Add Some Ribbon!" on page 276.

Families Are Fabulous!

Who are the most important people in your preschoolers' lives? Why, their families, of course! Invite little ones to focus on families for this selection of engaging learning opportunities!

ideas contributed by Roxanne LaBell Dearman, Western NC Early Intervention Program for Children Who Are Deaf or Hard of Hearing, Charlotte, NC

Counting on Families!
Counting and comparing numbers

Showcase the number of people in your youngsters' families with this picture-perfect idea! In advance, have each child bring in a photograph of his whole family. (To ensure the safety of the photos, place each one in a plastic bag or make a copy of the photo and send home the original.) Label each of six index cards as shown. Then display them in order at student eye level. Help each student count the total number of family members in his photo and then post it above the corresponding number. Encourage youngsters to compare the different family sizes using words such as *more, less,* and *same.*

| 2 | 3 | 4 | 5 | 6 | 7 or more |

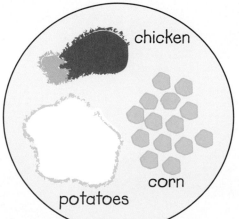

chicken

potatoes

corn

Mealtime!
Engaging in dramatic play

Have each child name a favorite family meal and then draw the food on a large paper plate. Help her label each food pictured. Then place the completed plates at a table along with plastic utensils, napkins, and plastic serving dishes. Encourage center visitors to sit around the table and act like a family as they serve and feast on some favorite foods!

Chores Galore
Recognizing differences among families

It takes an entire family to run a household! Color and cut out a copy of the picture cards on page 284. To begin, show youngsters a card and invite them to name the chore pictured. Then encourage each child to discuss which member or members of his family complete that chore. Continue in this manner with each remaining card, making sure to highlight differences in youngsters' responses.

F Is for *Family!*
Building connections between home and school

Send home with each child a large uppercase *F* cutout and a note similar to the one shown. Encourage each child to help her family decorate the cutout with items that have special meaning. For example, they might add drawings of the family pet or pictures from a family vacation. When youngsters bring their projects to school, invite each child to share her unique *F*. No doubt you'll want to display these nifty projects for all to see!

Dear Family,
F is for family! Help your child decorate the provided letter cutout with photos, drawings, and objects that have meaning to your family. Please return the project to school by December 16.

Thank you,
Ms. Dearman

All in the Family
Naming family members

For each child, gather two sheets of 9" x 12" construction paper. Cut a window in one sheet; then place it over the second sheet and staple them together at the top. Label the papers with the rhyme shown. Have each child draw a self-portrait in the window. Then, on the second page, encourage her to draw her family members around her. Finally, help each child label each member of her family.

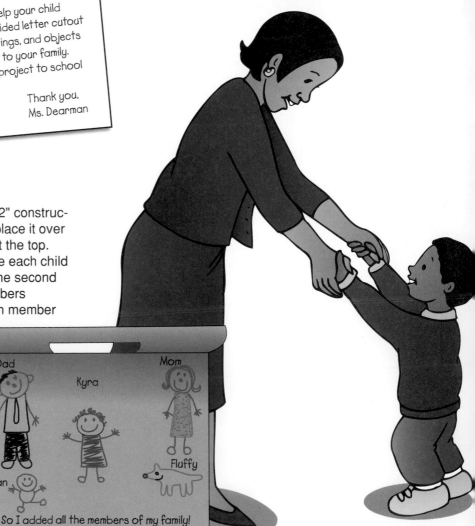

Gotta Have Caregivers!
Speaking and listening

Ask students to explain why it is important to have parents or caregivers. Then tell students that the book you are about to read is about a family without any grown-ups! Read aloud *Snow Family* by Daniel Kirk. After the reading, help youngsters conclude that caregivers are needed to take care of children and keep them safe. Then lead youngsters in reciting the rhyme shown, inviting one child at a time to substitute a family member's name or title.

[Nana] takes good care of me!
[She's] a part of my family!

So Many Members
Identifying people in a family

Encourage youngsters to name people who might be found in a family with this tasty idea! Give each child a construction paper house cutout and a small cup of Teddy Grahams crackers. Have a child name the title of a person who might be in a family, such as baby, aunt, grandpa, or stepdad. Then prompt each student to remove a bear from her cup and place it on her house to represent that person. Continue in the same way with several different family titles. Then have little ones nibble on their snack!

Thank You! Thank You!
Connecting spoken language with written words

Families are sure to treasure this note expressing thanks for all they do! Throughout the week, take brief moments to ask youngsters to explain ways that family members are kind and caring; write their thoughts on a sheet of chart paper. When each child has had a chance to respond, copy all the information on a sheet of paper. Then make copies of these kind words on decorative paper and send one home to each youngster's family!

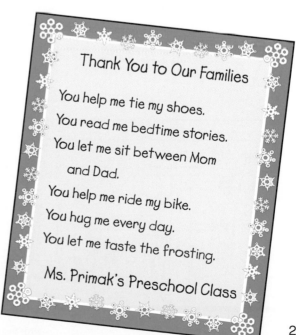

Thank You to Our Families

You help me tie my shoes.
You read me bedtime stories.
You let me sit between Mom and Dad.
You help me ride my bike.
You hug me every day.
You let me taste the frosting.

Ms. Primak's Preschool Class

Picture Cards
Use with "Chores Galore" on page 282.

TEC41022

TEC41022

TEC41022

TEC41022

TEC41022

TEC41022

Hooray for Valentine's Day!

Celebrate Valentine's Day in a big way with this colossal collection of ideas!

ideas contributed by Ada Goren, Winston-Salem, NC

Make a Match
Matching letters

When youngsters play this small-group game, they're in for a real treat! To prepare, gather an empty heart-shaped candy box and write pairs of letters on the inside in a random arrangement. Press a small ball of brown play dough (chocolate) on top of each letter. To begin, gather a small group of youngsters around the box. Each student takes a turn removing two chocolates. If the letters match, he keeps the chocolates. If they do not match, he returns the chocolates to the box. Play continues until all of the letter pairs are uncovered.

Dino Decor
Developing fine-motor skills

Cut out a large construction paper dinosaur for each child. Prepare a supply of small construction paper heart cutouts. Invite each child to glue the hearts upside down along the spine and tail of the dinosaur to resemble bony plates. Personalize each dinosaur and then display the completed projects on a bulletin board titled "Valentine's Day Is 'Dino-mite'!"

Hidden Hearts
Counting

Little ones are sure to dig this hands-on center! Remove the nine numbered heart cards from a deck of playing cards. Bury the cards in a tub of crinkled red paper shreds (or, if desired, bury them in your sand table). A youngster visits the center and searches through the shreds for the cards. As she finds each card, she removes it and counts the number of large hearts aloud.

"1, 2, 3, ..."

Hearts and Arrows
Matching sets

To prepare for this math center, make several heart cutouts and an equal number of arrow cutouts. Label each heart with a different numeral and a matching set of dots. Also label each arrow with a corresponding dot set. Place the arrows and hearts at a center. When a youngster visits the center, he chooses an arrow, counts the dots, and places it atop the matching heart. He continues in the same manner for each remaining heart.

Puppy Love
Listening for the beginning sound /p/

Make a copy of the puppy pattern on page 288 for each child. Have each student color his puppy, cut it out, and then glue it to a paper bag. To complete the puppet, have him glue a pink tongue cutout under the flap as shown. Invite each youngster to place his completed puppet on his hand. Then say a word. If the word begins with the /p/ sound as in *puppy,* students hold up their puppets and bark like a happy puppy. If the word does not begin with /p/, youngsters sit quietly. Continue in the same manner with several different words.

Tanya Tschombor, Childtime Learning Center, Brea, CA

Hugs and Kisses
Making a pattern

Place at a center a supply of construction paper strips, a shallow pan of tempera paint, and *X* and *O* sponge stamps (or use a stamp pad and *X* and *O* rubber stamps). Explain to students that *X*s and *O*s represent hugs and kisses. Then invite students to visit the center and stamp a simple pattern along a strip. Use the completed strips as bulletin board border or cut the strips into smaller pieces to make snazzy bracelets!

Leslie Boyett
Asbury Ark Academy
Bossier City, LA

Love Potion
Following directions

Give each child a scoop of raspberry sherbet in a clear plastic cup. Help her pour a half cup of lemon-lime soda over the sherbet. Then have her add a dollop of whipped cream to her drink. For added fun, invite each child to top her drink with a dash of heart-shaped sprinkles.

Please Be Mine
Participating in a song

No doubt little ones will just love this toe-tapping tune. It's perfect for a Valentine's Day celebration!

(sung to the tune of "Bingo")

My friend gave me a valentine.
Its message is so fine!
Won't you please be mine?
Won't you please be mine?
Won't you please be mine?
Please be my valentine!

adapted from an idea by Suzanne Moore
Tucson, AZ

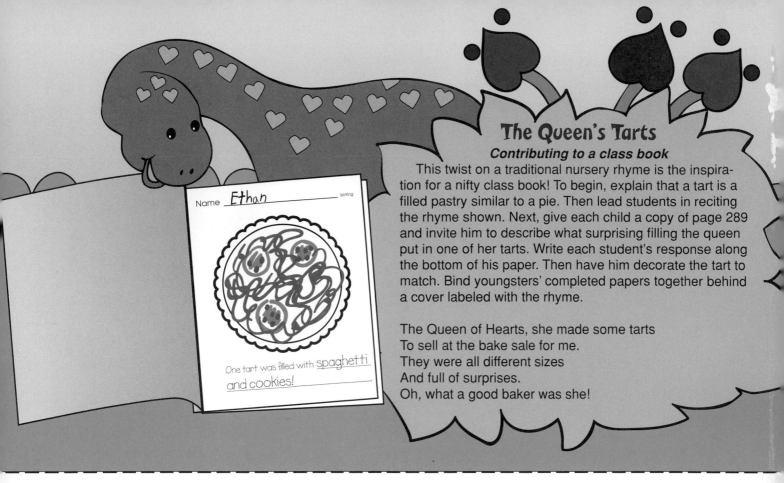

The Queen's Tarts
Contributing to a class book

This twist on a traditional nursery rhyme is the inspiration for a nifty class book! To begin, explain that a tart is a filled pastry similar to a pie. Then lead students in reciting the rhyme shown. Next, give each child a copy of page 289 and invite him to describe what surprising filling the queen put in one of her tarts. Write each student's response along the bottom of his paper. Then have him decorate the tart to match. Bind youngsters' completed papers together behind a cover labeled with the rhyme.

The Queen of Hearts, she made some tarts
To sell at the bake sale for me.
They were all different sizes
And full of surprises.
Oh, what a good baker was she!

Name _Ethan_ _____ Writing

One tart was filled with _spaghetti_
and cookies!

Puppy Pattern
Use with "Puppy Love" on page 286.

TEC41023

Time for Tarts

One tart was filled with_____

_____

Plentiful Puddles!

When spring showers fall from the skies, the ground is sure to be covered with lots and lots of puddles! That means it's the perfect time to make a splash with this selection of learning opportunities!

ideas contributed by Jana Sanderson, Rainbow School, Stockton, CA

Perfect Pairs
Matching letters

Familiarize little ones with uppercase and lowercase letters with this center! To prepare, make four yellow construction paper copies of the pair of rain boot patterns on page 293. Label one boot in each pair with an uppercase letter and the other boot with the matching lowercase letter. Then cut out the boots. Also label each of four puddle cutouts with corresponding letters to match each pair of boots. Then put all of the cutouts at a center. A child places each boot below the corresponding letter on each puddle. These boots are made for matching!

Amazing Absorption!
Predicting, observing

There's a puddle in the classroom! No doubt your youngsters will be eager to help clean it up with this small-group experiment. Pour a small amount of water on a tabletop to make a puddle. Place a piece of lamination film and a supply of paper towels nearby. Invite a small group of students to the table and explain that the puddle needs to be cleaned up. Have each student predict whether the lamination film or the paper towel will do a better job soaking up the puddle. Then place the film over the puddle and invite students to describe what happens. After repeating the process with a paper towel, encourage students to revisit their predictions. Those paper towels sure are handy!

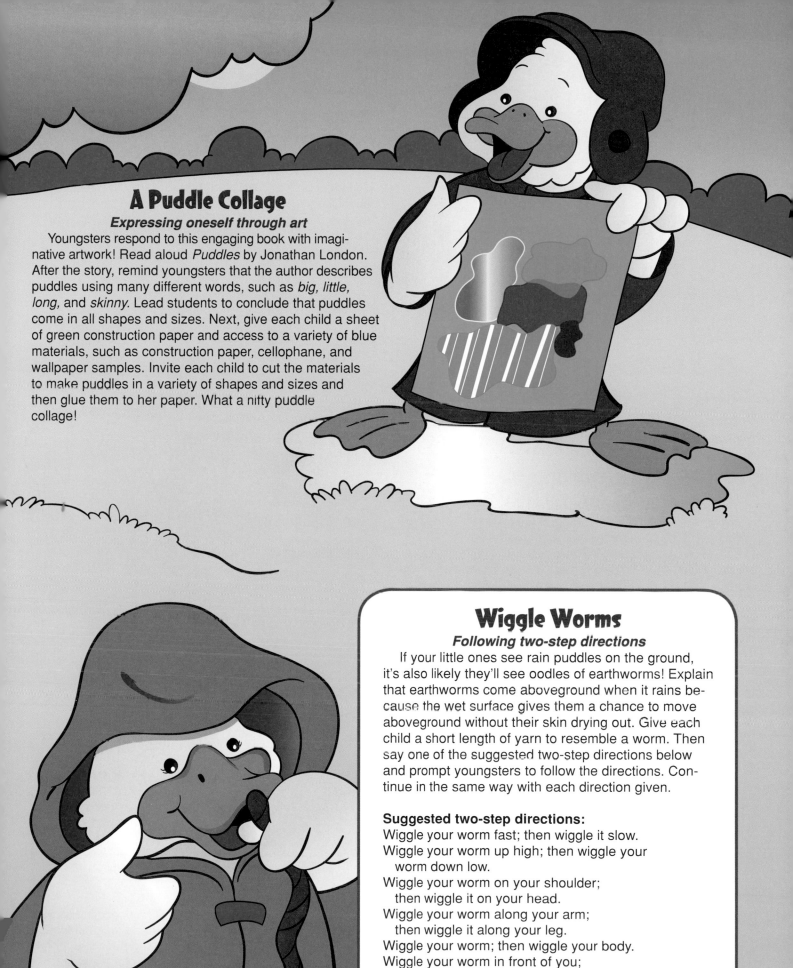

A Puddle Collage
Expressing oneself through art
Youngsters respond to this engaging book with imaginative artwork! Read aloud *Puddles* by Jonathan London. After the story, remind youngsters that the author describes puddles using many different words, such as *big, little, long,* and *skinny.* Lead students to conclude that puddles come in all shapes and sizes. Next, give each child a sheet of green construction paper and access to a variety of blue materials, such as construction paper, cellophane, and wallpaper samples. Invite each child to cut the materials to make puddles in a variety of shapes and sizes and then glue them to her paper. What a nifty puddle collage!

Wiggle Worms
Following two-step directions
If your little ones see rain puddles on the ground, it's also likely they'll see oodles of earthworms! Explain that earthworms come aboveground when it rains because the wet surface gives them a chance to move aboveground without their skin drying out. Give each child a short length of yarn to resemble a worm. Then say one of the suggested two-step directions below and prompt youngsters to follow the directions. Continue in the same way with each direction given.

Suggested two-step directions:
Wiggle your worm fast; then wiggle it slow.
Wiggle your worm up high; then wiggle your
  worm down low.
Wiggle your worm on your shoulder;
  then wiggle it on your head.
Wiggle your worm along your arm;
  then wiggle it along your leg.
Wiggle your worm; then wiggle your body.
Wiggle your worm in front of you;
  then wiggle your worm behind you.

From Small to Large
Ordering by size
Cut four puddle cutouts from blue bulletin board paper, making sure that each one is a different size. Laminate the cutouts and place them in a center. Youngsters arrange the puddles from smallest to largest on your floor. Then they walk through all the puddles. Splash, splash, splash, splash!

One Crowded Puddle!
Estimating
How many students can stand in a puddle? Little ones find out with this whole-group idea! Cut a piece of blue bulletin board paper to resemble a puddle. Then place the puddle on the floor in your circle-time area. Have youngsters estimate how many children can stand on the puddle; write each child's guess on a sheet of chart paper. Then invite students, one at a time, to come and stand on the puddle. When no more youngsters will fit, enlist students help in counting the number of children. Finally, instruct students to sit down and then help them to compare their estimates to the actual number of students that fit on the puddle.

A Splashy Snack
Following directions
This muddy little puddle is quite tasty! Give each child a chocolate sandwich cookie in a sealed plastic bag. Encourage her to knead and squeeze the bag to break up the cookie. Have her open the bag and pour the crumbs (dirt) into a disposable paper bowl. Then have her place a spoonful of blue-tinted vanilla pudding (water) over the dirt to make a muddy puddle. Finally, invite little ones to dive into this tasty treat!

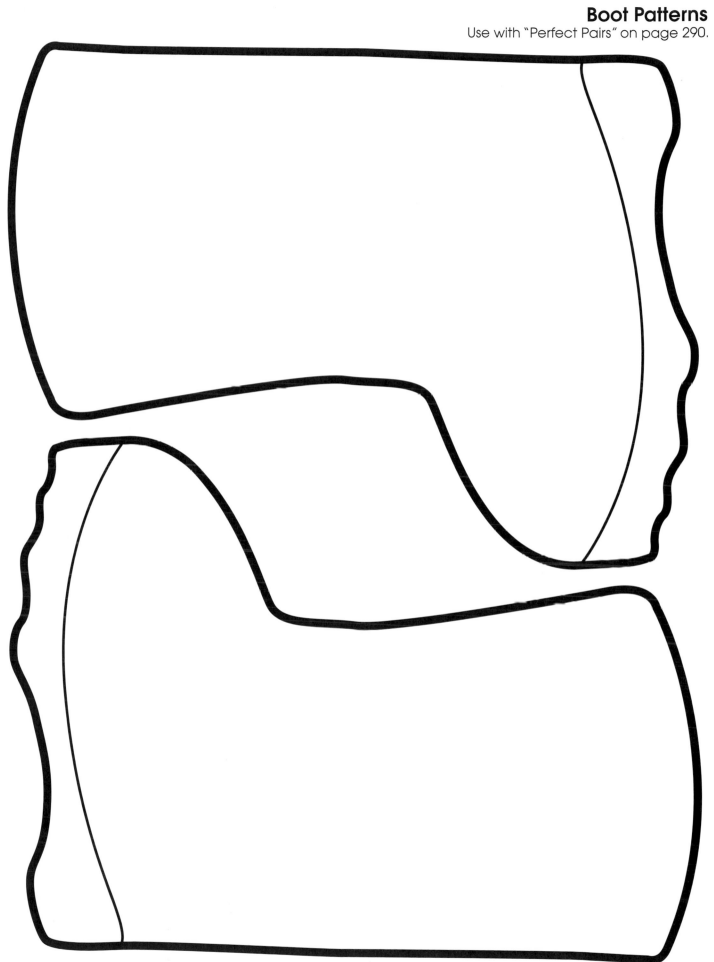

Fine-Feathered Friends!

These songbird-themed activities are a real "tweet" for your little ones!

ideas contributed by Jana Sanderson, Stockton, CA

A Nest of Facts

Extending prior knowledge
Youngsters share what they know about birds with this nifty nest display! Attach a supersize brown nest cutout to your classroom wall. Call students over one at a time and ask them to share what they know about birds. Write each child's words on a strip of tan construction paper to resemble a twig. Next, gather all your youngsters around the nest. Then read each child's strip and have him attach it to the nest. Have youngsters add to the display throughout your bird study by sharing new thoughts and by crafting birds and eggs to embellish the scene.

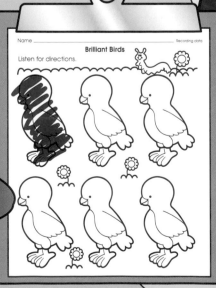

Bird-Watchers

Recording data
Your little bird-watchers will be all atwitter when they realize that several unique birds are hiding in the classroom! Make six copies of the bird pattern on page 297, making sure each copy is a different color. Cut out the birds and post them throughout the room. Make a class supply of the recording sheet on page 298. To begin, a child places a recording sheet on a clipboard and quietly searches the classroom for birds. When she spots a bird, she takes note of its color and then uses a crayon to color one of the birds on her sheet the same color as the one sighted. She continues in the same way with each remaining bird. Look! There's a red one!

294

Beautiful Blue!

Expressing oneself through art

Your youngsters may be surprised to find out that robin eggs aren't white but are instead a beautiful blue! If you have access to a picture of robin eggs, display it in your art center. Then place at the center the following items: scissors, glue, white egg cutouts, and a variety of blue craft items, such as tissue paper, wallpaper samples, markers, and magazine pictures. Invite youngsters to the center to trim the craft items as desired and then glue them to an egg cutout. These beautiful blue eggs would look lovely added to the nest display described in "A Nest of Facts" on page 294!

Super Singers

Participating in a song

Birds are known for their singing. Your little ones will be known for their singing as well when they perform this chirpy little chorus!

(sung to the tune of "Do Your Ears Hang Low?")

Do you hear birds sing?
They're so happy that it's spring!
Hear them cheep, cheep, cheep.
Hear them twitter; hear them peep.
Hear them at sunrise
When you open up your eyes.
Do you hear birds sing?

Looking for Worms

Making sets

For these birds to have a fair lunch, they each need to have an equal number of worms. Make two bird cutouts and ten worm cutouts (see the patterns on page 297) and then laminate the cutouts for durability. Nestle the worms in your sand table and place the birds nearby. Encourage students to search through the sand and remove all the worms. Then invite her to divide the worms fairly between the birds. Each bird has five worms!

Bath Time!

Listening for the beginning sound /b/

Here's a whole-group activity that's sure to make a splash! To make a birdbath, hot-glue a paper plate to the bottom of a disposable cup as shown. Cut out a colorful copy of the bird cards on page 299. To begin, give a card to a youngster and encourage her to identify the picture. Invite students to repeat the name of the picture, leading them to recognize that the picture's name begins with /b/, just like the words *bird* and *bath*. Then invite the child to place the bird in the bath. Continue in the same way with each remaining bird card. When youngsters are comfortable with the activity, place the props at a center for independent exploration.

bell

Nest Builders

Investigating characteristics of living things

Little ones can build a nest just like birds do! Gather items a bird may use to build a nest, such as yarn, leaves, sticks, strips of fabric, and torn paper. Before youngsters arrive, place the items in various locations around the room. To begin, explain that birds use many different items to build nests, such as those mentioned above. Have youngsters pretend to be birds as they "fly" around the room to search for items to use for nest building. Have children place their found items in a container. Then place the container at a center along with paper bowls and glue. Invite students to visit the center and glue items to a bowl to make a nest!

296

Bird Pattern
Use with "Bird-Watchers" on page 294, "Fun Feather Sort" on page 26, and "Looking for Worms" on page 295.

Worm Patterns
Use with "Looking for Worms" on page 295.

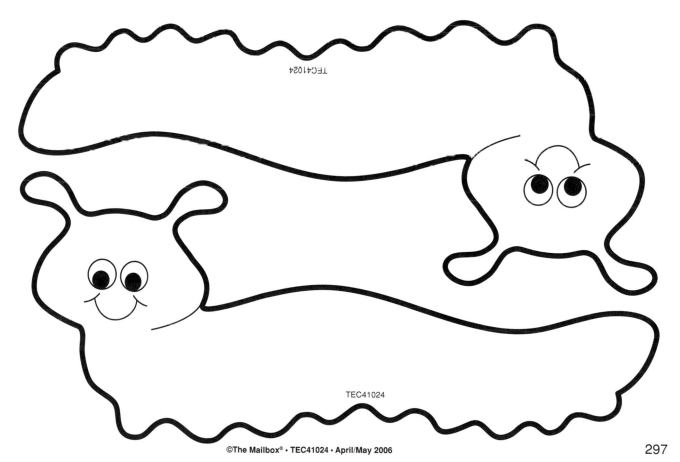

Brilliant Birds

Listen for directions.

Note to the teacher: Use with "Bird-Watchers" on page 294.

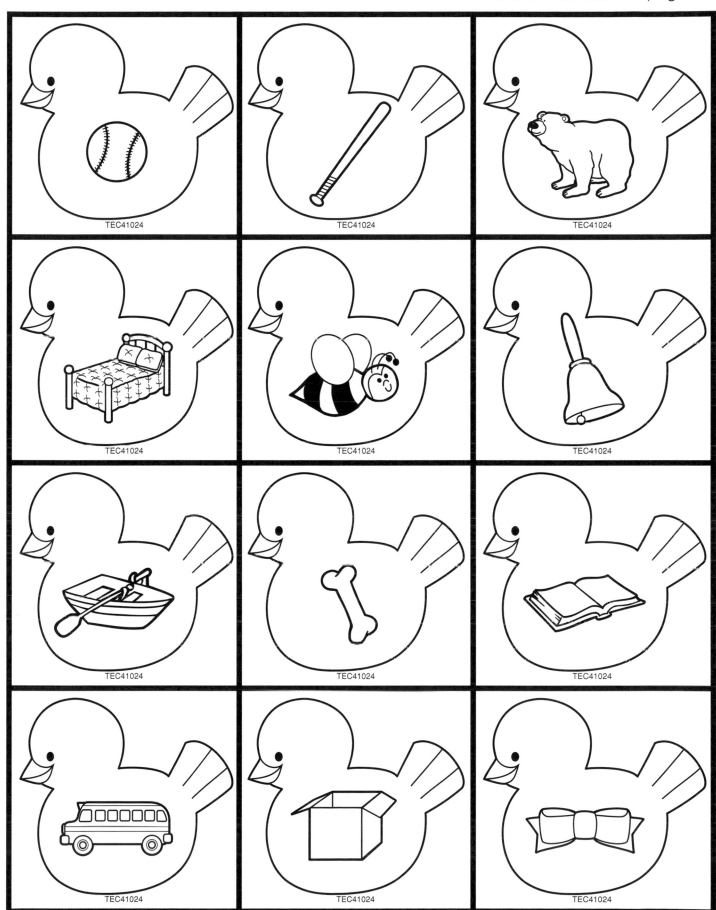

TEC41024

TEC41024

TEC41024

TEC41024

TEC41024

TEC41024

TEC41024

TEC41024

TEC41024

TEC41024

TEC41024

TEC41024

Beautiful Farm Babies!

Chicks, goslings, calves, and foals? It must be springtime on the farm!
Little ones are sure to delight in this adorable unit all about those new
arrivals to the farm community: baby animals!

ideas contributed by Lucia Kemp Henry, Fallon, NV

Down on the Farm
Developing new vocabulary

This toe-tapping song is a fun way to introduce names
for different farm babies! Color and cut out a copy of the
animal cards on pages 303 and 304. Place the cards
in your pocket chart. Then lead students in singing the
song shown. Encourage a child to find the card that
shows the corresponding animal. Then have her hold up
the card as you prompt youngsters to say the animal's
name. Continue in a similar way with the remaining cards,
altering the song to reflect a different animal each time.

(sung to the tune of "The Wheels on the Bus")

What baby on the farm says, "[Moo, moo, moo],"
"[Moo, moo, moo. Moo, moo, moo]?"
What baby on the farm says, "[Moo, moo, moo]?"
What is its name?

Woolly the Lamb
Exploring the sense of touch

Lambs have woolly coats just like adult
sheep do! Make a simple, large lamb picture
on white bulletin board paper. Laminate the
paper and then securely tape it to a tabletop.
Place several dollops of shaving cream on the
lamb. Then invite little ones to visit the center
and explore the shaving cream with their
fingers, encouraging them to spread it over
the lamb to resemble its woolly coat.

Melinda Blackwill
Hays Head Start
Hays, KS

Flossie and Bossie
Comparing sets

Help each youngster cut out two copies of the calf pattern on page 304 and glue them to a sheet of green construction paper to resemble a meadow. Label the calves with the names shown (or, if desired, have the child choose names for the calves). Have a child roll a die and count the number of dots. Then encourage her to press her thumb on a black ink pad and then place the corresponding number of fingerprints on a calf to represent spots. Have her repeat the process with the second calf. Finally, prompt her to compare the numbers of spots on the calves using words such as *more, less,* or *the same.* Then write her words on the paper.

Melinda Blackwill
Hays Head Start
Hays, KS

Lucy

Flossie   Bossie

Flossie and Bossie have the same number of spots.

Calves in the Corn
Developing fine-motor skills

Make several copies of the calf pattern on page 304 and label each one with a large dotted letter *C*. Laminate the calves and then nestle them in a plastic container of feed corn. Encourage children to visit the center, find each calf hiding in the corn, and then trace the letter *C* on each one with a wipe-off marker. For further fine-motor practice, students can remove the kernels from the ears of corn, placing the loose kernels back in the tub!

Chick Cuisine
Understanding needs of living things

Your little ones may be surprised to learn that chicks can eat the same foods as grown-up chickens: grains, insects, seeds, worms, and berries! This fun snack will remind youngsters of a chick's favorite foods. Place cereal, sunflower seeds, and dried cherries or blueberries in separate bowls. Have each child take a tablespoon of each food and place it in a cup. If desired, give each child a Gummy Worm candy to add to his treat.

Piglets in the Puddle

Counting to ten

To prepare for this whole-group activity, cut a large mud puddle shape from brown bulletin board paper and then place it on your classroom floor. Invite ten students to sit on the mud puddle and pretend to be piglets. Then lead youngsters in singing the first verse of the song shown as you gesture to each piglet on the puddle. Next, pretend to give each youngster a bar of soap. Then lead youngsters in singing the second verse of the song as the piglets pretend to wash with the soap. Those cute little piglets look squeaky clean!

(sung to the tune of "Ten Little Indians")

One little, two little, three little piglets,
Four little, five little, six little piglets,
Seven little, eight little, nine little piglets,
Ten little piglets in the mud.

Ten little, nine little, eight little piglets,
Seven little, six little, five little piglets,
Four little, three little, two little piglets,
One more—now they're clean!

Goodnight, Animals

Listening

Follow up a reading of Margaret Wise Brown's *Big Red Barn* with this sweet activity. Cut out enough copies of the animal cards on pages 303 and 304 for each child to have one card. Make a large barn cutout and place it on the floor. To begin, read aloud the book and then give each child a card. Tell youngsters that it's time for the animals to go to sleep just as they do at the end of the story. Say, "Goodnight, piglets," and then encourage all youngsters with piglet cards to place them on the barn. Continue in the same way with the remaining animal cards. Then have students move quietly to their next activity so as not to disturb the sleeping animals.

Use with "Down on the Farm" on page 300 and "Goodnight, Animals" on page 302.

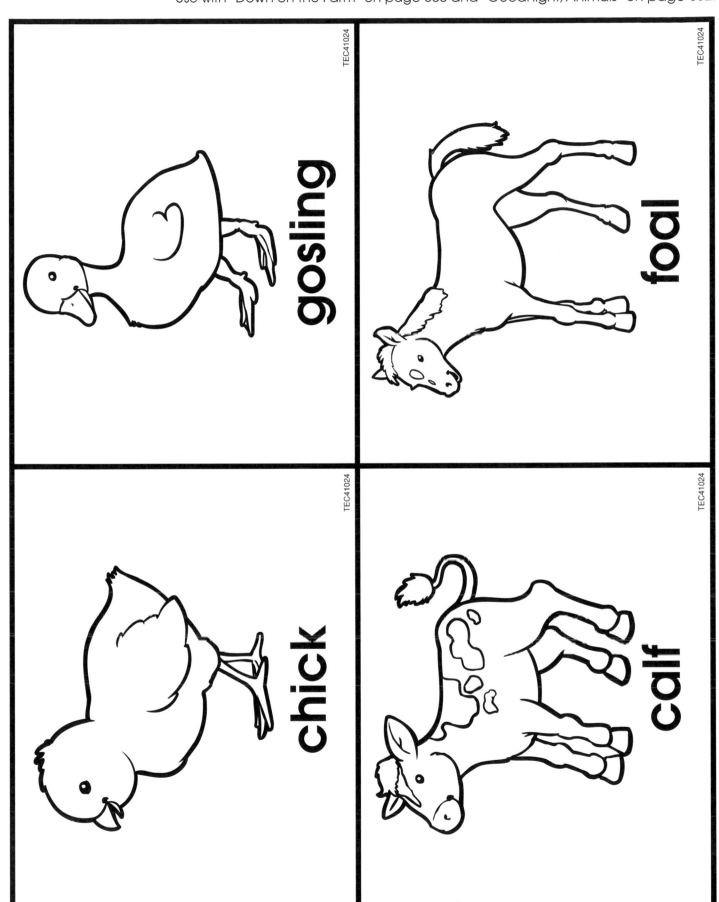

TEC41024

TEC41024

gosling

foal

TEC41024

TEC41024

chick

calf

Animal Cards

Use with "Down on the Farm" on page 300 and "Goodnight, Animals" on page 302.

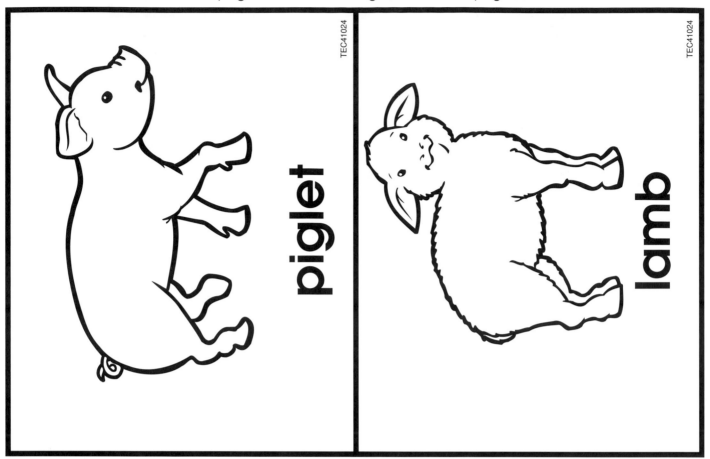

piglet

lamb

TEC41024

TEC41024

Calf Pattern

Use with "Flossie and Bossie" and "Calves in the Corn" on page 301.

TEC41024

Let's Go Camping!

Pitch the tent and load up that backpack. It's time for some camping-related learning fun!

ideas contributed by Angie Kutzer, Garrett Elementary, Mebane, NC

Good Packing, Bad Packing
Developing life skills

You're sure to see oodles of smiles when your happy campers evaluate items packed for a pretend camping trip! Place in a backpack objects you might take on a camping trip, including a few odd items that would not be practical choices. Then gather youngsters and present the backpack. Explain that you've packed some items for a camping trip. Pull out each item and ask students whether it was a wise item to pack and how it could be used on the trip. That fancy hat will just have to stay at home!

All Fired Up!
Developing fine-motor skills

Transform your large-group area into a campground with this crafty campfire! Glue cardboard tubes (logs) to a sheet of poster board as shown. When the glue is dry, place the poster board at a table along with scraps of red, orange, and yellow tissue paper. Provide access to a paintbrush and container of glue. Youngsters visit the center, brush glue on the project, and then place crumpled tissue paper on the glue. After each youngster has had the opportunity to visit the center and the glue is dry, place the resulting campfire in your circle-time area. Then have youngsters sit around the fire during the large-group activities on the following pages.

Stacie Scalisi, Capital District Beginnings, Troy, NY

305

Hiking Through the Woods
Listening to draw a conclusion

With this activity, little ones identify forest animals based on descriptions! Color and cut out a copy of the cards on page 308, and tape the cards to your board. Invite students to go on a pretend hike through a forest. Have them pat their hands on their legs to sound like walking feet. Then explain that you have spotted an animal. Quietly tell them that the animal you see has a long, furry tail; enjoys eating nuts; and likes to climb trees. Have students use the cards as a guide to help them guess the correct animal. Then repeat the process with a new animal and description as shown. You must have seen a squirrel!

Suggested animal descriptions:

raccoon: has a mask, has rings on its tail, and might get into the garbage at the campground

skunk: is black and white, has a white stripe on its tail, and might make the hiking trip very stinky

bird: builds a nest, lays eggs, and likes to sing

deer: has brown fur, has antlers, and is taller than the other animals

bunny: has long ears, hops, and has a fluffy tail

Simple S'mores

Give each child a plate with a spoonful of marshmallow cream, a spoonful of hot fudge ice-cream topping, and a few Teddy Grahams graham snacks. A youngster dips a teddy bear into the toppings and then nibbles on the resulting tasty treat. No doubt these bears are a welcome addition to this camping trip.

Flashing Fireflies
Developing preaddition skills

Flashing fireflies light up an evening at the campground! Color and cut out a copy of the firefly patterns on page 106. Ready the fireflies for flannelboard use. Then place two fireflies on the flannelboard. Lead students in reciting the chant shown below, adding one more firefly when indicated. Finally, help youngsters count the total number of fireflies on the board. Repeat the activity several times using different numbers.

[Two] little fireflies glimmer and glow,
Putting on a fancy summertime show.
[One] more firefly adds his light.
How many fireflies are out tonight?

Who's Camping?
Writing one's own name

This simple class book is sure to be popular in your reading center! Help each child cut out a brown construction paper copy of the tent on page 309. Encourage her to cut a slit in the tent where indicated. Have her fold up the resulting tent flaps and glue her tent to a sheet of construction paper programmed as shown. Invite each student to draw herself so it appears she is in the tent. After she adds any desired scenery, help her write her name in the blank at the top of the page. Stack the completed pages under a cover titled as shown. Then read the book aloud before placing it in your reading center.

Fabulous Flashlights
Identifying rhyming words

Collect a couple of flashlights and give each one to a different child. Say a pair of words, such as *bright–light*. If the words rhyme, encourage the youngsters to flash their lights. If they don't rhyme, prompt students to keep their flashlights off. Continue in the same way, using different rhyming words and passing the flashlights to new volunteers each time.

Buzz, Buzz, Buzz!
Participating in a song

Bugs are often a part of a camping experience. So why not make light of those pesky critters with a giggle-inducing song about mosquitoes! If desired, give each youngster a simple mosquito puppet similar to the one shown. Then encourage children to move their mosquitoes as you lead them in singing the song.

(sung to the tune of "Camptown Races")

> A mosquito is in my tent.
> Buzz, buzz. Buzz, buzz.
> A mosquito is in my tent.
> I don't want him here.
> He will buzz all night!
> Please, oh, please don't bite.
> A mosquito is in my tent.
> I don't want him here.

Animal Cards

Use with "Hiking Through the Woods" on page 306.

TEC41025

TEC41025

TEC41025

TEC41025

TEC41025

TEC41025

TEC41025

A Boat Bonanza!

Keep your small shipmates on course with this nautical collection of ideas!

ideas contributed by Jana Sanderson
Rainbow School, Stockton, CA

Beautiful Boats
Participating in a song

This catchy tune introduces little ones to different types of boats. To prepare, color and cut out a copy of the boat cards on page 313. Trim blue bulletin board paper to resemble a body of water, and post it at students' eye level. Attach the sailboat card to the water; then lead youngsters in singing the song. Continue in the same manner for each remaining card, replacing the boat name appropriately for each verse.

(sung to the tune of "If You're Happy and You Know It")

There's a [sailboat] bobbing in the sparkling sea.
Splish, splash!
There's a [sailboat] bobbing in the sparkling sea.
Splish, splash!
Oh, who wouldn't want to be
That [sailboat] in the sea?
There's a [sailboat] bobbing in the sparkling sea.
Splish, splash!

Porthole Patterning
Copying patterns

Invite little ones to cruise over to this center for some ship decorating fun! Draw a simple ship with six portholes, similar to the one shown. Then make a copy for each child. Also prepare several different pattern strips to resemble the portholes. Place the strips and ships at a center. When a child visits the center, he chooses a strip and colors the portholes on his ship to match the pattern. Finally, he decorates his ship as desired. Anchors aweigh!

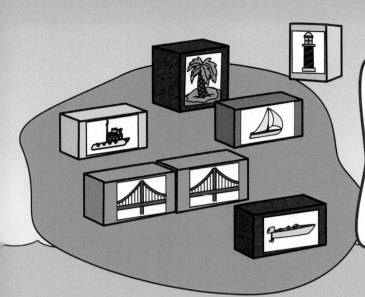

The Block Dock
Engaging in pretend play
Steer youngsters toward the block center for some engaging creative play! Color and cut out several copies of the cards on pages 313 and 314. Attach each card to a different block in your block center. Then trim blue bulletin board paper to resemble a body of water. Laminate the paper and place it near your block center. Invite youngsters to visit the center to engage in nautical-themed block play.

Herrily, herrily, herrily, herrily, Life is but a dream.

A Rowboat Review
Exploring phonemic awareness
Reinforce letter-sound association with this giggle-inducing version of a familiar song! Prepare a supply of letter cards that show familiar consonants. Seat students in lines to resemble the seating in a rowboat. Then hold up a letter card and help youngsters identify its sound. Next, have little ones pretend to row as they sing the song "Row, Row, Row Your Boat," substituting the /m/ in *merrily* with the sound of the letter on the card. Repeat the song several times, spotlighting a different letter and its sound each time.

Gail Marsh, St. Mark's Lutheran School, Eureka, MO

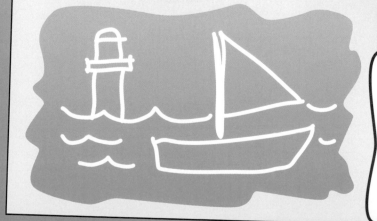

Lost and Found
Engaging in creative arts
Little ones find their boats in the deep blue sea with this supersimple art project! On a white sheet of paper, have each child draw a boat and water scene using a thick white crayon. Then have him paint over the paper with blue watercolor paint. He is sure to be surprised when his boat is found in the sea!

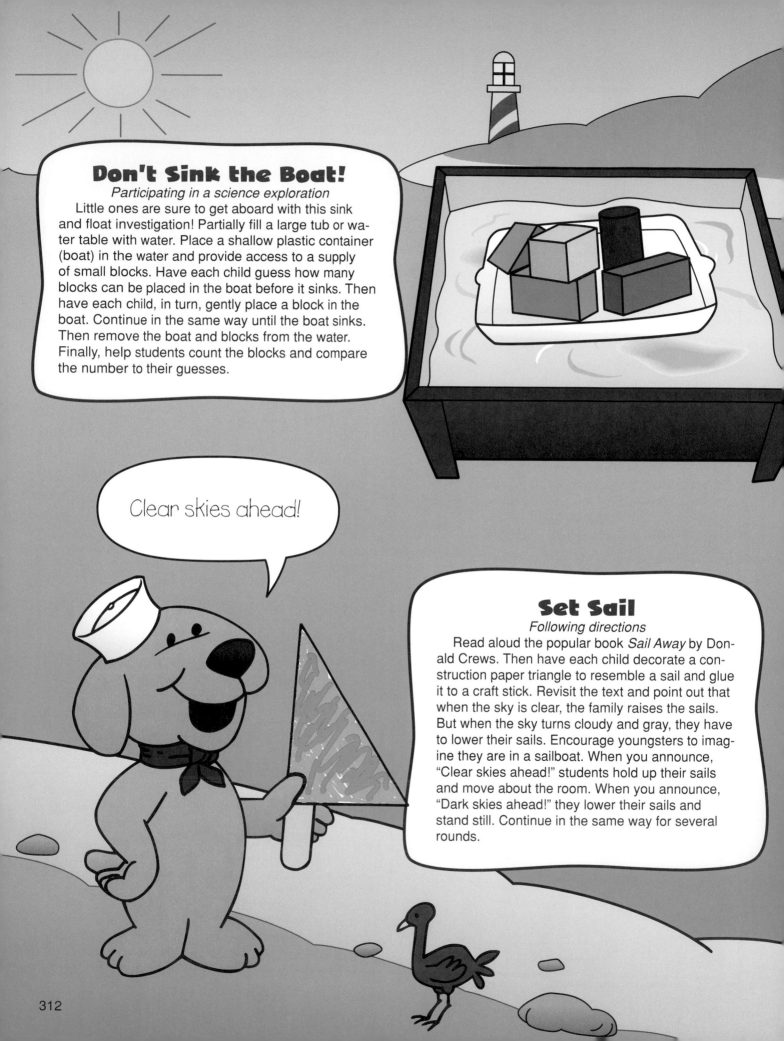

Don't Sink the Boat!

Participating in a science exploration

Little ones are sure to get aboard with this sink and float investigation! Partially fill a large tub or water table with water. Place a shallow plastic container (boat) in the water and provide access to a supply of small blocks. Have each child guess how many blocks can be placed in the boat before it sinks. Then have each child, in turn, gently place a block in the boat. Continue in the same way until the boat sinks. Then remove the boat and blocks from the water. Finally, help students count the blocks and compare the number to their guesses.

Clear skies ahead!

Set Sail

Following directions

Read aloud the popular book *Sail Away* by Donald Crews. Then have each child decorate a construction paper triangle to resemble a sail and glue it to a craft stick. Revisit the text and point out that when the sky is clear, the family raises the sails. But when the sky turns cloudy and gray, they have to lower their sails. Encourage youngsters to imagine they are in a sailboat. When you announce, "Clear skies ahead!" students hold up their sails and move about the room. When you announce, "Dark skies ahead!" they lower their sails and stand still. Continue in the same way for several rounds.

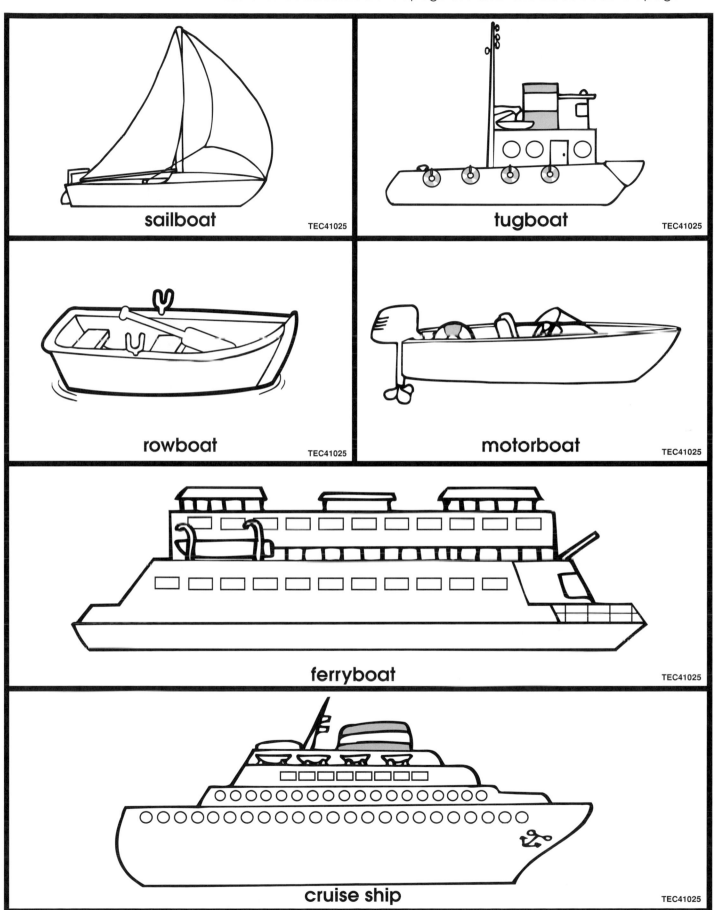

sailboat

TEC41025

tugboat

TEC41025

rowboat

TEC41025

motorboat

TEC41025

ferryboat

TEC41025

cruise ship

TEC41025

TEC41025

TEC41025

TEC41025

TEC41025

Index

Action Poems and Songs
  apples, 116
  beach, 250
  boats, 310, 313
  camping, 307
  cats, 198
  counting, 116, 239
  end of the year, 124
  fish, 162
  friendship, 68
  getting acquainted, 117
  gift giving, 277
  handwashing, 117
  letters, 224, 226
  letter-sound association, 311
  movement, 58
  pumpkins, 118
  rhyming words, 198
  sand castle, 256
  sleeping animals, 48
  spring, 122
  summer, 124
  washing machine, 120
Apples
  comparing, 261
  foam, 32
  letter matching, 263
  parts, 261
  patterning, 260, 263
  song, 116, 261
  tracking print from left to right, 260, 263
  unit, 260–263
Archambault, John, and Bill Martin Jr.
  Chicka Chicka Boom Boom, 99, 144
Arts and Crafts (see also Painting)
  apple crown, 260, 263
  apples, foam, 32
  bees, 43
  bingo dauber activities, 22, 23
  boat, 311
  bubble picture, 43
  class card, 25
  colorful caterpillar, 42
  colorful collage headband, 180
  dreidel painting, 36
  Easter card, 41
  fabulous flower garden, 42
  finger skating, 38
  fireworks, 44
  flyswatter painting, 104
  frosty windows, 37
  gift wrap collage, 277
  heart mouse, 39
  "Hickory, Dickory, Dock" clock, 33, 45
  holiday crayons, 110
  holiday lights, 36
  leprechaun, 40
  letters in envelopes, 24
  love letters, 24
  marbleized eggs, 42
  mazao project, 38
  microwave play dough, 114
  noodle art, 32
  packing materials, 25
  poinsettia center, 98
  Puddles, 291
  rainbow, 40
  sandcastle, 44
  shamrock, 39
  snoozing ladybugs, 35, 46

  spiderweb rubbing, 137
  stamps, 25
  three-dimensional fish, 255
  turkey, 35, 170
  wallpaper kites, 41
  wreath, 37
Authors
  Archambault, John, 99, 144
  Baer, Gene, 234
  Brett, Jan, 139, 231, 233
  Brown, Margaret Wise, 302–304
  Carle, Eric, 137
  Crews, Donald, 175, 312
  Degen, Bruce, 154–157
  Ehlert, Lois, 162, 163
  Ezra, Mark, 231, 233
  Freeman, Don, 138
  Henkes, Kevin, 146
  Hutchins, Patricia, 220, 222
  Kalan, Robert, 140
  Kirk, Daniel, 283
  Lionni, Leo, 143, 145, 148
  London, Jonathan, 291
  Martin, Bill, Jr., 99, 144
  Numeroff, Laura, 164–166
  Seuss, Dr., 110
  Steig, William, 136, 141
  Tafuri, Nancy, 142, 148
  Titherington, Jeanne, 204, 206
  Walsh, Ellen Stoll, 158–161
  Wood, Audrey, 150–153
Back-to-School
  bulletin board, 254, 257
  chant, 117
  getting acquainted, 117, 254, 258
  nametags, 256
  room decoration, 255
  school tour, 255
  school-year growth, 109
  unit, 254–259
Baer, Gene
  Thump, Thump, Rat-a-Tat-Tat, 234
Bears
  animal environment, 271, 274
  behavior, 272
  /b/ sound, 272, 274
  bulletin board, 271, 274
  circle time, 271
  following directions, 272
  independent interest in books, 270
  needs of a living thing, 270, 273
  song, 270
  unit, 270–275
Bees
  art project, 43
  cards, 105
  literacy center, 101
Beginning Sounds
  /b/ sound, 296, 299
  center, 211
  flannelboard sacks, 211, 213
  game, 78
  gift box objects, 210
  names, 210
  /p/ sound, 160, 161
  /p/ sound puppet, 286, 288
  /r/ sound, 220, 223
  unit, 210–213
  wordplay, 212
Big Red Barn
  Brown, Margaret Wise, 302–304
  listening skills, 302–304

Birds
  art center, 295
  beginning sound /b/, 296, 299
  characteristics of living things, 296
  display, 294
  expressing oneself through art, 295
  feather center, 26
  making sets, 295, 297
  prior knowledge, 294
  recording data, 294, 297, 298
  song, 295
  toucan, 246–249
  unit, 294–299
  whole-group activity, 296, 299
Birthdays
  balloon print, 193
  candle snack, 194
  color matching, 195
  connecting spoken language with written words, 195, 196
  name recognition, 192
  numeral matching, 194
  plate puzzle, 193
  reading area, 194
  unit, 192–196
  wrap and ribbon cutting, 192
Boats
  art project, 311
  creative play, 311, 313, 314
  following directions, 312
  letter-sound association, 311
  patterning, 310
  science exploration, 312
  song, 310, 313
  unit, 310–314
Bookmaking (see also Class Books)
  shapes, 235, 236
Books
  Big Red Barn, 302–304
  Chicka Chicka Boom Boom, 99, 144
  Chrysanthemum, 146
  Corduroy, 138
  Fish Eyes: A Book You Can Count On, 162–163
  Freight Train, 175
  Gingerbread Baby, 139
  Have You Seen My Duckling? 142, 148
  Hedgie's Surprise, 231, 233
  How the Grinch Stole Christmas, 110
  If You Take a Mouse to School, 164–166
  Inch by Inch, 143, 148
  Jamberry, 154–157
  Mouse Paint, 158–161
  Napping House, The, 150–153
  Pete's a Pizza, 136
  Prickly Hedgehog, The, 231, 233
  Puddles, 291
  Pumpkin Pumpkin, 204, 206
  Rain, 140
  Sail Away, 312
  Snow Family, 283
  Swimmy, 145
  Sylvester and the Magic Pebble, 141
  Thump, Thump, Rat-a-Tat-Tat, 234
  Very Busy Spider, The, 137
  Wind Blew, The, 220, 222
Brett, Jan
  Gingerbread Baby, 139
  Hedgie's Surprise, 231, 233
Brown, Margaret Wise
  Big Red Barn, 302–304

Bulletin Boards and Displays
    art show display, 114
    back-to-school, 254, 257
    baseball, 14
    behavior, 65
    birds, 11, 294
    cardinals, 8
    colors, 6
    creative caterpillar, 13
    Earth Day, 12
    Easter, 12, 65
    environmental print, 10
    family quilt, 6
    feather, 27
    fish, 162
    friendship, 9, 17
    holiday tree, 8
    I Spy, 7
    King, Martin Luther, Jr., 9, 17
    letter recognition, 215, 217
    names, 146
    New Year, 9
    ocean, 254, 257
    owl, 7, 16
    patriotic, 15
    polar bear's environment, 271, 274
    pot of gold, 11
    powder clouds, 101
    racecar, 15, 18
    rainy day, 13
    seasonal tree, 109
    sunshine, 14
    Valentine's Day, 10
    weather, 113
Camping
    developing fine-motor skills, 305
    developing life skills, 305
    drawing a conclusion, 306, 308
    name booklet, 307, 309
    preaddition skills, 106, 306
    rhyming words, 307
    snack, 306
    song, 307
Carle, Eric
    Very Busy Spider, The, 137
Chant
    fast and slow, 56
    fireflies, 306
    fish, 163
    letter recognition, 214
    Santa Claus, 121
    St. Patrick's Day, 123
    toucan chant, 247
    transition time, 65
Chicka Chicka Boom Boom
    holiday tree center, 99
    letter recognition, 144
    Martin, Bill, Jr., and John Archambault,
        99, 144
Christmas (see also Gifts)
    bulletin board, 8
    cake, 83, 84
    chant, 121
    Chicka Chicka Boom Boom tree center, 99
    holiday lights, 36
    jingle bell counting, 72
    lightbulb patterning center, 99
    poinsettia center, 98
    popcorn and cranberries center, 98
    Santa's cookies rhyme, 72
    wreath, 37

Chrysanthemum
    Henkes, Kevin, 146
    name flower, 146
    name introduction, 146
Circle Time
    alphabet game, 78
    body parts rhyme, 70
    butterfly activity, 76
    common sounds, 74
    emotions, 70
    emotions leprechaun, 74
    five senses, 69
    following directions, 71
    friendship chant, 68
    hidden pictures, 75
    I Spy game, 76
    jingle bell counting, 72
    letter recognition, 74, 144, 214, 217
    letter sounds game, 78
    mystery letter sing-along, 70
    name recognition, 68, 142, 148
    number matching, 77
    rhyming pairs, 155
    Santa's cookies rhyme, 72
    shape monster, 71
    shape search, 69
    song of letters, 76
    squish-and-bake cookies, 73
    star rhyme, 72
    transition chant, 65
    vacation rhyme, 78
    valentine song, 75
    weather, 68
    Who Has Your Fish? 271
    Who's My Friend? 73
Class Books
    covers, 113
    name booklet, 307, 309
    Napping House, The, 151
    Valentine's Day, 288, 289
Classroom Management
    animal imitations, 63
    artwork displays, 114
    artwork holders, 64
    attendance, 63, 65
    behavior incentive, 65
    boo-boo bag, 108
    book ordering, 112
    bulletin board, extra, 62
    bulletin board measuring, 66
    comfort bear, 109
    crayon holders, 62
    cutting tip, 66
    desktag, fabric paint, 109
    donation tree, 111
    dyeing pasta, 113
    easy cleanup, 66
    flannelboard, 64
    glue, 64
    microwave play dough, 114
    music, 64
    name labels, 110
    permanent marker removal, 62
    portable flannelboards, 114
    portfolios, 62
    reminder bracelets, 65
    rhyming reminder, 66
    sharing snowball, 63
    sink waiting line, 63
    small pieces, 64
    snacktime manners, 111

    storing calendar pieces, 65
    teacher bag, 62
    timer, 63
    title page tip, 66
    transition time chant, 65
Colors
    bulletin board, 6
    collage, 6
    colorful collage headband, 180
    handprints, 108
    matching, 26, 178
    mixing, 132, 158–160
    poem, 179, 181
    rainbow fruit snack, 179
    recognition, 159, 160
    recording, 294, 297, 298
    red, 27
    robin eggs, 295
    secondary, 132, 158
Cooking and Snacks (see also Learning
        Centers—Snack)
    "bear-y" cute cupcake, 80, 82
    beautiful butterfly snack, 89, 90
    chick cuisine, 301
    Christmas cake, 83, 84
    fish snack, 145
    fruit snack, 132, 179
    leprechaun pudding, 86, 87
    pumpkin spread, 80, 81
    s'mores, 306
    snail snack, 91, 92
    snowshoe hare, 83, 85
    squish-and-bake cookies, 73
Corduroy
    button search, 138
    Freeman, Don, 138
    positional words, 138
Correspondence
    reminder bracelets, 65
Counting
    action rhyme, 239
    cheese blocks, 237, 240
    circle time, 72
    comparing sets, 239
    concrete objects, 239
    families, 281
    gift ribbon, 276
    math center, 102
    set of five, 237, 241
    sets, 238
    song, 238
    strategy, 239
    to five, 238, 241
    to ten, 163
    unit, 237–241
    Valentine's Day center, 286
Crews, Donald
    Freight Train, 175
    Sail Away, 312
Degen, Bruce
    Jamberry, 154–157
Dramatic Play (see also Learning Centers—
        Dramatic Play)
    family meal, 281
    pancake breakfast, 22
    snack sequencing, 204
Earth Day
    display, 12
    water table activity, 103
Easter
    card, 41

display, 12, 65
plastic egg number match, 77
Ehlert, Lois
Fish Eyes: A Book You Can Count On,
162, 163
End of the Year
song, 124
Environmental Print
bulletin board, 10
Ezra, Mark
Prickly Hedgehog, The, 231, 233
Fall (see also Fire Prevention Week,
Halloween, Leaves, Pumpkins,
Thanksgiving)
bulletin board, 7, 16
Families
connecting spoken and written language,
283
counting and comparing numbers, 281
dramatic play, 281
home-school connection, 282
identifying people in a family, 283
naming family members, 282
recognizing differences, 282, 284
Snow Family, 283
speaking and listening, 283
unit, 281–284
Farm Animals
comparing sets, 301, 304
counting to ten, 302
developing fine-motor skills, 301, 304
developing new vocabulary, 300, 303, 304
listening skills, 302–304
sense of touch, 300
snack, 301
song, 300, 302
understanding needs of living things, 301
unit, 300–304
whole-group activity, 302
Feely Box
classroom surroundings, 69
Fine Motor (see also Learning Centers—
Fine-Motor Area)
campfire, 305
collage, 102, 277
cutting skills, 27
fabulous flower garden, 42
feather painting, 27
letter *C,* 301, 304
pot of gold, 86, 88
pumpkin prints, 266
Valentine's Day, 285
wallpaper kite, 41
weaving, 180
Fire Prevention Week
song, 118
Fish Eyes: A Book You Can Count On
Ehlert, Lois, 162, 163
Five Senses (see also Feely Box)
hearing, 74
Flannelboard
beginning sound, 211, 213
butterfly, 76
Jamberry, 154, 156
letter sounds, 226
portable, 114
rhyming words, 200
toucan, 247, 248
Flowers
plant parts, 101

Following Directions
bear behavior, 272
circle time, 71
clown hats, 183
fruit snack, 179
puddles, 291
Valentine's Day, 287
Fourth of July
fireworks art, 44
movement activity, 58
patriotic display, 15
patriotic rice center, 103
Freeman, Don
Corduroy, 138
Freight Train
Crews, Donald, 175
Games (see also Learning Centers—Puzzles)
alphabet game, 78
I Spy game, 76
letter sounds, 78
rhyming, 198
number recognition, 246, 248
small-group letter, 216–218
Valentine's Day letter matching, 285
Who's My Friend? 73
Gifts
action rhyme, 277
classroom, 110
collage, 277
counting, 276
descriptive words, 276, 279
fine-motor skills, 277
home-school connection, 278, 279
matching letters, 277
Mother's Day, 102, 114
ordering by size, 278
polite words, 278
unit, 276–280
Gingerbread Baby
Brett, Jan, 139
gingerbread house, 139, 147
Graphing
collecting data, 250
object graph, 251
organizing and interpreting data, 251
organizing data, 250–252
unit, 250–252
Gross Motor (see Learning Centers—Gross-
Motor Area)
dramatizing a story, 163
following directions, 312
Fourth of July activity, 58
movement song, 58
Groundhog Day
song, 122
Halloween
song, 119
Hanukkah
dreidel painting, 36
Have You Seen My Duckling?
before you read, 142, 148
circle-time activity, 142, 148
Tafuri, Nancy, 142, 148
Hedgie's Surprise
Brett, Jan 231, 233
Henkes, Kevin
Chrysanthemum, 146
How the Grinch Stole Christmas
Seuss, Dr., 110
Who Pudding, 110

Hutchins, Patricia
Wind Blew, The, 220, 222
If You Take a Mouse to School
Numeroff, Laura, 164–166
positional words, 165
predicting, 164
responding to literature through play, 165
science demonstration, 165
sequencing, 164, 166
Inch by Inch
center, 143, 148
Lionni, Leo, 143, 148
prereading activity, 143
Jamberry
building prior knowledge, 154, 156
circle time, 155
Degen, Bruce, 154–157
developing number recognition, 154, 156
dictating information to complete a
sentence, 155, 156
flannelboard, 154, 156
poem, 154, 156
rhyming pairs, 155
sorting, 155, 157
Kalan, Robert
Rain, 140
King, Martin Luther, Jr.
friendship bulletin board, 9, 17
Kirk, Daniel
Snow Family, 283
Kwanzaa
mazao project, 38
Language Development (see also Learning
Centers—Literacy, Letters, Name
Recognition)
beginning sound /p/, 266, 269
/b/ sound, 272, 274, 296, 299
dictating information to complete a
sentence, 155, 156, 162
using descriptive words, 265, 267, 276, 279
using vocabulary specific to a living thing,
261
Learning Centers—Art
balloon prints, 193
bug web, 96
car tracks, 29
colorful collage headband, 180
feather painting, 26, 27
flyswatter art, 104
poinsettia, 98
powder clouds, 101
robin eggs, 295
watermelon, 188
Learning Centers—Block
boats, 311, 313, 314
building a train, 175–177
clown formations, 183, 185
foil blocks, 94
Learning Centers—Dramatic Play
beginning sounds, 211
restaurant, 94
watermelon shopping, 188
Learning Centers—Fine-Motor Area
building railroad tracks, 173
campfire, 305
clown hair, 183
cutting skills, 27
feather painting, 27
flower collage, 102
identifying letters, 215

lacing, 97
popcorn and cranberries, 98
robin eggs, 295
toothbrushing, 100
turkey feathers, clip-on, 170
watermelon lacing, 188
weaving, 180
wrap and ribbon cutting, 192
Learning Centers—Flannelboard
matching shapes, 265, 268
Learning Centers—Games
color matching, 175–177, 195
letter recognition, 216–218
matching, 95
nose throwing, 184
Learning Centers—Gross-Motor Area
letter recognition, 215, 218
rainbow tossing toy, 180
tightrope, 182
Learning Centers—Literacy
alphabet soup, 97
beginning sounds, 211, 296, 299
birthday, 194
Chicka Chicka Boom Boom tree, 99
hearts matching, 100
identifying the letter c, 184, 185
identifying the letter w, 187
letters, 104, 169, 171, 178, 214, 215, 217
name recognition, 95, 192
name writing, 307, 309
rhyming, 101
sorting letters, 173, 176, 177
Learning Centers—Math
clown color matching, 182
color matching, 26, 178
comparing sets, 301, 304
counting, 102, 163
lightbulb patterning, 99
matching numerals, 189, 194
measurement, 143, 148
one-to-one matching, 103, 106, 163
patterning, 310
sets, 174, 176
shapes, 95, 96
sorting, 169, 172, 187, 190
Valentine's Day counting, 286
Valentine's Day matching sets, 286
Learning Centers—Play Dough
car tracks, 29
pumpkins, 97
sparkly snowfolk, 99
Learning Centers—Puzzles
birthday plate, 193
Learning Centers—Science
bubbles, 104
hot or cold, 98
nest building, 296
plant parts, 101
seasonal tree, 94
turkey nest, 20
Learning Centers—Sensory
feathers, 27
patriotic rice, 103
smell, 189
soft objects, 96
texture, 29, 174, 176, 177, 251
touch, 179, 189, 300
Learning Centers—Snack
caboose, 175
clown hats, 183
crunch and munch candles, 194

rainbow fruit, 179
turkey taco salad, 170
Learning Centers—Thematic Units
birthdays, 192–196
clowns, 182–186
rainbows, 178–181
turkeys, 168–172
watermelon, 187–191
Learning Centers—Water Table
birdbath, 171
buoyancy, 312
car wash, 28
litter, 103
St. Patrick's Day, 100
Learning Centers—Writing
connecting spoken language with written
words, 179, 181, 189, 191, 195, 196
Mother's Day gift, 102
prewriting, 174
Leaves
painting, 21
rubbing, 21
Letter Recognition
center, 214, 215, 217, 218
chant, 214
circle-time game, 214, 217
first initials, 215, 217
game, 216–218
unit, 214–218
whole-group rhyme, 216
Letters
circle time, 74
grouping, 76
identifying c, 184, 185
letter of the week, 108
love letters, 24
matching, 263, 277, 285, 290, 293
recognition, 77, 144
snowflake center, 219
Letters and Sounds
flannelboard, 226, 228
identification, 224, 225, 227
puppet, 226
song, 224, 226
unit, 224–228
Lionni, Leo
Inch by Inch, 143, 148
Swimmy, 145
Literacy Development (see also Beginning
Sounds, Bookmaking, Class Books,
Learning Centers—Literacy, Print
Concepts, Rhyming)
building prior knowledge, 154, 156
letter recognition, 77
letter-recognition center, 219
letter-sound association, 224–228, 311
predicting, 164
prewriting, 220
raindrop /r/ sound, 220, 223
responding to literature, 165
rhyming, 220, 222
sequencing, 164, 166
song, 219, 221
unit, 219–223
Wind Blew, The, 220, 222
words with similar meanings, 221
writing, 221
London, Jonathan
Puddles, 291
Martin, Bill, Jr., and John Archambault
Chicka Chicka Boom Boom, 99, 144

Math (see also Counting, Graphing, Learning
Centers—Math, Measurement With The
Three Billy Goats Gruff, Number
Recognition, One-to-One Correspondence)
comparing sets, 301, 304
counting to ten, 302
estimating, 292
measurement, 143, 148
number matching, 77
number recognition, 57, 154, 156, 246–249
ordering by size, 278, 292
ordering numerals, 264, 267
preaddition skills, 306
Measurement With The Three Billy Goats Gruff
blocks, 243, 244
bridge, 242
capacity, 243, 245
goats in meadow, 243, 244
length, 242
unit, 242–245
Mother's Day
gift, 102, 114
poem, 114
Mouse Paint
beginning sound /p/, 160, 161
camouflage, 158, 160
expressing oneself through art, 158
prior knowledge, 158, 160
secondary colors, 158
unit, 158–161
Walsh, Ellen Stoll, 158–161
word connections, 159, 160
Movement (see also Action Poems and Songs,
Gross Motor)
action spinner, 48, 59
beanbag toss, 53
buzzing bees bracelet, 56
candy cane lane, 52
circle of friends, 50
fast and slow chant, 56
fun frog hop, 57
letter-recognition rhyme, 216
lovebugs, 54
phone number hop, 54
pretend nap, 52, 57
Rainbow Pokey, 55
reach the teacher, 50
ribbon streamers, 51
shamrock parachute, 55
snowflake dance, 53
to music, 49, 58, 158
turkey nest, 51
whimsical walking, 49
Name Recognition
birthday cake, 192
circle-time activity, 142, 148
getting acquainted, 68
Names
beginning sounds, 210
identification, 254
writing, 108
Napping House, The
class book, 151
identifying characters, 150, 152, 153
personal connection, 150
reviewing story through song, 151
Wood, Audrey, 150–153
National Dental Health Month
toothbrushing center, 100
New Year
display, 9

song, 121

Number Recognition
 flannelboard, 247, 248
 game, 246, 248
 identify the numeral, 247
 number match, 247, 249
 small-group activity, 246
 unit, 246–249

Numeroff, Laura
 If You Take a Mouse to School, 164–166

Ocean
 bulletin board, 254, 257
 nametags, 256, 259
 rhyme, 256
 room decoration, 255
 seashell search, 254, 258
 three-dimensional fish, 255
 unit, 254–259

One-to-One Correspondence
 cheese blocks, 237, 240

Painting (see also Arts and Crafts, Learning Centers—Art)
 bingo daubers, 22, 23
 boat, 311
 display, 13
 fabulous flower garden, 42
 feather, 26, 27
 flyswatter prints, 104
 golf ball, 33
 handprints, 108
 ice pops, 111
 leaves, 21
 peg puzzle, 112
 pie slice, 34
 potato masher prints, 34, 43
 pumpkin prints, 266
 sandcastle, 44

Patterning (see also Learning Centers—Math)
 apples, 260, 263
 bracelet, 230
 floor pattern, 232
 hedgehogs, 231, 233
 parent note, 232
 snack, 231
 sounds, 230
 strips, 230
 textures, 231
 unit, 230–233
 Valentine's Day, 287

Patterns
 action spinner, 59
 animal cards, 303, 304, 308
 apple, 263
 banana, 217
 banana peel, 218
 barn, 171
 bedtime picture cards, 208
 bee cards, 105
 beginning sound /p/, 161
 berries, 156
 bird, 148, 297
 bird cards, 299
 boat cards, 313
 boot, 293
 bows, 280
 boxcar, 177
 boy and girl cards, 252
 bread, 157
 builder, 17
 calf, 304
 car, 186

clockface, 45
clown cards, 185
cupboard, 241
daily activity picture cards, 209
duckling, 148
engine, 176
firefly, 106
food cards, 228
gift, 279
gift tag, 279
gingerbread house, 147
goat cards, 244
hedgehog cards, 233
If You Take a Mouse to School sequencing cards, 166
jack-o'-lantern cards, 268
leaves, 30
log, 46
lovebug cards, 60
monkey, 217
mouse, 45, 160, 241
mouse manipulatives, 240
Napping House, The, 152, 153
octopus, 259
owl, 16
parent note, 232, 244
picture cards, 213, 269, 284, 314
pumpkin, 267
pumpkin life cycle pages, 206
puppy, 288
racecar, 18
rainbow rhyme, 181
raindrop cards, 223
recipe cards, 81, 82, 84, 85, 87, 90, 92
rhyming-picture cards, 202, 203, 222
seashell, 258
shape booklet, 236
snail cards, 227
squirrels, 30
starfish, 257
tent, 309
toucan, 248, 249
troll pattern, 244
turkey body, 170
turkey food, 172
turkey profile, 171
watermelon slices, 190
worm, 263, 297

Pete's a Pizza
 being a pizza, 136
 Steig, William, 136

Play Dough (see also Learning Centers—Play Dough)
 identifying letters, 215
 microwave, 114

Poems and Rhymes (see also Action Poems and Songs, Songs)
 body parts, 70
 color, 159
 friendship, 68
 Jamberry, 154, 156
 letter recognition rhyme, 216
 Mother's Day, 114
 rainbow rhyme, 179, 181
 Santa's cookies, 72
 shapes, 69
 toucan rhyme, 246, 247
 vacation rhyme, 78

Positional Words and Concepts
 Corduroy, 138
 If You Take a Mouse to School, 165

Prickly Hedgehog, The
 Ezra, Mark, 231, 233

Print Concepts
 tracking print from left to right, 219, 260, 263

Puddles
 art, 291
 estimating, 292
 experiment, 290
 following directions, 291, 292
 matching letters, 290, 293
 ordering by size, 292
 Puddles, 291
 unit, 290–293

Puddles
 London, Jonathan, 291

Pumpkin Pumpkin
 Titherington, Jeanne, 204, 206

Pumpkins
 action rhyme, 118
 beginning sound /p/, 266, 269
 descriptive words, 265, 267
 emotions, 70
 life cycle, 204, 206
 matching shapes, 265, 268
 ordering numerals, 264, 267
 play dough, 97
 prints, 266
 Pumpkin Pumpkin, 204, 206
 song, 264, 266, 269
 unit, 264–269

Rain
 game, 140
 Kalan, Robert, 140
 writing prompt, 140

Reading (see Language Development, Learning Centers—Literacy, Literacy Development)

Reproducibles (see also Patterns)
 investigating living things, 273
 pot of gold, 88
 recording sheet, 298
 rhyming words, 201
 sequencing, 207
 Valentine's Day class book, 289
 watermelon writing, 191
 writing, 196

Rhyming
 action rhyme, 198
 circle time, 72
 flannelboard activity, 200
 game, 198
 hat and *cat,* 199, 201
 literacy center, 101
 pairs, 155, 200, 203
 pictures, 199, 200, 202, 203
 poem, 199, 201
 unit, 198–203
 Wind Blew, The, 220, 222
 words, 198, 307

Sail Away
 Crews, Donald, 312

Sand Table
 birds and worms, 295, 297
 letter matching, 104
 seashells, 250

Science (see also Bears, Learning Centers—Science, Pumpkins)
 bubble-blowing experiment, 104
 buoyancy, 312
 butterfly nutrition, 89
 comparing apples, 126, 127

evaporation, 130, 131
experiment, 132, 290
lava demonstration, 165
mixing colors, 132–134, 158–160
nest building, 296
plant parts, 101
same and different, 126, 127
secondary colors, 132, 158
thumbprints, 128, 129
Seashells
  song, 250
Sequencing
  bedtime ritual, 205, 207, 208
  daily routine, 205, 209
  familiar activities, 205
  pumpkin life cycle, 204, 206
  snack, 204
  unit, 204–209
Seuss, Dr.
  How the Grinch Stole Christmas, 110
Shapes
  booklet, 235, 236
  identification, 234
  matching, 265, 268
  recognition, 235, 236
  search, 69
  sorting, 235
  Thump, Thump, Rat-a-Tat-Tat, 234
  unit, 234–236
  vehicle parade, 234
Small Group
  colors, 132
  letter recognition game, 216–218
  letters and sounds, 224, 225, 227
  number recognition activity, 246
Snow Family
  Kirk, Daniel, 283
Songs (see also Action Poems and Songs)
  apples, 261
  birds, 295
  cleanup time, 116
  counting sets, 238
  counting to ten, 302
  farm animals, 300
  Fire Prevention Week, 118
  Groundhog Day, 122
  Halloween, 119
  Napping House, The, 151
  New Year, 121
  Old MacDonald Had a Farm, 76
  pumpkin, 264, 266, 269
  rainbow Hokey-Pokey, 55
  rainy day words, 221
  Thanksgiving, 119
  Valentine's Day, 75, 123, 287
  winter clothes, 120
Sorting
  jam flavors, 155, 157
  shapes, 235
Spring (see also Birds, Puddles)
  action rhyme, 122
  butterfly flannelboard, 76
  butterfly snack, 89, 90
  displays, 13
  Earth Day display, 12
  Easter card, 41
  Easter display, 12, 65
  fabulous flower garden, 42
  flower center, 102
  flower parts, 101
  Inch by Inch, 143, 148

Mother's Day gift, 114
Mother's Day poem, 114
powder clouds, 101
wallpaper kites, 41
Steig, William
  Pete's a Pizza, 136
  Sylvester and the Magic Pebble, 141
St. Patrick's Day
  chant, 123
  emotions leprechaun, 74
  leprechaun, 40
  leprechaun pudding, 86
  parachute shamrock shake, 55
  pot of gold, 88
  pot of gold hunt, 113
  shamrock, 39
  water table, 100
Student Photos
  matching game, 95
  name recognition, 68
  school-year growth, 109
Summer
  alphabet ant game, 78
  baseball display, 14
  beach, 250–252
  boats, 310–314
  firefly counting, 103
  fireworks art, 44
  Fourth of July center, 103
  Fourth of July movement activity, 58
  patriotic display, 15
  postcard from teacher, 109
  sandcastle art, 44
  snail snack, 91–92
  song, 124
  sunshine display, 14
  watermelon centers, 187–191
Swimmy
  fish snack, 145
  Lionni, Leo, 145
  teamwork, 145
Sylvester and the Magic Pebble
  magic stone, 141
  Steig, William, 141
  wishes, 141
Tafuri, Nancy
  Have You Seen My Duckling? 142, 148
Thanksgiving
  song, 119
  turkey, 35, 168–172
Thematic Units (see also Learning Centers—
      Thematic Units)
  apples, 260–263
  back-to-school, 254–259
  beach, 250–252
  boats, 310–314
  camping, 305–309
  gifts, 276–280
  ocean, 254–259
  pumpkins, 264–269
  watermelon, 187–191
Three Billy Goats Gruff, The (see Measurement
      With *The Three Billy Goats Gruff*)
Thump, Thump, Rat-a-Tat-Tat
  Baer, Gene, 234
Titherington, Jeanne
  Pumpkin Pumpkin, 204, 206
Train Learning Centers
  building a train, 175–177
  fine-motor skills, 173
  following directions, 175

Freight Train, 175
  matching colors, 175–177
  prewriting, 174
  sets, 174, 176
  sorting letters from other symbols, 173, 176,
      177
  texture, 174, 176, 177
  unit, 173–177
Turkeys
  leaf, 35
  learning centers unit, 168–172
Valentine's Day
  bulletin board, 10
  class book, 288, 289
  counting center, 286
  fine-motor skills, 285
  following directions, 287
  kindness notes, 112
  lacing cards, 112
  matching, 100, 285, 286
  mouse, 39
  patterning, 287
  /p/ sound puppet, 286, 288
  song, 75, 123, 287
  unit, 285–289
Very Busy Spider, The
  Carle, Eric, 137
  daily schedule, 137
  spiderweb rubbing, 137
Visual Discrimination
  matching letters, 104, 214
  matching colors, 26, 178, 180
  matching numbers, 77, 189
Walsh, Ellen Stoll
  Mouse Paint, 158–161
Whole-Group
  /b/ sound activity, 296, 299
  counting to ten, 302
  graphing, 250, 252
  letter recognition rhyme and activity, 216
  letter sounds song, 226
  number recognition game, 246, 248
  /p/ sound activity, 160, 161
Wind Blew, The
  Hutchins, Patricia, 220, 222
Winter
  cardinals bulletin board, 8
  finger-skating painting, 38
  frosty windows, 37
  snowman, 111
  snowpal center, 99
  snowshoe hare snack, 83, 85
  winter clothes song, 120
Wood, Audrey
  Napping House, The, 150–153

ISBN-13: 978-156234723-9
ISBN-10: 156234723-3

9 781562 347239